W9-BAS-430

The Way of Confucius

The Way of
Confucius

Jonathan Price

COMPENDIUM

I dedicate this book to all my Chinese students, past, present, and future.

Text Copyright © Qilu Press 2010 All Rights reserved
Extracts from the *Analects of Confucius* from the translation by Charles Muller 1991/2004
Extracts from the *Shi Jing* (*Book of Songs*) from *The Chinese Classics*, vol. 4 translated by James Legge (1898)
Extracts from *Shi Ji* (Sima Qian, *Records of the Grand Historian*) translated into German by Richard Wilhelm (1931) [English translation by George H. Danton and Annina Periam Danton]
Extracts from the *Book of Zhuangzi* from *The Chinese Classics* translated by James Legge (1891)
Extracts from the *Dao Dejing* (*The Way of Being*) from the translation by Charles Muller 1991/2004
Extracts from the *Book of Mencius* from *The Chinese Classics* translated by James Legge (1891)
Numbering of *Analects* according to *The Analects of Confucius (Bilingual Edition)* Qilu Press 2004

Photography: Hou Xinjian, Kong Xianglin,
                    Jonathan Price
Design: Ian Hughes
Picture Research: Zhang Suxue, Lei Jie, Liu Jiaxu,
                    Wang Yinuo, Wang Yuxiang
Picture Editor: Huang Weizhong
International Project Directors: Paul Richardson,
                    Zhang Lisheng
Executive Editor: Gong Xiaowei, Zhang Xiaodong
Editor: Yan Menghui
English editor: Donald Sommerville

Published in 2010 by Compendium Publishing Ltd,
43 Frith Street, London W1D 4SA

Copyright © 2010 by Compendium Publishing Ltd,
43 Frith Street, London W1D 4SA

ISBN:978-1-90634-700-0

All rights reserved. With the exception of quoting brief passages for the purposes of review, no part of this publication may be reproduced, stored in a retrieval system, or transmitted in any form or by any means, electronic, mechanical, photocopying, recording, or otherwise without prior written permission from the Publisher.

The information in this book is true and complete to the best of our knowledge. All recommendations are made without any guarantee on the part of the author or Publisher, who also disclaim any liability incurred in connection with the use of this data or specific details.

We recognize, further, that some words, model names, and designations mentioned herein are the property of the trademark holder. We use them for identification purposes only. This is not an official publication.

Designer: Compendium Design/Ian Hughes, Mouse-mat Design

All Internet site information provided was correct when provided by the Author. The Publisher can accept no responsibility for this information becoming incorrect.

Explanation: Quotes from the *Analects of Confucius* are identified in blue text, and quotes from other sources are in red.

Printed and bound in China

Contents

The largest statue of Confucius in China, outside the Confucius Temple in Nanjing. *Photo: Jonathan Price*

Confucius' People

Name	Other names/ nicknames
Kong Family	
Confucius	Kong Qiu, Kongzi, Kongfuzi, Kugni, "the Master"
Kong Shuliang	
Yan Zhengzai	Yen Tsengsai
Qi Guan	
Kong Li	Bo Yu
Name unknown	
Zisi	Kong Ji
Dukes of Lu	
Duke Zhao the Prominent	Duke Chao
Duke Ding the Settler	Duke Ting
Duke Ai the Lamentable	
Duke of Qi [Chi]	
Duke Jing	Duke Ching
Ji Family of Lu	
Ji Pingzi	Lord Ji, Ji Sun
Ji Huangzi	Chi Huan
Ji Kangzi	Chi Kang Tzu
Yang Huo	Yang Ho
Meng Family of Lu	
Lord Meng the Elder	
Meng Yi	
Nangong Jingshu	

Relationship to Confucius	Dates/ Comments
	551–479
Confucius' father.	618–548
Confucius' mother	566–538
Confucius' wife	Separated from Confucius 527?
Confucius' son	529–483
Confucius' daughter	Born 527; married 508?
Confucius' grandson	487–425; author of *Book of Zisi*

Ruled 541–510
Ruled 509–495
Ruled 494–467

Employed Confucius as his advisor	Died 489

Confucius' first sponsor	Died 505; prime minister of Lu 518–505
Lord Ji 504–491	Died 491; prime minister of Lu 501–491
Friend of Confucius; Lord Ji 491–?	Born 531?; prime minister of Lu 501–?
Chief steward to Ji Family; dictator of Lu 505–501	known as "Confucius' double"

Head of the Meng family; died 502?
Eldest son of Lord Meng the Elder. Lord Meng himself 501–?
Younger son of Lord Meng the Elder; Confucius' best friend.

Name	Other names/ nicknames
Confucius' Students (only the most prominent listed)	
The Big Three: "The Wandering Scholars" (All three accompanied Confucius in exile 497–484 BC)	
Zilu	"Yu"; Tzu Lu; family name Zhong You
Yan Hui	"Yu"; Yen Yuan
Zigong	"Su"; "Si" (Ci) Tzu Kung; surname Duanmu
First Generation Students	
Hsia	Zixia;Tzu Hsia; family name Bu Shang
Min Ziqian	Min Tsze Chien
Ran Yu	"Qiu"; Zan Yu; Chiu,Yen Qiu
Zai Wo	Tsai Wo
Second Generation Students	
Zengzi	Tseng Zu; Zeng Shen
Zhonggong	Chung Kung; family name Ran Yong

Dates/ Comments

542–480. Confucius' oldest and most faithful student. Originally from a poor family he attended Confucius' first classes and continued attending throughout his life. Worked for Ji family as a steward then as an administrator for several state governments. Accompanied Confucius on his final exile. Killed in a coup in state of Wei 480.

513–483. Confucius' best and favorite student, who came from a very poor family. Was only sixteen when he first became a student of Confucius. Accompanied Confucius for the whole of his thirteen-year exile towards the end of his life.

520?–455? One of Confucius' brightest students. Came from a merchant family and was himself a successful businessman, but dedicated his life to supporting Confucius both in his lifetime and after his death. Stayed by Confucius' tomb for six years. Later became a successful diplomat.

Prominent first-generation student. Later attributed several of Confucius' most famous sayings to himself. Famous for his "filial piety." Later became a local government administrator.

Talented first-generation student who went on to work as a steward for the Ji family. Expelled by Confucius from students' circle for over-taxing the poor to benefit the nobility. Later reconciled with Confucius. Army commander for Lord Ji from about 498.

Notorious for "asking stupid questions". Later worked as a government officer for the Duke of Qi.

505–436. Young student of Confucius in the Master's final years. Principal biographer of Confucius and source for the *Analects*. Most Prolific writer of Confucian works after his teacher's death including *Book of Zengzi* and *Da Xue* (*The Great Learning*). Teacher of Zisi, Confucius' grandson. First person in the world to suggest the earth is round.

Another prolific writer and second main source for the *Analects*; author of *Book of Zhonggong*. Compiled Confucius' sayings on politics and law. Worked in the administration of the Ji family.

Preface

The picture of Confucius' life and ideas as presented in this book may come as a surprise to many readers both in China and the West, as it is so different from the conventionally received ideas about him.

I make no apology for this, and claim only, as Confucius claimed about himself: "I am a transmitter not a maker." What he meant by this famous statement was that he was simply transmitting the wisdom of ancient China to future generations. In the same way the aim of this book is to transmit to modern readers the "real" Confucius, to let him speak from his own time directly to our own age. Over two and a half thousand years his ideas have been reinterpreted and revised to such an extent that what is conventionally understood as "Confucianism" has almost nothing to do with what he actually said.

I believe, strongly, that we still need to listen to what he really said, and that of all the great thinkers the world has produced he is the most relevant to our world today.

Yes, I am an unashamed "Confucius fan"—but having said this I still insist I am a "transmitter not a maker," and have not created a Confucius of my own making to suit my own preconceptions, as many others have done over the past two and a half millennia, but have tried to present him, as far as is humanly possible, as he actually was. We have so little verifiable information about his life that it is very difficult to create an authentic picture of what he did and when, and every biography is completely different. In this book of course I have had to speculate about the exact chronology of the events of his life, but I have done this by looking at the historical records and then deciding whether these accord with the primary source we have for Confucius' life and ideas, which is the work known as the *Lun Yu*—in English the *Analects of Confucius*—a collection of his sayings supposedly compiled by his students after his death.

In presenting Confucius' ideas, I have relied almost exclusively on the *Analects*, which all scholars agree is basically authentic. There are many collections of the so-called "Sayings of Confucius," both in books and on the Internet, but unless these derive from the *Analects*, it is very doubtful whether he actually said anything like that at all,

especially when he appears to be stating the obvious.

For example in many collections of his sayings he is supposed to have said: "Everything has beauty, but not everyone sees it." Nothing even remotely resembling this can be found anywhere in the *Analects*, and it is the sort of thing that somebody waxing philosophical in a bar might come up with—just before he passes out. It is hardly worthy of one of the greatest thinkers who ever lived, and it is best to just ignore all these pseudo-Confucian homilies and stick with the *Analects* which contain true wisdom:

> **Confucius said: "When three men are walking together, there is one who can be my teacher. I pick out people's good and follow it. When I see their bad points, I correct them in myself.**
>
> *Analects*, 7:22

Even some of the best-known sayings which are based on the *Analects* are paraphrases of the original text in which the true meaning has been lost, so that Confucius appears to be delivering trite little homilies which more properly belong on a greetings card. This one, for example, appears in many collections of his so-called sayings: "If you shoot for the stars and hit the moon, it's OK. But you've got to shoot for something. A lot of people don't even shoot."

Confucius said this in 500 BC? I hardly think so. This appears to be a crass modernization of Saying 34 in Chapter 7 of the *Analects*:

> **"A sage or a man of perfect virtue? How dare I describe myself like this? It may simply be said of me, that I strive to become such a man without giving up."**

In order to understand what Confucius actually meant by this we have to understand the historical context in which he said these words, and then decide whether his idea still has relevance in the context of our own times. This is what I have tried to do in this book, relying on the best modern translations of the original Chinese texts and not trite modernizations like "shooting for the stars."

The "modernization" refers to ambition *per se*, and could be applied to anybody who wants to realize their dream, whether as a successful pop singer or president of the United States. The original, in the wonderful modern translation into English by Charles Muller, refers exclusively to somebody who strives to be a good person. What Confucius was saying is that perfection is impossible, but we should still try to attain it; he was, however, talking about moral perfection not the achievement of worldly career goals, and we should therefore ignore all these attempts to bring him into the greetings-card school of philosophy, and listen to what he actually said.

This is more difficult than might be imagined as, for some reason, Confucius has always been fair game for people who want to put their own words into his mouth; this has been going on for thousands of years and to such an extent that he has become the most misunderstood of all the ancient thinkers. For example during the Han Dynasty about 400 years after he died, a scholar named Sun Hsing-yen, writing an introduction to the classic work on military strategy *The Art of War* by Sun Tzu (a contemporary of Confucius) made the absurd claim that Confucius had said: "When I fight I always win."

Since Confucius was an avowed pacifist who actively campaigned for disarmament, this is as ridiculous as saying that Buddha's last words were "Take no prisoners" or that during the Sermon on the Mount Jesus said "The poor are losers—that is why they are poor." Yet Sun Hsing-yen presented Confucius' gung-ho remark as gospel; he wanted Confucius as a militarist and in the absence of any recorded remark about anything remotely martial he simply made something up—no scholar has ever tracked down the source of "I always win."

In a similar way the commonly held perception of Confucius as an ultra-conservative misogynist also derives from misquotations and much later interpretations of his sayings. In the following pages I have quoted almost all of Confucius' most important statements as recorded in the *Analects*. As a rule of thumb, readers may confidently assume that if it does not appear in this book, he did not say it; no matter what anybody else may tell you.

The Confucius you will meet in this book is, I hope, the real man, and the ideas are his real ideas. I also hope that, like me, you will feel that he still has so much to say to us today …

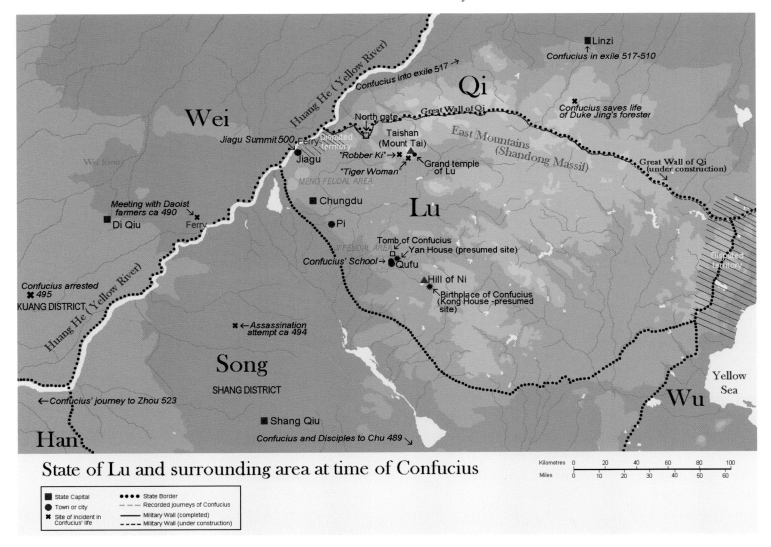

State of Lu and surrounding area at time of Confucius

Who Was Confucius?

onfucius has probably had a greater influence on more people, and over a longer period of time, than any other comparable figure in the history of the world. In his own day and for many centuries afterwards he was known as Kong-Fu-Tzu, *"Fu-Tzu"* being an honorary title meaning "great" or "master" teacher.

He is known in China today as Kong Zi—"Master Kong"—following the modern spelling system known as Pinyin which is used to transliterate Chinese into the western alphabet. Sometimes this system works and sometimes it does not—"Peking" has become "Beijing" and "Shantung" (where Confucius lived) is now "Shandong" and these are better approximations to the actual Chinese pronunciation than the older versions. *"Zi,"* however, (which means "master") is not pronounced "zee" but something like "zzzuh," so to all Chinese people he is "Kongzzzuh." In the rest of the world he is known by the Latinized version of his name which was first coined by Matteo Ricci, a Jesuit missionary to China in the seventeenth century, who heard the sound "Kong-Fu-Tzu" and transliterated this into "Confucius."

His true name was Kong Qiu (pronounced "chioo") and he was born into fairly humble circumstances in 551 BC in the state of Lu in China (now part of Shandong Province), and died there in 479.

The most reliable source for Confucius' sayings has always been the *Lun Yu*, known in English as the *Analects*—or "Sayings"—of Confucius. Although the work was not finally compiled until at least three centuries after Confucius' death, this collection of 492 of the Master's sayings and dialogues is known to be based on much earlier works written by Confucius'

Portrait of Confucius. Painting on paper, Qing Dynasty. *Qilu Press*

"disciples," in which they set down for posterity their recollections of what he had actually said, as accurately as they remembered.

In 1993, archaeologists discovered a tomb in Guodian, China, dating from around 300 BC (about 170 years after Confucius' death) which contained a collection of "bamboo-slips"—books at this period were written on strips of bamboo bound together with leather—which turned out to be works by many of Confucius' known students, and even a book written by Confucius' grandson Zisi. The following year, the Shanghai Museum acquired another 1,400 bamboo slips also dating from the same period, which had been stolen from a tomb near Guodian and ended up in Hong Kong; these also contained many Confucian texts. The bamboo manuscripts were found to contain many passages that were identical—sometimes word-for-word—to the records of the same sayings which were compiled into the *Analects of Confucius* several centuries later.

This means that the *Analects* must after all be an extremely reliable source for Confucius' sayings. Even though they were not "published" until many centuries after his time, they are clearly based, as most people had always thought before the discovery of the tomb manuscripts, on "eyewitness" recollections set down on bamboo slips by his students shortly after he died.

When we come to the life of Confucius, however, we are on much less sure ground. His earliest "biographer" in any sense could be said to be the philosopher Meng Zi ("Master Meng"), also commonly known by the Latinized version of his name, Mencius. He was born in 371 BC, just over a century after the death of Confucius, and he included many stories about the man he regarded as his "Great Master," together with records of his sayings and discussions of his philosophy, in his main work the *Meng Tze* or *Book of Mencius*. Although not a contemporary of the Master, Mencius lived not only in the same part of China but in the same kind of world, and he claimed in his book that this gave him the right to be taken seriously as his biographer and interpreter:

> From Confucius downwards until now, there are only 100 years and somewhat more. The distance in time from the sage is so far from being remote, and so very near at hand was the sage's residence. In these circumstances, is there no one to transmit his doctrines?
>
> Mencius, Book 7, Part 2, Chapter 38:4

Mencius saw his role as the transmitter of Confucius' ideas to future generations, rather than as a historian, so we have no way of knowing whether his accounts of the Master's deeds and sayings are historically accurate, although we can say that probably most of them are, at least in essence.

Apart from the *Analects* (which do contain many reliable biographical details) and the *Book of Mencius*, the other prime source for Confucius' life is the work entitled *Shi Ji* (*Records of the Grand Historian*) by Sima Qian, who lived during the Han dynasty from 145 to 85 BC, more than 300 years after Confucius' death. Devoted to scholarship, Sima Qian sacrificed more than most people in the cause of his art. In 98 BC he deeply offended his ruler, the Emperor Wu Di, by attempting to defend a general accused of sedition, and he was ordered to choose either castration or death. The emperor assumed that death was obviously preferable to the humiliation of castration, and expected his historian to take the honorable course and commit suicide. Sima Qian, however, was made of sterner stuff. At this time he had not completed his monumental work of history, and instead he chose the way of shame and dishonor in order to give himself time to finish it.

> I have examined the deeds and events of the past and investigated the principles behind their success and failure … but before I had finished my rough manuscript, I met with this calamity. It is because I regretted that it had not been completed that I submitted to the extreme penalty without rancor. When I have truly completed this work, I shall deposit it in some safe place. If it may be handed down to men who will appreciate it then though I should suffer a thousand mutilations, what regret would I have?
>
> Sima Qian, *Records of the Grand Historian*

However much we may admire the stoicism of the Grand Historian, unfortunately his accounts of Confucius' life as they appear in the *Records* have to be taken with much more than a pinch of salt.

Sima Qian's accounts of Confucius' movements are probably fairly accurate, since his records of other events several centuries before his own time can in many cases be corroborated from other sources. So it is probably safe to assume that, if he says Confucius was in such and such a place at such and such a time, this is probably true. Many other details are very suspect and Sima Qian was fond of embellishing his narrative with fanciful details and small anecdotes that very often do not ring true. For example, many of his stories about Confucius' wanderings during his years of exile are duplicated in other Chinese poems and stories of the period, but featuring completely different people. He also includes many literal fairy tales, like his story of Confucius' discovering a unicorn.

There are many other stories about Confucius which derive either from Sima Qian or later sources—Chinese children even today are brought up on them and know them by heart—but most scholars now insist that we should discount almost all of them as fiction. They usually feature Confucius outwitting others by his

Mencius (372-289 B.C.) and his disciples. *Qilu Press*

"The beautiful maidens of Qi". Ming Dynasty Painting.
Qilu Press

extreme cleverness, but this type of story belongs to the genre of the folk tale rather than history. Sima Qian's descriptions of Confucius' career as a government minister, for example, as described in the *Records*, are almost like something out of a Chinese version of the *Arabian Nights*.

The Grand Historian relates that a neighboring state sent a large number of beautiful dancing girls to distract the Duke of Lu, who was Confucius' ruler, while soldiers prepared a surprise attack. While the Duke and his courtiers wallowed in orgies of sensuality, the wily Confucius naturally saw through the ruse and saved the day. Like many writers from time immemorial, Sima Qian seems to be spicing up his tale with generous helpings of sex and violence, and while it all makes for a gripping read it is questionable history.

In general Sima Qian's account of Confucius' life is based on the premise that he was a sage sent by the gods to earth, who was recognized as such from a very early age. Thus he has Confucius starting his teaching while still in his teens, after rumors reached the rulers that a divine sage descended from the ancient kings had been born in their state. This is entirely inaccurate and pure mythologizing: Confucius by his own account in the *Analects* had a very hard struggle before he was noticed, and had to do a variety of very mundane jobs before he was finally able to start teaching around the age of thirty.

Many of Sima Qian's "folk stories," and those written

by others many centuries after Confucius' lifetime, were in fact designed to counteract the influence of the many "anti-Confucian" stories which were bandied about by Confucianism's main rivals, the Daoists. Thus, the Confucian writers portrayed their idol as a semi-divinity, the embodiment of wisdom and all human virtues, while the Daoists represented him as a semi-idiot.

One of the principal Daoist writers, Zhuangzi, in his *Book of Zhuangzi* uses Confucius as a fictional character in a novelistic world of his own creation in which the rival sage appears as a liar, coward, and sometimes an outright buffoon. In Zhuangzi's stories not only is Confucius constantly humiliated intellectually by the number-one Daoist sage, Lao Tze, but he is also made to look extremely stupid by a series of humble but naturally wise individuals such as "The Old Fisherman," and "The Man with no Toes."

Zhuangzi himself admitted that his portrayal of Confucius was literary rather than historical in the famous passage where he says that "Confucius is a dream":

Confucius and you are both dreams; and I who say you are dreams—I am but a dream myself …

Once upon a time, I, Zhuangzi, dreamed I was a butterfly. Suddenly I awoke, and there I lay, myself again. Now I do not know whether I was then a man dreaming I was a butterfly, or whether I am now a butterfly dreaming I am a man.

Zhuangzi, 2:9 and 2:11

As literature this is knockout stuff—many people consider Zhuangzi to be the greatest Chinese writer of all time, who stands beside Homer, Shakespeare, Tolstoy, and Euripides (almost his exact contemporary) in the pantheon of the all-time greats. Confucius, however, was never a dream; he was a real person with real ideas who lived in a historical period, and somehow we have to separate the fact from the fiction if we are to get any idea of what he really stood for, and decide if he still has something to say to us today. Fortunately this is still possible. The *Analects*, supported by the recently discovered bamboo-manuscript texts, provide an authentic record of his thought, while if we sift judiciously through the writings of both the Confucian and anti-Confucian schools, we can begin to construct a reasonably reliable portrait of the man and his ideas.

Though this is not, alas, a portrait in the literal sense. Sima Qian in the *Records of the Grand Historian* gives us a "fairy-tale" version of his appearance: "Confucius was nine feet six inches tall. All the people called him a giant and marvelled at him." This is laughably unlikely since

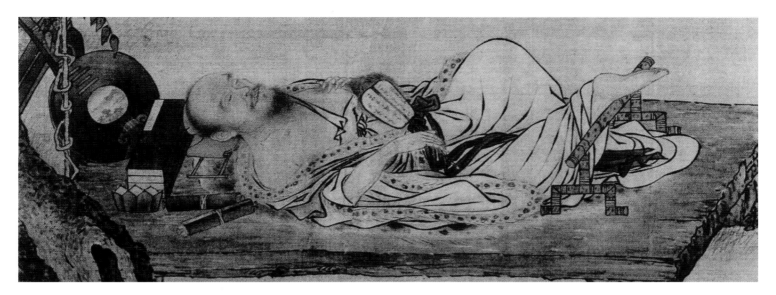

nobody who actually knew him ever recorded this astonishing fact—so let us just say he was a tall man.

Everybody *thinks* they know what Confucius looked like, because his physiognomy in the thousands of drawings and paintings of him is so consistent and so familiar; but unfortunately the truth is that we do not know if they are a genuine likeness, since the earliest surviving portraits of him date from many centuries after his death. Perhaps they are a true portrait, certainly the face and expression of the Confucius we see in the earliest paintings seem to be those of the man we know from the *Analects*. The humor is there in the eyes, and in the mouth which seems always ready to break into a smile. Perhaps the artists of those early portraits simply based their rendering of his features on their own reading of the *Analects*, or maybe there were even earlier portraits which are authentic and have now been lost. We will never know.

If the portraits of Confucius seem to accord with our idea of the man we form from the written sources—and they certainly appear to—then we might as well accept them as a true likeness. It does no harm, and they are the best we have. The smiling eyes and wry expression of the traditional paintings seem to fit perfectly with the humorous self-portrait Confucius provided of himself in that most reliable of written sources, the *Analects*:

> **The Duke of She asked Zilu about Confucius, but Zilu did not answer him.**
>
> **Later the Master said to Zilu, "Why did not you just tell him: he is simply a man who in his eagerness to study forgets his food, who in the joy of attaining knowledge forgets his sorrows, and who does not notice that old age is coming on?"**
>
> *Analects*, 7:19

Yes, this is certainly a man we can know …

Portrait of Zhuangzi dreaming. *Qilu Press*

Portrait of Confucius. Ming Dynasty Painting. *Qilu Press*

~Confucius in Time~

Before we look at Confucius' life and consider his ideas, it is useful to fix his dates into the timeline of history. His thinking often appears so modern that it is sometimes difficult to believe that he actually existed in a world that appears to be so very different from our own, but as we look closer at this world it becomes clearer that it was not so very different, at least in essence. Having just emerged from the twentieth century, arguably the most barbaric and inhumane in human history, perhaps we should once again begin to listen to Confucius as we continue heading into the twenty-first. Indeed Confucians from every century have always maintained that this was a man far ahead of his time, who in fact had more relevance to their own period than his own, so perhaps he really is a man for all times and all ages, and this is how we should look at him.

To start with let us look at him in the context of his own time …

Date BCE	Chinese Dynasty	Events in China
ca. 1766–1040	Shang	
1027–771	Western Zhou	1027 King Wu usurps power. So-called "Golden Age" of the Zhou 771 Sack of Hao: Zhou Dynasty flees to Luoyang
770–476	Eastern Zhou: Spring and Autumn Period	770– Break-up of Zhou Empire into autonomous states 685 Construction of Qi Great Wall started between states of Qi and Lu 521 All contact lost between Lu and the Zhou capital
475–221	Eastern Zhou: Warring States Period	281 Great Wall of Qi finished
221–206	Qin	221 China united under the "First Emperor" Shi Huangdi 220 Great Wall of China started
206 BC–220 AD	Han	

Despite the astonishing coincidences and parallels, it does not really help our understanding of Confucius to relate the events in China at his time to what was happening simultaneously elsewhere in the world because, as far as we know, there was no real contact during this period between China and the other civilizations in Europe, the Middle East, and Asia.

Systematic and regular contact along the Silk Road, which allowed not only trading but the exchange of ideas and technologies in both directions, did not really start until at least two centuries after Confucius, so it is of no real significance that the great battles of Marathon (490 BC) and Thermopylae (480 BC), when the 300 Spartans defeated the might of the Persian army, happened during his lifetime.

It is indeed astonishing that Buddha, who was born in India in 480 BC, was also alive at the same time as the Chinese Sage—just—while Socrates was born in 476 BC,

only three years after his death. This means that within the space of fifty years Buddha achieved "enlightenment" under the fig tree of Bodh Gaya, Confucius gave lessons to his students in the shade of the cypress trees of Lu in ancient China, and Socrates together with his disciple Plato debated philosophy with their followers in the olive groves of Athens. At this distance away in time, they can all be considered to be contemporaries. It is even theoretically possible that a young student of Confucius could have journeyed to India to sit at the feet of Buddha, moving on by way of Persia to Greece where he could have heard Socrates, finally ending up in his old age as a member of Plato's Academy—all within the space of one lifetime. It is possible—but unlikely.

However, the parallels between Socrates and Confucius are indeed uncanny. Even the worlds in which they lived were similar, since neither "China" nor

Confucius and Confucianism	India	Middle East/ Greece
551 Confucius born in state of Lu		569 Pythagoras born
ca. 523 Confucius begins teaching		
ca. 501–498 Confucius works as a minister in Lu government		
ca. 496–484 Confucius' 13 years period of exile	490? Buddha born	490 Battle of Marathon
484 Confucius' final return to Lu: edits classics		480 Battle of Thermopylae
479 Death of Confucius		476 Socrates born
		475 Pythagoras dies
		427 Plato born
Mencius (371?–288?) develops Confucianism	410? Buddha dies	399 Socrates dies
Xunzi (298–238) develops Confucianism		384 Aristotle born
		356 Alexander the Great born
		347 Plato dies
	326 Alexander reaches India	323 Alexander dies
		322 Aristotle dies
Confucianism repressed—burning of the bamboo scrolls		
Analects of Confucius compiled from surviving manuscripts		
Confucianism becomes major state philosophy		*ca.* 150 Regular trade between
Sima Qian (145–85) writes first biography of Confucius		the West and China begins along
65 AD Buddhism arrives in China		the Silk Road

"Greece" existed at this time as united countries, and both areas were instead a collection of feuding city-states: Athens, Sparta, and the rest in the western world, Qi, Chu, and Lu (Confucius' home), and many other small states in the east. Both came from relatively humble circumstances; both were considered the greatest teachers who had ever lived, and are the acknowledged fathers of philosophical thought in Europe and China respectively. Neither wrote down anything he said but left others to do it, Plato in the case of Socrates and the anonymous compilers of the *Analects* in the case of Confucius. Both of them challenged their followers to look at everything in a new way, and both fell foul of the leaders of their time, who considered their free-thinking ideas subversive. There were many calls for Confucius' execution, several unsuccessful attempts on his life, and he was driven into exile on numerous occasions, while Socrates was actually forced to commit suicide.

What are we to make of this? To all intents and

purposes Confucius, Buddha, Plato, and Socrates might as well have been living on different planets, and yet here was this amazing flowering of original thought in different parts of the globe at almost exactly the same moment. By another amazing coincidence, one of Confucius' students, Zengzi, was the first person to suggest the earth is round, beating Eratosthenes by about a hundred years. Perhaps it is after all just a coincidence, or maybe there was just "something in the air" at the time. Who knows?

Placing Confucius in the context of Chinese history on the other hand does really help us to understand why he suddenly emerged as the voice of reason and humanity during the period in which he lived. Confucius' dates, 551–479 BC, will be seen from the timeline to place him in the middle of the Zhou Dynasty, which lasted for 900 years from 1027–221 BC, the longest-lasting single dynasty in Chinese history and probably in the history of the world. However, it is quite wrong to imagine Confucius living in a "dynasty" such as those which

The Great Wall of Qi (contemporary with Confucius).
Photo: Jonathan Price

existed in later times with an emperor, a court, and a governmental bureaucracy, since by his time the Zhou "empire" had been reduced to a petty kingdom which had lost power not only over the state of Lu, one of its neighbors to the east where Confucius was born, but over almost all of the other areas it once controlled.

It is true that for its first 300 years, the Zhou Dynasty controlled quite a large area of what is now modern China from its capital, Hao, which was very near to the site of the later city Chang'an (Xian), which in time became the capital of Imperial China. The Zhou nation was made up of a large number of provinces, of which Lu, Confucius' home state, was one of the smallest.

Then, in the year 771 BC, the Zhou capital was sacked by barbarian tribes out of the west, aided by rebel lords who wanted power for themselves. The Zhou king was killed, and the remnants of the Zhou aristocracy retreated much further east to Luoyang, in what is now Henan province. Very quickly the original Zhou state disintegrated into a collection of much smaller independent states, which in turn rapidly fragmented themselves into areas controlled by clans based on ethnic origin. The Zhou Dynasty continued within its own tiny borders, but for the next 450 years it was a "Chinese dynasty" only in name. After the break-up of the original Zhou kingdom, the Zhou dynasty ceased to be a major player and the center of gravity of Chinese culture and civilization shifted even further eastwards into their former states in the area which now forms the province of Shandong.

Thus the Zhou Dynasty is clearly divided into two parts—the period of the Western Zhou (1027–771 BC) when the dynasty controlled a large area as a united country, and the Eastern Zhou (770–221 BC), when it was reduced to relative insignificance and its former kingdom was a collection of feuding city states. Historians also subdivide this later period—during which Confucius lived—into two distinct eras the Spring and Autumn Period (770–476 BC) and the Warring States Period (475–221 BC), and it will be seen from the timeline that Confucius lived at the very end of the first period and died only three years before the start of the second.

If this seems confusing do not worry, it was probably equally confusing for the people living at the time, who often never really knew where they were actually supposed to be living, or to whom they owed ultimate allegiance: the faraway king of Zhou; the leader or "duke" of their own city-state; or their local warlord.

Since Confucius lived at the transition point between these two periods, we might expect some sort of momentous change to have been taking place during his lifetime, but this was not in fact the case and it was, generally speaking, chaos as usual. Anybody living in China in 475 BC (the start of the "Warring States Period") would hardly have noticed any change from the previous year, and in fact the whole period from the fall of the relatively stable Western Zhou dynasty in 770 BC until the unification of China in 221 BC shares the same characteristics—disunity and constant warfare.

Twice a year, in the spring and autumn, the events of the previous six months in each state were set down for posterity onto bamboo scrolls. The records for Confucius' home state of Lu, which were supposedly edited and indexed by Confucius himself towards the end of his life, are known as the *Spring and Autumn Annals*. The last entry in this work is for the year 476, and for this reason, rather than because of any specific historical event, the period covered in the annals became arbitrarily known as the Spring and Autumn Period.

The only real difference between the Spring and Autumn and Warring States eras is that the struggles for power in the earlier period were largely between warlord clans, whereas from the fifth century onwards the warfare was mainly between the small states themselves. Nevertheless, this is still a fairly arbitrary distinction, and especially so at the time of Confucius, when both the states and the warlords were constantly coming to blows.

Confucius' home state of Lu, which had its own "duke" and several areas controlled by warlords, was very small compared to the others, even though the largest of them were not much bigger than present-day "counties." As a result Lu was under constant threat of being gobbled up by its more powerful neighbors, and many of Confucius' political and social ideas were based on a longing for a return to the kind of society which had existed under the Western Zhou (1027–771 BC), before the break-up of that kingdom into warring states and clan fiefdoms. From the perspective of their own chaotic times, Confucius and many of his contemporaries regarded the Zhou period as a "golden age," when society was harmonious and stable, allowing the arts, literature, and culture to flourish as never before.

Confucius' admiration for this lost "golden age" was the subject of many of his tirades against the anarchic and self-seeking rulers of his own time, and there is some historical justification for his stance on this. Although starting out as just another clan which seized power, the Zhou rulers had ended slavery in China (2,500 years before Abraham Lincoln) and evolved a highly centralized system of government which still allowed a large measure of autonomy to the various states which made up their domain. Though not as large as the first "Chinese Empire" under the Qin, and certainly not as large as the great empire under the Yuan (Mongol) Dynasty 2,000 years later (which is still the largest single geographical area controlled by one government in the history of the world) the Zhou nevertheless controlled a significant part of what is now modern China, which is no mean feat. Since it is extremely difficult to achieve this kind of stability over very large areas—then or now—the type of government they practised must contain some sort of example for students of politics everywhere and in any period.

So what were the features of this government that Confucius emphasized? Apart from the idea of centralized government but relatively autonomous regions, the other main principle developed by the Zhou was the concept of the "mandate of heaven." Although at first sight this appears to be a variation of the "divine right of kings"- the basis for the monarchies of medieval Europe—there was a crucial and uniquely Chinese difference. This was the idea that the mandate was not irrevocably given by the gods to a particular family or individual to rule *in perpetuo*, but was provisionally granted and was dependent upon the good behavior of the monarch. If a ruler proved unworthy of the mandate of heaven, and ruled tyrannically or against the interests of the people as a whole, he could therefore be overthrown and replaced without disturbing the stability of the system as a whole, and this indeed happened many times not only under the Zhou but at later periods of Chinese history when the Imperial dynasties presided over a "Confucian" system of government. In this way Confucius can certainly be credited with handing down the wisdom of the ancients to future generations, which was in fact all he himself claimed to be doing:

Confucius said: "I am a transmitter, rather than an original thinker. I am passing on the teachings of the ancients."

Analects, 7:1

This then was the so-called "golden age" of the Zhou, the passing of which Confucius so bitterly lamented. Why had it passed away? This is the question which

Confucius often asked himself, and the answer was that the Zhou system had an inherent flaw: human nature. By granting so much power to the individual regions of their empire to govern their own affairs, the Zhou kings opened the way for self-seeking and greedy local leaders to assume absolute power for themselves in the areas they controlled. The feudal system as developed under the Zhou required the inhabitants of each region to swear allegiance to their local clan leaders, and the clan leaders to swear allegiance to the leaders of each state, while the state leaders were in turn bound in fealty to the king of the whole empire.

This system worked for several hundred years, but gradually the state leaders began to ignore the dictates of the king, naturally hogging all the taxes for themselves, and eventually the local clan leaders began to do the same. By the time of Confucius the whole of the Zhou empire had disintegrated into a myriad collection of tiny areas controlled by powerful warlords who milked their own domains for all they could get. The feudal clans were all-powerful, setting fire to any town or village that resisted them, hacking off the limbs of the men before decapitating them, and raping the women.

Zhuangzi the "anti-biographer" of Confucius describes one of these warlords:

Tao Kih had 9,000 followers, who marched at their will through the kingdom, assailing and oppressing the different princes. They dug through walls and broke into houses; they drove away people's cattle and horses; they carried off people's wives and daughters ... he halted on the south of Mount Tai, mincing men's livers, which he gave to his followers to eat.

Although the cannibalism is probably an exaggeration the general picture is likely correct. Might had become right, and there was no effective central authority, nothing to restrain the inhuman savagery of the warlords and the unbridled greed of those in power. This was a world largely without morals or common feelings of humanity, in which horses were considered to be more worthy of compassion than ordinary people, since horses pulled the chariots of the powerful.

And this was the world into which Confucius was born ...

Zhengzai's Child

As has already been pointed out, the primary source for Confucius' biography is the *Records of the Grand Historian* by Sima Qian, and since much of this work is what we would now call a "novelization" of his life, written centuries after his death, it is often difficult to separate fact from fiction. We have to try, however, because to a large extent it is all we have.

First of all we have to ignore all the tales of supernatural portents surrounding Confucius' birth: mysterious birds landing on the roof, dragons breathing fire in the sky, unicorns outside the door, and the appearance of magical symbols on the baby's body. Sima Qian himself did not include all of these details in the *Life of Confucius* section of his book, but he started the trend by representing Confucius as a nine-foot giant who consorted with unicorns, and over the centuries more and more fabulous events were incorporated into the Confucius legend.

These mythological events belong in a legendary tale of the appearance of a divine sage upon the earth, and not in any kind of serious biography of a man who really existed. Sima Qian also includes a detailed genealogy which later Confucians extended to show that Confucius could trace direct descent from the royal house of Shang, the ancient dynasty which preceded the Zhou. This too can probably be discounted as fanciful, since a royal pedigree was also a required element in the type of legendary tale in which the hero emerges from poverty and obscurity to claim his rightful kingdom.

What then do we really know about Confucius' birth and parentage? Hard facts are difficult to come by. Even the year of his birth, 551 BC, has been disputed, and is given in some sources as one year later. Certainly he was born in the state of Lu, somewhere near the town of Qufu in present-day Shandong Province, but visitors to the area are often bewildered to find several places referred to as the "birthplace." Sima Qian recorded his birth as having taken place in the town of Chou in Chang Ping district, although nobody knows exactly where this was. The so-called "Cave of Confucius" is now claimed as the authentic birthplace, but this seems too much like another myth—the birth of a legendary hero of divine descent in a humble cave (or stable) is another stock element in folk tales and many religions, and it is much

Confucius' mother with baby. *Qilu Press*

more likely that Confucius was born at home like everybody else.

Sima Qian is the only source we have for the name of Confucius' father, Shuliang He, a member of the Kong family who originally came from the village of Kong in the state of Song, Lu's immediate neighbor to the south. In their original home the Kong family seems to have belonged to the aristocracy, or at least the upper class—this much we can accept as Confucius was educated as a member of this class even though by then the family had fallen on hard times. Confucius great-grandfather, however, was killed following some sort of dispute with the Song leaders, and the rest of the family were forced to move north to the state of Lu.

Leaving behind their privileged existence in their home state, the Kong family found it increasingly difficult to survive. Strangers in a strange land, they found no immediate entrée into the halls of the mighty and, while still maintaining their pretensions to gentility, were forced to live on the periphery of power in a small town. Confucius' father seems to have made a living as a mercenary soldier, working mainly for the Lu government, rather than as a permanent member of the military as a bona-fide member of the ruling class would have done. We know this because he is mentioned in several independent records (by scribes other than Sima

"A unicorn appears to Confucius' mother". Ming Dynasty Painting. *Qilu Press*

The "Cave of Confucius" near Ni Hill – so-called birthplace of Confucius. *Qilu Press*

Bronze soldier's helmet (Spring and Autumn Period) as worn by Confucius' father.
Capital Museum Beijing. *Photo: Jonathan Price*

be proud of. If you skin a tiger and a dog, he once said, there is little difference, yet dogs are our friends. It is as if they have chosen not to be wolves, and we as human beings can make the same sort of choices: we can refrain from killing while a tiger cannot.

The brave man is not necessarily possessed of humaneness.

Analects, 14:4

Confucius' father was certainly brave; whether he was also humane we do not know, perhaps he was—on occasion—although he is on record as having killed a large number of people as part of his job. Despite these heroic achievements, however, he was never given any sort of honor or official salary, which he would no doubt have considered his due, and it can be well imagined that he must have turned into a very bitter old man.

Even the small dwelling where he lived may only have been granted him for his lifetime by his unappreciative government—this was a common practice at the time—and as a result he would have had little to pass on his son, not even the house he lived in. Assuming he had a son, which he did not, at least no son capable of continuing the Kong family line.

This was the greatest humiliation of all for a man of his time. After two wives and a lifetime of hardship, he had produced only daughters and one son who is variously described as "disfigured" or "lame" (possibly he may have been retarded), and was therefore incapable, in Shuliang's view, of ever marrying and producing sons of his own. By the time he was in his late sixties, Kong Shuliang was becoming a desperate man, facing not only his own imminent extinction but the total extinction of his family name. His second wife was past the age of child-bearing, so his only hope was to find a young concubine and hope against hope that she did not give him yet another daughter.

To understand what he did it must be remembered that the Chinese system of inheritance was different from that in the West, then and later. The family fortune and name was inherited by the eldest son, irrespective if whether he was born in or out of wedlock. For this reason it was common practice for the sons of concubines to inherit if the official wives had failed to produce a male heir—this practice continued until the beginning of the twentieth century.

Shuliang finally managed to find a prospective mother for his longed-for "proper" son when he was almost

Qian) as having distinguished himself in various minor skirmishes, not, however, as a commander but as one of several officers.

During one encounter, a detachment of Lu soldiers managed to force their way into the town of Biyang, which was at the time under the control of a rebel warlord. Unfortunately the warlord's men started to lower the gate, attempting to trap the Lu soldiers inside the city before finishing them off. Confucius' father saw what was happening and, Samson-like, single-handedly held up the gate with his bare hands, thus enabling his comrades to beat a hasty retreat unharmed.

The success of these heroic exploits seems to have depended on brawn not brain, and it is difficult to credit such a tough individual with having sired one of the greatest philosophers the world has ever known; it seems to be his mother's genes we have to thank. His son, then unborn, was to grow up singularly unimpressed by boasts of military prowess. He considered the sort of petty skirmishes his father had been involved in, and which continued throughout his own lifetime, to be completely pointless; and he never tired of pointing out that bravery without humanity is a distinguishing quality of wild beasts, and is nothing to

seventy: her name was Yan Zhengzai and she was only fifteen. Sima Qian describes this (with his usual eye for salacious detail) as a "wild union," thereby implying that the old goat had somehow managed to force his attentions on some sort of hormone-crazed village girl who would fall willingly into any man's arms whether he was sixteen or sixty-nine. This is completely misleading. Zhengzai was a cultured and literate girl from a good family, described in many records as from a "family of scholars." Even without these records we can deduce with complete certainty that this must have been true, because her son Confucius is on record as saying:

"At fifteen my heart was set on learning."

Analects, 2:4

This love of scholarship must have come from his mother and her family, since she was alone responsible for his upbringing (his father died when he was three). Why then would a girl from such a family have submitted herself to the embraces of an "old goat" like Shuliang? The reason was probably economic, and Shuliang may have done some sort of deal with Zhengzai's family. Although we do not know what this was, we do know—as will be seen—that it turned sour very quickly. The members of the Yan family to which Zhengzai belonged, were, like the Kong family, originally immigrants from another state and like them they had also fallen on hard times, presumably even harder or their daughter would never have been forced to submit to the "wild union."

The Yan family, however, although cultured and scholarly, were in fact the social inferiors of the Kong family because they originally came from the state of Zou, which was outside the borders of the original Zhou Empire, in the area known as the Yi. Although the Zhou exercised no political power at this period over the Warring States, which were to all intents and purposes completely independent, the inhabitants of the now defunct empire regarded all those who lived—or had lived—outside its former borders as "barbarians."

As a result Yan Zhengzai's family—"barbarian" immigrants struggling to survive and facing prejudice at every turn—were in no position to refuse any sort of deal offered by the Kongs, so Shuliang bedded his young mistress, but at first with no result—Zhengzai failed to become pregnant. Increasingly desperate, the "spring and autumn" couple made regular visits to the sacred hill of Ni, near their home, to pray to the gods for a child. This sacred hill may still be visited and there are many

The Confucius Temple on the Hill of Ni. *Qilu Press*

shrines to Confucius on its wooded slopes; it is one of the few places associated with him that seems untouched by time. Because such prayers and offerings were very public, this must mean that the rest of Shuliang's family—including his wife—must have accepted the situation, albeit reluctantly. This was no hole-in-the-corner affair, tolerated though never spoken of, but right out in the open.

In some accounts Shuliang is supposed to have divorced his wife and married Zhengzai, but this is unlikely, and it is much more probable that the future mother of his expected son would simply have been accepted into the family as "Number Three Wife," as was the custom in China until recent times. The young wives who were brought into a family simply for the purposes of child-bearing were often treated appallingly by the "senior wives," and this was probably what happened in Shuliang's household. Zhengzai, still very young, found herself in the unenviable position of junior wife, hated by the other wives and daughters, living in a household without books or music or anything she was used to, her "husband" a rough soldier with whom she had nothing in common, who only visited her for the purposes of procreation. A wonderful depiction of the plight of one of these young wives is Zhang Yimou's classic film *Raise the Red Lantern*. Although this film is set in the early twentieth century, Chinese society had changed very little over thousands of years and it is not unreasonable to imagine a similar situation in Confucius' day.

At last, at the beginning of 571 BC, Zhengzai had good news—she was expecting a baby. The child, to the immense relief of Shuliang, was a boy, and is traditionally celebrated as having been born on September 28th (according to the Western calendar), although there is no evidence that this was the exact date. In any case according to the Chinese lunar calendar the date varies from year to year, like the Chinese New Year.

Where he was born is equally uncertain, presumably in the household of Shuliang He, the "proud father." The new baby was named "Qiu," which means "sacred hill," after the hill of Ni where his parents had prayed so fervently for a son. In fact his family name "Kong" meant "answer to prayer," and therefore Confucius' full name Kong Qiu reads as "answer to a prayer at the sacred hill," so his given name is a clever play on the existing family name.

How proud a father Shuliang actually was is debatable. There are many stories about the family's great disappointment at the "ugliness" of the new baby. Some of the stories feature the "nine elder sisters" who are supposed to have tormented the child on account of his "grotesque appearance." Although these stories are reminiscent of folk tales, there may still be a grain of truth in them—little Kong Qiu's tormentors would have been his step-sisters, the daughters of Shuliang's previous wives. Number Two Wife would no doubt have been seething with fury at Zhengzai's successful delivery of a son, because the infant Kong Qiu was now his father's heir and the future head of the family, effectively disinheriting her own "lame" son who by now would have been almost an adult. Supported by the daughters, she would have spared no effort in trying to turn Shuliang against his new young wife and son, and drive them out.

In this she was very soon successful.

Confucius' mother praying for a child on the Hill of Ni. Ming Dynasty Painting. *Qilu Press*

Growing Up

We know that Zhengzai left the Kong household some time not more than three years after the birth of her son, taking her baby boy with her and ceasing all communication with his father. What had gone wrong?

We can only speculate: maybe Shuliang reneged on his deal with Zhengzai's family, or more likely Number Two Wife and her family finally succeeded in turning Shuliang against her and had the "lame" son reinstated as the official heir. For whatever reason, by the time Confucius' father died three years after he was born, his family had ceased all contact with both the mother and the son. We know this because Sima Qian records that neither Confucius nor his mother knew where his father was buried, and when Zhengzai died she was interred not beside her "husband" but beside the "Way of the Five Fathers" near Qufu.

Although Confucius was not yet three when his father died, and so could be excused for not remembering where he was buried, it is impossible that his mother would not have known had she been living in the household at the time. The ignorance of both mother and son about the whereabouts of the Kong tomb is such an odd fact that it is unlikely that Sima Qian or anybody else would have made it up, so we can conclude with almost absolute certainty that Confucius was taken away

'Ritual utensils' used in religious ceremonies (Zhou Dynasty). *Qilu Press*

from his father before he died, and was brought up as a child not in the household of his father's family, but somewhere else.

Where was this? Almost certainly Zhengzai would have returned with her little boy to the home of her own family, the Yans, since the idea of a "single mother" bravely bringing up a child on her own would have been unthinkable in China at this time. The Yan household can be assumed to have been somewhere near Qufu—which was a small city at that time—while his father must have lived some distance away since there was no communication between the two families after Zhengzai left.

The Yan family, as has already been noted, was scholarly and cultured, though by no means well-off. Accounts of Confucius living as a child in extreme poverty are wildly exaggerated, and designed to fit his life into the framework of a folk-tale. His mother somehow managed to give him an education, instill in him a love of reading, and teach him music and traditional rituals, and this would not have been possible if her family were dirt-poor farmers trying to scrape a living off the land.

Their household would have been modest enough,

Child Confucius playing with utensils. *Qilu Press*

Altars in the Confucius Temple Qufu (Western Side hall) showing traditional positions of 'ritual utensils'. *Qilu Press*

with mud-brick dwellings surrounding a small courtyard, and rough-hewn wooden pillars supporting the timber roofs. There may well have been chickens pecking the dust in the yard, and ducks swimming in a small pond nearby, but inside the house one room would have been full of books, with another small outhouse serving as the family temple.

This was in fact the ideal environment for the future philosopher to spend his formative years, and indeed, had his early life been different, we may never have had a "Confucius" at all. If he had been born into a rich and powerful family, he might not have been so eager to castigate the ruling class for their shortcomings. On the other hand if his mother had stayed with the Kong family she would have found it very difficult to pass on the Yan love of scholarship to her son—Shuliang sounds like the sort of rough-hewn soldier who would have boasted that he had never read a book in his life. Had he lived longer,

What Confucius' books looked like: this example of a page from a 'bamboo-slip' book (dating from less than two centuries after Confucius' time) was stolen from a 4th Century B.C. tomb and acquired by Shanghai Museum in 1994. The slips were bound together at top and bottom by leather straps. *Photo courtesy Shanghai Museum.*

The "Bridge of Heaven" on the summit of Mount Tai. The ancient rock, eroded into fantastic forms, persuaded people of Confucius' time that Mount Tai was the realm of the gods. Confucius' childhood home would have been somewhere in the hazy distance below the mountain. *Photo: Jonathan Price*

and if his little son had remained in his household, he would surely have wanted him trained as a soldier.

Fortunately, and thanks to his young mother, his childhood turned out very differently. Instead of playing soldiers, Confucius as a boy played "rituals." In all the later biographies he is described as having spent hours arranging the sacred utensils in their traditional order on the family altar, and this became the subject of countless paintings and drawings in later times. This

important of which, Mount Tai, was not far from Confucius's home—were believed to emanate colossal spiritual power. Every district also had its own sacred hills, and of course it was at the local hill Ni Qiu that Confucius' father and mother had prayed for a child.

Although all the gods were often represented in quasi-human form in paintings and statues, their appearance was never standardized, and the practice of religion at this time

The so-called "Confucius stone" on Nine Immortals Mountain, near Qufu in ancient state of Lu. *Qilu Press*

may be apocryphal, but the image is so charming and seems so right that we might as well accept it.

These "utensils," of earthenware or bronze, were used in various household rituals and sacrifices. Many examples from the period have survived and may be seen both in Chinese museums and all over the world. The objects were used for cooking sacrificial meat, or holding the blood of sacrificed animals, and the procedure followed prescribed rituals which dated back to even more ancient times. The actual ceremonies (which little Kong Qiu imitated in his childhood games) would have been conducted by his grandfather or one of his uncles.

There was no organized religion at this time in the sense of a hierarchical church. There were people who looked after the temples at various sacred sites, but they are never mentioned in any of the contemporary records as having been important or powerful; instead it was up to the head of each family to conduct the rituals in the correct manner. The gods or unseen presences to whom the sacrifices were made were many and various, with one god for the crops (Hou Ji, the god of millet) another for the kitchen and so on, but even then these beings were not organized into a recognizable pantheon, but were simply "there." In addition to this the spirits of the family's ancestors were also honored in the small family temples.

Outside the house there were also believed to be strong spiritual forces in nature, so that wind, rain, thunder and lightning, and disasters like flooding were seen as actual movements of unseen gods. Immobile geographical features, especially the Five Sacred Mountains—the most

Sacred mountain: the northern frontier of ancient Lu was the towering massif of Mount Tai. Now protected as a National Park, the landscape is unchanged from Confucius' day. *Photo: Jonathan Price*

seems to have depended more on a sense of powerful but invisible forces, and thus inclined towards mysticism. The religion of Daoism (Taoism), which has many mystical elements, was growing in popularity during Confucius' time, but the Yan family, including Confucius himself, were traditionalists. Indeed Confucius in his later sayings often dismissed mystical thought as an idle indulgence, and considered speculation about religious questions such as "Is there life after death?" as a complete waste of time since we can never know the answers anyway:

Ji Lu asked about serving the spirits.

Confucius said, "If you can't yet serve men, how can you serve the spirits?"

Lu said, "May I ask about death?"

Confucius said, "If you don't understand what life is, how will you understand death?"

Analects, 11:12

So even as a child, Confucius is unlikely to have been precociously religious and his fascination with the sacred utensils would have been more a cultural and social experience than a spiritual one.

On the first day of each lunar month—at the full moon—one of his uncles would sacrifice a sheep, and it was for ceremonies like this that the ritual utensils were kept; little Confucius merely borrowed them for his mock rituals with his playmates. Later in his life he discussed this ceremony with one of his more "modernist" students:

> **Zigong wanted to do away with the sacrifice of the sheep on the first of the month. Confucius said, "Zi, you love the sheep; I love the ceremony."**
>
> *Analects*, 3:17

Realm of the Jade Emperor: view from the summit of Taishan (Mount Tai). *Photo: Jonathan Price*

It is significant that he did not say "the gods require it," as a fervent religious believer would have done, or even "that is what it says in the *Book of Rites*, so we have to do it," like a died-in-the-wool conservative (something Confucius is often unfairly accused of being). Just, in a very good humored way, "I love the ceremony." There is no reason for thinking that he would have felt any different as a child. The antique ritual objects and garments opened a magical door into a beautiful traditional world, while the ceremonies themselves united the family and gave all its members, even the youngest, a sense of continuity and security.

The Yan household would also have been full of books, their library becoming the most important influence on the development of the young Confucius. He later described himself to his students as a voracious reader dedicated to study by the time he was in his teens, so he must have started reading at a much earlier age. His mother, or perhaps one of his uncles, would have started his education at home by teaching him to read

and write, then they would have moved on to reading together some simpler passages from the Chinese classics.

"Books" at this period meant bound volumes of bamboo slips, which were made from strips of bamboo attached together into "pages" (the same technique is used for modern bamboo blinds and mats), and then bound together by leather straps. The characters were inscribed vertically down each slip.

Among the books in the Yan household would have been the so-called "five classics." The *Book of Rites* (*Li Ji*) not only contained instructions for rituals but also included ways of correct behavior, something which certainly found its way into Confucius' later thinking, while the *Book of History* (*Shu Jing*) recorded the events of the Zhou dynasty and the earlier Shang period. Confucius had an encyclopedic knowledge of history and was always ready to cite historical examples to support his arguments, so he must have known this book too from an early age.

The *Book of Changes* (*Yi Jing*) was in fact a divination manual, designed to be used with divination sticks (milfoil stalks) to predict the future. Confucius did not become interested in this book until he was in his sixties, so it is unlikely he knew it as a child.

The *Book of Music* (*Yue Jing*) would certainly have been in the house. The Yans must have been a musical family since they passed on their love of music to the boy—Confucius' own proficiency as a player of the Chinese zither is legendary and is mentioned many times in the *Analects*. Unfortunately the *Book of Music* has been lost, although it is referred to in the Guodian Tomb bamboo manuscripts, so must have still existed at Confucius' time.

The most important of these bamboo-book classics, however, at least for Confucius, was the *Book of Songs* (*Shi*

The Hall of Great Accomplishments, first built in the Tang Dynasty to honor Confucius' skills in music and the other arts. *Qilu Press*

Jing), a collection of poems and folk songs which encapsulated the whole culture of the Zhou dynasty and earlier, and can even be said to have defined Chinese literary culture, because the great poets of later centuries, for example those of the Tang dynasty, consciously imitated its style. Certainly it was Confucius' favorite book, as he constantly used it in his teachings, and he was possibly responsible for handing it down to posterity, since according to tradition he edited the work towards the end of his life, selecting 300 of the best poems from over 3,000 in the original, and arranging them in the anthology that we now have. All the poetry abounds with depictions of beautiful scenery, colorful details of everyday life in town and country, and charming descriptions of the behavior of birds and animals, which turns the whole work into a kind of encyclopedia in verse.

The young Confucius would have been introduced to some of these poems and songs during his childhood in his mother's house, and his great love for the *Book of Songs* continued throughout his life. Many of the songs are similar to modern nursery rhymes, using repeated sound syllables like ding-ding and ting-ting, and we can well imagine his young mother (when he was four she herself was only nineteen) bouncing little Kong Qiu on her lap and singing this charming ditty:

> On the trees ring the axe ding-ding;
> With the birds crying out ying-ying.
> *Book of Songs*, Minor Odes of the Kingdom—Fa
> Mu

In the *Book of Songs* there is music and joy. His mother's family, though relatively poor, were rich in culture, and Confucius always maintained that this was the mark of true "gentility," for this was the world of his childhood …

> Hoo, hoo, cry the deer, nibbling the wild garlic of the fields.
> I have a lucky guest. I play my zithers, small and big. Play my zithers, small and big.
> Let us make music together,
> Let us be merry, and delight the heart of a lucky guest.
> *Book of Songs*, The Minor Odes, 1st Decade
> "The deer cry"

The melodious notes of the Chinese zither, the *guqin*, would have been one of the best-remembered sounds of Confucius' childhood, for certainly his family must have owned one of these ancient instruments, since Confucius was passionately devoted to its playing almost to the point of obsession—he is on record as having spent three months in his middle age practising a single piece until he was satisfied that he rendered its true spirit. He also commented later on the importance of starting to practise music at as early an age as possible:

Confucius said: "Ordinary people develop their understanding of music and ritual earlier. The nobility develop these later. In terms of practicality, earlier development is better."

Analects, 11:1

So he must have been introduced to the *guqin* when quite young, and the Yan household would have echoed to the often discordant notes produced by the young perfectionist, annoyed with himself for not producing perfect harmony.

Performance on a modern reproduction of the ancient Chinese zither – the *guqin*. *Jonathan Price*

The instrument was a seven-stringed zither—in other words it was played in a horizontal position, unlike the lute or guitar, and did not have a bridge. The sound it produces is quite unique. The guitar or lute renders distinct and separate chords, so that Spanish guitar music for example has a strong rhythm, while the harp—the principal instrument of early European music—produces a blended "river" of sound. The Chinese *guqin* on the other hand, which Confucius played, produces distinct chords but with a lingering resonance that has an almost ethereal quality, and it is this resonance that Confucius, all his life, was trying to achieve.

The echoes of the notes from the *guqin* have an unutterable sadness, a poignant longing for something we cannot quite grasp, yet which somehow exists in the resonance of the notes. This longing, for Confucius, was for the lost golden age of the Zhou, when society itself mirrored the harmony of music, and to which he hoped society would one day return. Indeed, according to legend, the sixth string of the *guqin*, which produces the sad note, was added by the first king of the Zhou dynasty in order to mourn the death of his son.

So, to understand Confucius, we not only have to listen to his words, we have to listen to his music, at least in our imaginations. This is not as fanciful as it sounds, since in ancient Chinese education (as in ancient Greece), music was considered to be as important as literature or mathematics; indeed it was held that the other subjects could not be truly understood without an understanding of musical harmony. This is an idea which today has been lost, with musical education relegated in almost all cultures to the status of an extra, rather like carpentry or horse-riding. So it is important to understand that the music which Confucius began to learn in childhood was not for him a hobby but an intrinsic part of his whole view of the world; he suggested that not only can harmonious music help us achieve social and spiritual harmony but that the reverse is also true—it is actually impossible for a brutish person to produce beautiful music:

Confucius said: "If a man has no humaneness what can his music be like?"

Analects, 3:3

All accounts of Confucius' life describe his having spent his boyhood in a village rather than a town, so as well as learning to read and write and play the *guqin*, he would have enjoyed the usual pastimes of a country childhood—fishing in the streams and lakes, and playing in the woods and fields. Lu was for the most part a country of gently rolling hills and small valleys,

Ancient Map of north part of the State of Lu, showing Taishan (Mount Tai) and surrounding mountains. *Qilu Press*

criss-crossed by many rivers and streams, and with a number of quite large lakes. It was a fertile, pastoral landscape, sheltered by mountains from the harsh winds which blow down from the Asian steppes across the northern part of China in winter, whipping up the dust and freezing the muddy roads. Even today the area is famed for its cultivation of flowers, especially the Chinese national flower, the peony, and the fields and the hillsides of ancient Lu would have been dotted with color every spring. Such a mellow landscape is perhaps the ideal environment for a budding philosopher—indeed Lu's neighbor to the north, Qi, with its harsher climate, became the Sparta to Lu's Athens, producing warlike sons and becoming known as the "State of a Thousand Chariots."

Lu, on the other hand, developed as the center of culture for the whole Eastern Zhou area and, as a result of its central position and good roads, the other states would often send deputations to its capital, Zhong Du, to study ritual and ceremonial. For a son of Lu there was less pressure to seek a military career than in the other states, and the world of the mind was an equally strong tradition. While the gentle valleys of Lu gave birth to Confucius, and the philosopher Mencius was born in another small state in the same area, their much larger and stronger neighbor Qi produced only military generals whose names are almost forgotten. Confucius himself pointed this out to his students:

> **"Duke Jing of Qi had a thousand teams of horses, but when he died, there was nothing for which the people could praise him. What meaning can you glean from this?"**

> *Analects*, 16:12

The Duke Jing whom Confucius mentions was somebody he knew well—he had acted as his advisor on several occasions. When he died in 489 BC, ten years

The 'Chariot Burial' of Duke Jing of Qi, underneath the Jinan-Qingdao expressway, Shandong. *Photos: Jonathan Price*

before Confucius, he had himself buried with 600 of his war horses and chariots. This grandiose burial site remained forgotten for nearly two and a half thousand years until it was excavated in 1964. Duke Jing and the skeletons of his war horses now lie somewhat ignominiously underneath the main expressway which runs all the way from Beijing to the seaside town of Qingdao.

In complete contrast, huge temples and other memorials to Confucius began to be built in Lu shortly after he died, and have stood there ever since. The world of the mind has triumphed, and tiny little Lu, now the district of Qufu in Shandong, is still one of the most important artistic and cultural sites in the world since it is the birthplace of Confucianism and its modern center.

As well as being a cultural center, there was another reason why the small state of Lu was important, then as now, and this was because the most sacred of the six sacred mountains in China, Mount Tai (Taishan), lay just within its northern borders. It is very likely that as a child Confucius would have been taken to the mountain by his mother's family; it is still a place of pilgrimage for all Chinese people, and there can be few children from Shandong even today who have not climbed to the summit at least once before they leave school.

In Confucius' time it was even more significant, since the mountain itself was regarded as a spiritual being, radiating ancient power, and the Grand Temple of Lu was built on its slopes. Ancient Lu's northern border was

the range of mountains now known as the Shandong Massif which stretches right across the land from the Yellow River (Huang He) to the sea, and forms a natural frontier. Raised up into the sky by tectonic forces aeons ago, the hard basaltic granites of Taishan and its neighboring mountains have resisted erosion by rain and wind for millions of years and still stand, eternal and unchanging, looking down upon the ceaseless flux of the world below.

As the young Confucius first gazed across his homeland from the heights of Mount Tai, he must have been struck by the thought of how small and insignificant the affairs of men appear when viewed from the perspective of the gods.

> Confucius ascended the eastern hill, and Lu appeared to him small. He ascended the Tai mountain, and all beneath the heavens appeared to him small.
>
> *Book of Mencius*, Book 6, Chapter 24:1

During his lifetime more and more people thought the same, embracing the doctrines of mystical religions like Daoism which espoused withdrawal from the corrupt world and a life of contemplation. How tempting it has always seemed to stay on top of the mountain, and throughout Chinese history many people have done just that. Even today many mountains have monasteries, where one may listen to the tinkling of the bells, the chanting of the monks and the song of the birds, and for a brief time escape the bustling world and all its problems.

Even when he stood on the summit of Mount Tai as a boy the young Confucius would have known that his place was not on the mountain. Instead he must have longed for the time when he would be a real part of that bustling world far below. It is an imperfect world, often a cruel one, but in Confucius' view it is our duty to try and change it, not flee from it and talk to the birds.

The Way of Confucius always leads *down* the mountain.

Sunrise seen from the Jade Peak on the summit of Taishan.
Photo: Jonathan Price

Schooldays

As Confucius entered his teens, his mother would have been growing increasingly worried about his future.

He was a big, strong boy, and by now would be lending a hand around the farm, which today would more likely be called a small-holding, where they raised their own pigs and used the manure to grow grain, vegetables, and even the hemp and flax which was used for making clothes and mats. There would always have been something to do—mending gates and fences, helping to build walls from mud brick and stone, or even lending a hand to push a fat sow off her litter of new-born piglets to prevent them being smothered. A true "gentleman" of this time would naturally have never had to do any of these things, as they had armies of servants and laborers to do everything for them, but the Yan family were not so lucky, and although they would have had a few servants any extra pair of hands was always welcome.

"As a youth my family was poor so I had to learn many ordinary skills."

Analects, 9:6

Zhengzai did not want her son to live like this for the rest of his life, however. Although, as a member of the Kong family, the young Kong Qiu could claim to belong to the lowest rank of the upper class, known as the *shi*, there had been no contact between the Kongs and the Yans for over ten years, and in any case his father's family were not very influential and could probably have done little for him except perhaps enrol him in some powerful man's army.

His mother's family were even lowlier and, although they still claimed *shi* status, would not have had the necessary connections to ensure Kong Qiu a successful career in the government or the military. Realistically, all she could hope for her clever son was some sort of career as a minor civil servant, or perhaps a clerk or steward in the employ of a wealthy nobleman. Not "high office" but at least on the bottom rung of the ladder.

Even for this humble type of career the boy would need a formal education, and just how the Yan family were going to get him one was something of a challenge. At this time there were no schools as such where students could be registered by their parents, nor were there any private tutors; instead all teachers were attached to one or other of the noble families. Through some tenuous connection with one of these powerful clans—the Ji family—Confucius' uncles eventually arranged for Kong Qiu to be educated by their family tutors in exchange for the promise that the boy would be indentured into the service of Ji Sun—Lord Ji—after

Status symbols: male dress ornaments from Spring and Autumn Period, as worn by the sons of the nobility at Confucius' school. Left: Stone tunic ring and crystal and agate dress ornament. Right: Bronze horse-brooch. Capital Museum Beijing. *Photos: Jonathan Price*

The sport of gentlemen: 4-horse chariot (Warring States Period). Life-size model based on archaeological finds. Museum of Chariots, Linzi. *Photo: Jonathan Price*

2-horse chariot (Spring and Autumn Period). Life-size model. Museum of Chariots, Linzi. *Photo: Jonathan Price*

his schooling was completed. The family probably had to promise that Kong Qiu would remain in the Ji service for life.

So it was that at the age of fourteen or fifteen, Kong Qiu was taken to the Ji mansion where he would be living and attending classes for the next three years, returning to his mother's home perhaps only once every six months for the harvest and lunar new year festivals. He was very much in the position of what we might now call a "scholarship boy"—belonging to the ranks of "gentlefolk"—the *shi*—but only just, his clothes hand-me-downs and a little threadbare, surrounded by the sons of the rich in their fine robes and golden ear-rings, who would have looked down upon him with arrogant disdain. It would certainly have been difficult, especially in the first days, and as he himself said later:

Confucius said: "To be poor without resentment is difficult. To be rich without arrogance is easy."
Analects, 14:10

There would have been many other boys in the same position as Confucius, although he was probably the poorest of them all. Education in the Ji household would have been a two-tier affair, with an upper level made up of the privileged sons of the nobility, and then a larger number of "ordinary" boys, destined for careers as clerks, keepers of records, custodians of temples, overseers of granaries and estates, and quartermasters of military supplies. These "ordinary" students, though educated members of the *shi* class, nevertheless only existed to serve the rulers. They would hardly have been acknowledged by their more dashing contemporaries, the gilded youth of the nobility. It was to this second group, the "ordinary boys" or *shi*, that Confucius most definitely belonged, and even among these boys he would have been considered the lowliest. As such he

Bronze axle-cap from chariot (Spring and Autumn Period). Capital Museum Beijing. *Photo: Jonathan Price*

would have been expected to know his place.

A traditional story recorded in many sources including the *Records of the Grand Historian*, relates that Lord Ji held a "graduation banquet" for all the students in his household when they had completed their studies. When Confucius turned up at the door he was refused admittance, and was told by the steward: "I'm sorry sir, knights only." In other words he was not a member of the upper-level group who were being groomed for greatness as military "knights"; he was not a "gentleman." Confucius' reaction is not recorded but it was no doubt just a nod and the ironical smile so familiar from the portraits; outright confrontation was never his way.

According to Sima Qian the person who refused him admittance was Yang Huo, Lord Ji's chief steward. Crawling and obsequious to his masters, Yang Huo was at the same time ruthless and cruel to anybody below him—just the sort of qualities to recommend him to Lord Ji, who had his eye on supreme power in Lu. Curiously, Lord Ji's steward and Confucius were very similar in appearance—Sima Qian writes that "Confucius resembled Yang Huo in form"; and many years later

Confucius enduring disparaging remarks about his abilities. Ming Dynasty illustration of Analect 9:2. *Qilu Press*

Confucius was arrested by mistake by soldiers who thought he was the other man. Since "Yan" was Confucius' mother's name they were possibly related, which would explain the resemblance, and it could even have been Yang Huo who first arranged for his "cousin" to be brought into the service of the Ji family.

Doors must have closed in Confucius' face many times like this during his youth, and these early humiliations may have forged his passionate belief in equality of opportunity, one of the cornerstones of Confucianism.

Although refused admission to banquets, the second-level students still needed a good grounding in reading, writing, and mathematics, since most of the jobs open to them involved the keeping of records of some kind. The curriculum also included ritual studies, history, poetry, divination, and the "gentlemanly" sports: archery and charioteering. It seems that Confucius, as an "ordinary"

射雙相圖
孔子習射于雙相圓
觀者如堵使于路枕
弓矢喻之曰貢軍之
將亡國之大夫與為
人後者不得入焉弟
好禮不從流俗者立
此去者大半

Confucius competing in a 'gentleman's archery contest'
(note the musical accompaniment). *Qilu Press*

student, was either not selected to participate in these elite sports or, if he was, proved not very good at them—he would always have preferred to read a book. Later in life, when criticized for his lack of gentlemanly accomplishments, he made a joke about knowing nothing whatsoever about either skill, adding that perhaps it was not too late for him to take up charioteering:

A man from Daxiang said: "What a know-it-all Confucius is! He knows so much about everything—but I never heard he excelled at any particular skill."

When Confucius heard this, he said to his students: "What shall I take up? Shall I take up charioteering? Shall I take up archery? I think I will take up charioteering!"

Analects, 9:2

If not chariot-racing, he may at least have participated in archery at school, since he once made a reference to the sport which indicates a fair degree of technical knowledge (in this saying he is suggesting that it is expertise, not brute strength which counts in any field):

Confucius said: "In archery it is not important to pierce through the leather covering of the target, since not all men have the same strength. This is the Way of the ancients."

Analects, 3:16

This sounds like a memory from his schooldays, since the boys from the nobility who were destined to become soldiers would no doubt have applauded wildly when one of their number sent his arrow clean through the leather and thudding into the wood—"killing" the target rather than simply hitting the mark.

Archery was one "gentlemanly" sport of which Confucius heartily approved. There would have been many archery contests held during his schooldays, which he would have been required to watch if not actually participate in. These competitions were accompanied by music and ritualized ceremonial and emphasized skill and fair play rather than martial strength.

Confucius said: "The Superior Man has nothing to compete for. But if he must compete, he does it in an archery match, wherein he ascends to his position, bowing in deference. Descending, he drinks the ritual cup. This is the competition of the Superior Man."

Analects, 3:7

Relief showing archers competing in an archery contest. Han Dynasty. *Qilu Press*

Highly civilized—and indeed all his life Confucius seems to have admired the qualities of what we would now call "a good sportsman":

"When the Master went fishing, he did not use a net; when he hunted, he would not shoot at a perched bird."

Analects, 7:27

Among all these activities there was still plenty of time for reading, and the library of bamboo-slip books available to the students would have been much more extensive than the modest collection of volumes Confucius had devoured so eagerly at home. We can imagine him tucked away in the corner reading while the other boys hurried out to practise archery during their leisure time. This does not mean that he was lonely and isolated, but he would have avoided joining one of the gangs that inevitably form in the monastic environment of a boarding school, preferring to seek his friends among those who shared the same interests as himself:

Confucius said: "The 'true gentleman'… has friends, but doesn't belong to a clique."

Analects, 15:22

Confucius said: "If you are virtuous, you will not be lonely. You will always have friends."

Analects, 4:25

At school he formed a lasting friendship with the most unlikely person imaginable, a boy who was not only in the upper level but at the very top of that level in status: Nangong Jingshu. Nangong was the younger son of the other powerful feudal lord in Lu, Lord Meng, but seems to have attended Lord Ji's school with his brother at the same time as Confucius. Sima Qian in the *Records* says that when Confucius was only seventeen Nangong Jingshu and his elder brother Meng Yi "learned rites" from him. Since Confucius did not begin his teaching career until he was nearly thirty this is highly unlikely and seems to be just another example of Sima's mythical portrayal of him as a prodigy who was acknowledged as a sage almost from birth. It does indicate, however, that almost certainly all three boys were at school together at this age, and that they shared an interest in ritual.

The other young scions of the nobility would only have been interested in chariot-racing, archery, and martial arts, and no doubt paid scant attention to their other classes. When they finally attained positions of power they could simply ask a *shi* (like Confucius) to advise them about how to behave on ceremonial occasions, so they could afford to sleep through the ritual classes and save their energies for the chariot field where they could truly excel.

Confucius' new friend was different. Nangong Jingshu was genuinely interested in Zhou ritual, since he later arranged for the two of them to travel to the Zhou capital to study the subject at first hand. He remained a loyal friend to Confucius throughout their lives, and later on helped him to start his classes. Without Nangong Jingshu's help, Confucius almost certainly would have been unable to achieve what he did.

Confucius later gave this prescription for lasting friendship:

"Have no friends not equal to yourself."

Analects, 1:8

Since Nangong Jingshu, the son of a lord, was his lifelong friend, Confucius clearly did not mean social equality—"only make friends with people from your own class"—but equality of spirit and character, and it is one of his core beliefs that all human beings are born equal, and if some people can be called "superior" to others, this should derive from their behavior and not their social status.

Confucius said: "People are similar by nature, only by habituation do they become quite different from each other."

Analects, 17:2

Although, as a noble, Nangong Jingshu would have been required to spend lots of time galloping his chariot-and-four around the practice track, as soon as he had finished he would hurry back to the library to spend precious hours with his friend Kong Qiu. There they would discuss Zhou history, literature and music, debate the finer points of ceremonial ritual and proper behavior, and argue about the best way to govern a country.

All too soon their schooldays were over. Both boys would by now have been about seventeen years old. Nangong Jingshu departed to take up a responsible position in the administration of the Meng family's affairs, while it was now time for Confucius to honor his own family's pledge and start work at the bottom of the heap in the service of Lord Ji. Once again they were unequal, but Confucius would not have minded. They were still equal in spirit and always would be—for him that was what mattered—so he threw himself into preparing for his first lowly job, which was to be as a steward on the Ji family's large estate.

It was time for him to make his way in the world, but before he was able to start doing this heaven dealt him a cruel blow and for the first time in his life he knew the true meaning of sorrow: his beloved mother died young at the early age of thirty-two. After doing so much for him, Zhengzai was never to see any of his achievements; he would never be able to thank her by becoming a scholar or even a minister of state as he secretly dreamed of doing. He would never be able to make her proud of him and see the result of all her sacrifices.

Confucius had been forced to grow up very quickly, to "know himself":

"If a man has not yet fully experienced himself, he will when his parents die."

Analects, 19:17

He would mourn her, and then he would make her proud of him, if only from heaven.

In Memoriam: This beautiful bronze wine vessel from the Spring and Autumn Period has a very clear inscription dedicating it to a deceased young woman. Found in a tomb in Shandong Province not far from Confucius' home. Shandong Museum. *Photo: Jonathan Price*

~Three Quiet Years~

According to many sources Confucius' mother had found him a prospective wife from the Qi family just before she died. This is very likely; he was about to start work and it was time for him to set up his own household. Sima Qian records Yan Zhengzai's death as having taken place when Confucius was seventeen and since the mourning period was three years, he would not have been able to celebrate his own wedding during this time.

Many people of the day wanted to cut the mourning period down to one year, but Confucius never agreed, and often got into arguments with people about it:

Zai Wo asked about the three years' mourning for parents, saying that one year was long enough.

Confucius said, "If you were, after a year, to eat good rice, and wear embroidered clothes, would you feel at ease?"

"I should," replied Wo.

Confucius said, "If you can feel at ease, do it. But a superior man, during the whole period of mourning, does not enjoy pleasant food which he may eat, nor derive pleasure from music which he may hear."

Analects, 17:21

This exchange took place much later in Confucius' life, but he would certainly have felt the same when he was young, so when his mother died he would have scrupulously observed the full three-year mourning period, which means he would not have finally got married and started work until he was about twenty, and this tallies with the accepted chronology of significant events in Confucius' life.

Some later biographers implied that the young Confucius was severely criticized for giving his mother a full funeral according to the ancient Zhou rites. While this is not certain, he certainly went into mourning as if the head of his family had died and not simply his mother; this in itself was a defiance of convention. Although many have taken his mother's grandiose funeral as further evidence of Confucius' "excessive conservatism," in fact it was the exact opposite. By giving his mother an official funeral appropriate to the head of a family, Confucius was demonstrating to the world that he considered her to be the most important person in his life, who had taken the place of the father who had in fact given him nothing except his name.

Sadly, Zhengzai's funeral was to be the last honor ever paid to her. In the patriarchal and male-dominated society of China at this time, the idea of a single mother who bravely brought up her clever son by herself, effectively giving him to the world, simply did not fit. Everything, including genius, had to be transmitted

The 'Pavilion of Joy' in the Confucius Temple complex, Qufu, close to the site of Confucius' original home.

Honouring the dead: objects found in tombs from the time of Confucius.
Above right: Red-painted '*hu*' pottery vessel (Spring and Autumn Period).
Photo: Jonathan Price
Above left and below right: Decorated pottery '*ding*' tripod vessel (Spring and
Autumn Period). Capital Museum Beijing. *Photo: Jonathan Price*
Below left: Painted pottery '*dou*' stemmed vessel (Spring and Autumn Period).
Capital Museum Beijing. *Photo: Jonathan Price*

Performance on reproduction of ancient "*Se*" zither.
Huaxia Ancient Music Ensemble, Henan Museum.
Photo: Jonathan Price

down the male line. Confucius himself later stated that he had not been "born wise"; everything he had attained was achieved through study, and it had been his mother who had given him the opportunity to do this.

Confucius said: "I was not born with wisdom. I love the ancient teachings and have worked hard to attain to their level."

Analects, 7:20

When his life story came to be written down after his death, however, his mother's important—in fact crucial—role in his life was ignored. His "sagehood" was either attributed to some sort of divine visitation, or the importance of the Kong family was magnified so that it appeared that the "sage genes" (which included "royal blood") had passed down to Confucius through his father. Either way, Zhengzai's only role in this official version of Confucius' life was simply to give birth to him.

Even today biographers often trot out the received version as if it were fact, and Zhengzai has never been accorded the honor to which she is due. It is easy to see why his near contemporaries would have found the story of Confucius' early life so unconventional that a

more sanitized version would have been preferred. In our own day, however, there is no longer any excuse, and we should start admiring her, not ignoring her.

Her son at least honored her, performing the rites at her graveside himself according to the ancient rituals of the Zhou, but she now lies forgotten beneath some unknown grassy mound, while only a short distance away the carved roofs of great temples and mansions rise into the sky, all resounding to the glory of the name of Kong. Many accounts describe Confucius as going into "total seclusion" during the three-year mourning period for his mother. In view of his later comments about the importance of honoring deceased parents, this must certainly have been the case. He would have spent these years of seclusion back in the Yan family home where he grew up, as his schooldays now were over. After the mourning period was complete he knew he had to start life in earnest; his marriage had already been arranged and a job had been found for him in the

Carved roof of Stele Pavilion – Confucius Temple complex, Qufu. *Qilu Press*

household of Lord Ji, where he would use his training to perform his duties as a steward.

Meanwhile these three years were a golden opportunity for Confucius to devote all his time to what he liked doing best of all—studying.

Confucius said: "In a hamlet of ten families there must be someone as loyal and trustworthy as I. But I doubt there will be someone as fond of study."

Analects, 5:28

This period was in a way Confucius' own "three years at university." Tertiary education did not exist at this time, so it was a rare privilege to be able to follow several years of general schooling with a further three years of specialized study, even though his university professor had to be himself. The fact that he was forced to teach himself was perhaps the biggest bonus of all, because he had to invent his own methods of learning and these became the basis for his own unique teaching methods later in his life. As he taught himself during those three quiet years, so later he taught others.

Luckily he had none of the distractions students usually have to put up with. As we have seen, it was forbidden for a mourning son to attend feasts, listen to musical performances, wear "embroidered clothes," or even to eat

Unmarked grave: A burial mound from the Warring States Period in the 'Confucius Forest' Qufu. *Photo: Jonathan Price*

any richly prepared food. Nevertheless, this monastic kind of existence was exactly what Confucius desired, and his years of study were the last gift his beloved mother gave to him, although in a very sad kind of way.

We can imagine him dressed in a simple robe, sitting by the window or in the shade of an apricot tree and making notations in his bamboo-scroll books for hour after hour, pausing only for simple and frugal meals with the rest of the Yan family, who were also mourning the passing of a beloved daughter and sister. Far from feeling deprived by this enforced monasticism, and the simple fare he had to eat, Confucius relished this simple scholarly life. Later in his life he expressed his admiration for his favorite student, Yan Hui, who had similar habits:

Confucius said: "Hui was indeed a worthy! With a single bamboo bowl of rice and gourd-cup of water he lived in a back alley. Others could not have endured his misery, but Hui never changed from his happy disposition... he loved to study!"

Analects, 6:11/6:3

So too did Confucius love to study, and this enthusiasm kept him going for the three long years he was closeted at home with his books:

Confucius said: "Knowing it is not as good as loving it; loving it is not as good as delighting in it."

Analects, 6:20

Three years may have seemed like a long time at first, but Confucius soon began to realize that really it was not long enough—there was so much to learn and so little time to learn it. However, at least he understood that the crucial first step was to acknowledge honestly the current limits of one's own knowledge:

Confucius said: "Shall I teach you about knowledge? What you know, you know, what you don't know, you don't know. This is knowledge."

Analects, 2:17

He also knew that if he was to achieve anything, he was going to have to select carefully which areas of study to concentrate upon, and look at them in depth, not just charge indiscriminately into his pile of books:

Confucius said: "... not thoroughly discussing what has been learned, not using new knowledge for self-improvement... this makes me uneasy."

Analects 7:3

Any student will know exactly what he meant by this. There simply is not enough time to read *everything*, and by the end of the mourning period, Confucius definitely

felt that that he had used his time well and achieved something. Later in life he made this comment to his students, significantly using the words "three years":

Confucius said: "It is quite rare to see someone who applies himself to the study of something for three years without improving his prospects and salary."

Analects 8:12

So what was this "something" he had studied for those three years, and which proved to have had such a "noticeable result"? Almost certainly, he would have meant above all the *Book of Songs*. He considered this to be the basis of all knowledge and later used it as the foundation for his teaching, but he would also have spent some time studying the *Book of History*, and also the *Book of Rites*—which is often called the *Book of Propriety*. "Propriety" in Confucius' day meant the application of the traditional Zhou ritual and custom to everyday life and government—so in discussing this with his later students he would have been interpreting the original book's relevance rather than simply making them "learn the rules."

Although the *Book of Rites* was a compendium of the ancient rituals and customs, many of these had changed by Confucius' time. The only real way to study modern thinking about rituals was to make a pilgrimage to Luoyang, the ancient Zhou capital, but for Confucius this would have been only a distant dream at this early stage in his life. In any case he was not allowed to travel or even stray very far from his house while he was in mourning, so even research trips to temples were out of the question and a proper study of ritual would have to wait. In the meantime, he could certainly concentrate on the *Songs* and the *History*, since copies of both these books would have been in the possession of the scholarly Yan family.

Confucius had been familiar with the *Book of Songs* since childhood, and must have still known many of the nursery-rhyme songs by heart—"On the trees rings the axe ding-ding, with the birds crying out ying-ying!" or "Hoo, hoo, cry the deer, nibbling the wild garlic of the

Above: Heir of Confucius: the famous scholar Zhang Jian studying hard for the Imperial Civil Service Examinations during the Qing Dynasty. The importance of studying is a Confucian principle which has survived in China for thousands of years. Tableau in Shanghai Jiading Museum. *Photo: Jonathan Price*

Left: Part of a 4th century B.C. manuscript of a philosophical work from the Shanghai Museum Bamboo Slip collection. *Photo courtesy Shanghai Museum*

fields. I have a lucky guest!" Indeed the whole work opens with a famous example of this style of poem, actually the charming love song of a young man pining for his faraway maiden:

> Guan-guan go the ospreys,
> On the islet in the river …
> Waking and sleeping, he sought her
> That modest, retiring, and virtuous young lady:
> He sought her and found her not,
> And waking and sleeping he thought about her.
>
> *Book of Songs*, 1. Guan Sui

Seductive as it must have been simply to study the work as literature and just enjoy it, Confucius knew that it was now time to research the work in real depth, and look for the lessons and meanings which underlay the undeniably beautiful flow of the language in all of the poems. Many of the Odes are overtly political, calling upon the Zhou rulers, who had become corrupt and self-seeking, to return to the ways of their dynasty's "golden age" and once again govern justly and for the good of all the people. These poems are the foundation for all of Confucius' later political ideas, and so it is the political odes that he must have found particularly interesting. What he had to do was start what he called "sifting" the material, ignoring all the love poems and nursery rhymes, and start concentrating on the more serious poetry… but how exactly was he going to do this? He later told his own students that memorizing whole texts was a waste of time—the important thing was to cut to the heart of a topic, then everything else falls into place:

Confucius said, "Si, do you think that I am a person who studies widely and memorizes all of it?"

Si (Zigong) replied, "It seems that way. But perhaps not?"

Confucius said, "The answer is no. I penetrate to the single idea which expresses the whole."

Analects, 15:3

Confucius' idea of study was: first read the text, and then

analyze it from every possible angle, after clearing your mind of all preconceptions:

Confucius said: "Do I possess knowledge? No, I do not possess it … I clear my mind completely and thoroughly investigate a matter from one end to the other."

Analects, 9:8

What he found when he penetrated to the heart of the texts of the *Book of Songs* was a critique of government in an age of corruption and chaos, which he recognized as very similar to the situation in his own day. He could see that none of the rulers had ever listened to the poets, and this gave birth to his own ideas, which were to a large extent identical to those found in the *Book of Songs*, but with the crucial difference that he was to urge that these ideas should actually be put into practice. He never claimed to be an original thinker ("I am a transmitter not a maker"); on the contrary what was truly original about his philosophy was his insistence on *doing* not *saying*. This has made Confucius' ideas very uncomfortable for most people, right up until our own day, and is one of the main reasons why they have been so distorted. Most people are far happier talking about something than actually doing it, and for this reason he kept saying to his students, to the rulers of his own day, in fact to anybody who would listen, that it was no good spouting lofty humanitarian ideals, or even writing poems about them, if nobody ever acts upon your words:

"Speech must translate into appropriate actions."

Analects, 13:3

At this early period of his life, still a teenager, he would probably have been somewhat naïve and idealistic, quite sure he could change the world—for after all are we all not like this at the same age? Indeed he once said, with truly astonishing naivety:

"If any of the rulers were to employ me, I would have control of the situation within twelve months, and would have everything straightened out within three years."

Analects, 13:10

He eventually got his wish many years later and was indeed employed by the rulers of Lu—for a little longer than three years in fact—but he signally failed to get anything straightened out. At this age, however, during the years of quiet study when he believed anything was possible, Confucius still had the burning idealism that most of us lose as we grow older:

Confucius said: "We should be in awe of the younger generation. How can we know that they will not be equal to us?"

Analects, 9:23

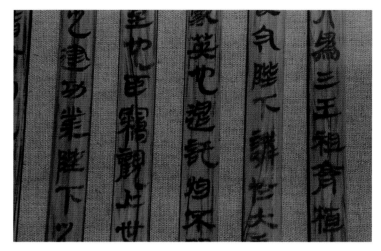

Bamboo Manuscript of the *Book of History*. Replica in Shanghai Jiading Museum. *Photo: Jonathan Price*

Later in his life he became, like all of us, a little more cynical and wary:

Confucius said: "At first I used to listen to what people said and expected them to act accordingly. Now I listen to what people say and watch what they do."

Analects, 5:10

While still an idealistic teenager, however, he discovered with the force of a revelation that the *Book of Songs* was in fact a recipe for good government and the way we should live our lives, and if only its principles could be acted upon he fervently believed the world would return to its golden days. A constant refrain in the *Book of Songs* is a longing to return to the order and prosperity which the people enjoyed under the first kings of the house of Zhou:

Ah me! I awake and sigh,
Thinking of that capital of Zhou.
Beautifully grew the fields of young millet,
Enriched by fertilizing rains.

Book of Songs, 153, Xia Quan

Confucius was to take up this refrain himself, both in his teaching and in his many attempts to get the leaders of his time to model themselves on the Zhou monarchs, who in his opinion did not rule tyrannically but almost let society "run itself":

Confucius said: "How sublime was the manner in which old Zhou rulers handled the empire, almost without taking part in its administration!"

Analects, 8:18

This "golden age" was contrasted by the poets of the *Book of Songs* with the misery of their own day:

Heaven is continually redoubling its afflictions;
Deaths and disorder increase and multiply;

Cracking the meaning of traditional poems: These 4th Century B.C. bamboo slips from the Shanghai Museum collection form part of an anthology of folk songs which were included in the *Yue Jing* (Book of Music). Confucius attached great importance to the study of both poetry and music. *Photo courtesy Shanghai Museum*

And yet our Grand Master does not correct nor bemoan himself!
It is not right he should reduce us all to such misery!

> *Book of Songs*, 191, Jie Nan Shan
> Ode written for King of the Zhou urging him to correct his ways

The same idea, that rulers should "correct" their behavior recurs again and again in Confucius' own sayings.

Confucius said: "If a minister can correct himself, what problem will he have in governing? If he can't correct himself, how can he correct others?"

> *Analects*, 13:13

Even some of Confucius' more specific ideas, such as his belief that governments should reduce punishments and concentrate instead on ruling by example, are foreshadowed in some of the poems in the *Book of Songs*.

Let the criminals alone—
They have suffered for their offenses;
All ye officers,
Let each of you reverently attend to his duties.

> *Book of Songs*, 194, ??? Yu Wu Zheng

Confucius reproduced almost exactly the same thought when advising one of the dukes of his own "warring states" many years later:

Confucius said: "First organize your administration; then grant pardon to all the petty offenses and then put virtuous and able men into positions of responsibility."

> *Analects*, 13:13

He took this idea even further, however, saying that strict law and order policies actually do no good in the long run, because the criminals will simply act out of a desire to avoid being caught rather than correcting their behavior:

Confucius said: "If you govern the people legalistically and control them by punishment, they will avoid crime, but have no personal sense of shame. If you govern them by means of your own good example, they will gain their own sense of shame, and thus correct themselves."

> *Analects*, 2:3

Whether this would actually work in practice, and criminals be shamed into good behavior, is another question, but it can be seen that Confucius was not simply copying the political advice he found in the *Book of Songs* into his own philosophy of government, instead he was using the poems as a basis to develop his own ideas, so that when he claimed to be merely a "transmitter not a maker" this was not strictly true. Nevertheless the poems were clearly the seeds which allowed his own thoughts to flower, and he continued to use them when he started teaching, taking a passage from the *Book of Songs* as the jumping-off point for discussions with his students on a whole range of topics.

All too soon this blissful period of quiet and uninterrupted study drew to a close. When his twentieth birthday arrived, he knew that the three-year mourning period would soon be officially over, and he would have to start making his way in the world. That meant getting married and moving into a new house, which would be provided by the Ji family near his place of work. And of course very soon he would have to start his first job—as a steward not a scholar. From now on, he would not have so much time for books.

The Wedding Feast

At last, and probably rather reluctantly, Confucius came out of mourning, putting aside his books and facing the realities of life.

First up was his wedding, and the scholarly quiet of the Yan household was now replaced by a noisy clattering and banging from morning till night as pots were cleaned, dishes prepared, trees felled to provide fuel for the open-air barbeques, and the house swept from top to bottom. Everybody loves a wedding—except perhaps in this case the bridegroom, who probably stayed in his room with a book while the servant girls shrieked and giggled and swept the floor around him. According to tradition, Confucius would probably have met his bride-to-be only once before the wedding (if at all) and in the event he only stayed with her for four years. Clearly this was an arranged marriage, as was the universal custom at the time:

In taking a wife, how do you proceed?
Without a go-between it cannot be done.

Book of Songs, 158, FA KE

Also from the *Book of Songs* we have a wonderful description of the preparations for a feast:

Xu-xu they go, as they fell the trees.
I have strained off my spirits, till they are fine,
And the fatted lambs are provided …
Oh! Brightly I have sprinkled and swept my courtyard,
And arranged my viands, with eight dishes of grain, along with my fatted meat,
I have strained off my spirits in abundance, the dishes stand in rows …

Book of Songs, 16, FA MU

At last the big day arrived, and the Yans' courtyard was filled with a noisy crowd of friends and relatives of both families, all seated at long tables and chattering noisily while servants hurried around refilling their drinking cups. The drink served at ceremonial feasts at this time was a strong spirit which is described in the *Book of Songs* as being clear (like its modern descendant which is still popular in China) and was made from

Preparations for the feast: Above left: Painted pottery food container (Spring and Autumn Period) – Capital Museum Beijing.
Above right: Bronze wine jar (Warring States Period) - Shandong Museum. *Photos: Jonathan Price*
Left: Girl with Lute.

"Jolly guests at the wedding". Han Dynasty pottery figurines, Capital Museum Beijing. *Photo: Jonathan Price*

Above: Bronze food container with 'elephant-trunk' handles. Below: Decorated bronze vessel with ornate handles also in the shape of elephants" trunks and inscription in ancient Chinese characters. The vessel is dedicated on the inscription to a woman named 'Lu' and is thought to have originally been a wedding gift. Shandong Museum. *Photos: Jonathan Price*

distilled black millet and flavoured with herbs.

The feasting would have followed the wedding ceremony, which would have been conducted in the Yan family temple. The traditional Chinese marriage, then as now, was as much a uniting of two families as the joining of two people, and Confucius' bride would have had to bow down before the spirits of her husband's ancestors during the temple ceremony. This would have presented a slight problem as Confucius' paternal family, the Kongs, were obviously not present—there had been no contact with them for eighteen years—and neither was his mother who had died three years earlier. As a result his stand-in father (if he was still alive) would have been grandfather—his mother's father—who would have been about sixty years old at this time. The men whom Confucius later referred to as his "elder brothers"—who were expected to play a leading role at his wedding— would have been the sons of his mother's older brothers, and in fact his cousins.

As a result the whole wedding ceremony must have seemed slightly artificial to Confucius, and he probably felt he was only going through with it because that was what was expected of him. He owed his mother's family, the Yans, for taking him in and bringing him up. If they had now found him a suitable bride, well so be it. Thus, as the smoke from the sacrifices wafted to the roof, his mother's father, representative of "the ancestors," recited the ceremonial words to unite them for ever:

"We confer on you great blessings," says the
representative of the dead,
"And may your descendants also be happy!"
Book of Songs, 220, Bin Zhi Chu Yan

For better or for worse (and it appears to have been for the worse) the knot had now been tied, and so now it was on to the feasting:

The stools are given, and there are plenty of servants.
The guests are pledged, and they pledge the host in return;
He rinses the cup, and the guests put theirs down.
Sauces and pickles are brought in,
With roast meat and broiled.
Excellent provisions there are also of tripe and cheek;
With singing to lutes, and with drums.

Book of Songs, 246, Xing Wei

Then there were fine speeches. One after another the more important guests rose unsteadily to their feet (for by now everybody had partaken of a little too much of the herb-flavoured spirits) and proposed a toast to the "happy couple":

May you enjoy myriads of years!
May your bright happiness ever be increased!

Below: Confucius meets the infamous concubine Nanzi in Wei while his disciple Zilu (left) looks on with disapproval. Ming Dynasty Painting. *Qilu Press*

Right: **"Happy wedding guest"** - Han Dynasty pottery figurine, Shanghai Museum. *Photo: Jonathan Price*

You have made us drink to the full of your spirits
…
There is given you a noble wife,
And from her shall come the line of descendants.

Book of Songs, 247, Ji Jui

Confucius would have received all these good wishes with his usual smiling politeness, but inside he must have been full of foreboding. We do not know why his marriage broke up so quickly, or even if it really did—many biographers have claimed that he divorced her after four years but there is no evidence for this in the form of records. Although divorce was possible in Confucius' day it is more likely that they simply chose to live apart. The main reason for thinking this is the case is that there is absolutely no mention of Confucius' wife in any of the contemporary records after the birth of their second child, and he appears from the *Analects* to have seen his son only rarely and with no affection. We know that Confucius certainly was never a widower. Had his wife died he would have had to go into mourning, as he had done for his mother, and there is no evidence of this either; she simply drops out of sight as if she no longer existed for him, so certainly this was no love match. A

marriage which lasts only four years is even today a little unusual; in 530 BC it must have been something of a record.

Loveless though his marriage turned out to be, the idea of romantic love did exist at this time, and there are many beautiful love poems in the *Book of Songs*, Confucius' favorite book. However, the more passionate odes in the *Book of Songs* often describe a "meeting by chance" (as opposed to an arranged marriage which was the universal custom) and the poets must therefore be talking about illicit (and probably extra-marital) love affairs:

> On the moor is the creeping grass,
> And how heavily is it loaded with dew!
> There was a beautiful man,
> Lovely, with clear eyes and fine forehead!
> We met together accidentally,
> And so my desire was satisfied.

Book of Songs, 94, Ye You Man Cao

Confucius in love? All the existing records come up a complete blank on this. The only mention of his having had any kind of relationship with a woman apart from his wife is an incident which appears in both the *Analects* and the *Records of the Grand Historian*. This is the story of Confucius' visit to the house of the number three wife of the Duke of Wei, Nanzi, who was a notorious libertine and was reputed to have slept with all the prominent members of her husband's court. Whether she fancied adding a sage to her list and summoned him, or whether Confucius visited her of his own accord we do not know, since the two accounts differ, although they both agree on the fact that he visited the temptress behind closed doors. Sima Qian as usual is trying to present his hero in the best possible light so maintains that Confucius was "obliged" to pay a call on the Duke's wife and nothing untoward occurred:

> He wished to refuse, but he was not successful, and was obliged to visit her. The lady sat behind a curtain. Confucius entered the door and bowed in the direction of the North. The lady returned the salutation twice behind the curtain, and as she did so her jade ornaments gave forth a clear sound.
>
> Confucius said afterwards: "I really did not wish to see her. I have seen her, and she returned my greeting with proper decorum."
>
> His disciple Zilu was displeased. Then Confucius implored him: "Whatever I have done wrong, Heaven forced me to do, Heaven forced me to do!"

Sima Qian, *Records of the Grand Historian*

The other version is almost identical in wording, so Sima Qian must have been using the same original source material. In the *Analects*, however, instead of claiming he was forced to visit the sex-goddess of Wei, Confucius implies that his own conscience is clear; whatever people might have thought had happened (or hadn't happened) behind those closed doors wasn't their business anyway:

> **The Master visited Nan Zi and Zilu was displeased. The Master dealt with this, saying: "If I have done wrong, let Heaven reject me! Let Heaven reject me!"**

Analects, 6:28

His student Zilu often acted as his Master's conscience like this, usually when Confucius intended to do something which would make it appear as if he was compromising his principles. Since Confucius never made any sort of statement about sexual morality he is clearly telling Zilu that this is not something for him to judge but is between himself and heaven.

Did he or didn't he? From the original Chinese text it seems that he didn't but it looked as if he had (Zilu's point). Needless to say, the later Confucians glossed over all this and accepted Sima Qian's clearly bowdlerized version as gospel; indeed the whole story of his failed marriage was fudged so that Kong-Fu-Zi could appear not only as a divine sage but a strictly conventional husband and therefore an example to us all. Although the idea of Confucius as a mythical sage and sexist paterfamilias is still widely accepted, I think I prefer the real human being.

Why he never talked about "love" except in the sense of a generalized love for humanity nobody has ever been able to explain, and in fact his immediate successors— his surviving students and those they themselves taught—recognized this gap and attempted unsuccessfully to fit the idea of human love into the general framework of their Master's thought. On the bamboo-slip manuscripts of writings by Confucius' followers which were discovered in the Guodian tomb, the character-element "*xin*"—a pictographic image of the human heart—appears many times incorporated into other word-characters thus modifying the meaning to apply to human as well as humanitarian love. In the *Analects* or other recorded sayings of Confucius, this character element does not appear at all.

Perhaps it was simply because he was "unlucky in love" as much as he was certainly unlucky in marriage. Since even in China today many marriages are effectively arranged by parents, with the couple themselves holding to the belief that they will "fall in love" after they are married, it is unlikely that things were any different two and a half thousand years ago. Confucius and his wife simply failed to get on in any way except perhaps in bed (they produced two children, a boy and a girl) and in this they were little different from countless married couples before or since.

Accordingly readers of the *Analects* will look in vain for any recipe for true love or a happy marriage; he makes no mention of either topic. Indeed it will come as a surprise to many people that he never spoke about marriage at all as such; his comments about family life were exclusively about the relationship between parents and children and he certainly never said anything about the "duties of a wife." Most people still seem to think (wrongly) that he decreed that "wives should obey their husbands"—this is a misunderstanding based on the writings of later Confucians and originated with Mencius, who was the first to take it upon himself to put words into his Master's mouth which he had never actually uttered:

When you go to your husband's house, you must respect him and be careful not to be disagreeable. To be properly obedient is the way of wives and concubines.

Book of Mencius, Book 3, Part 2, Chapter 2

Confucius may well have thought this too, since this was the prevalent belief at his time, but on the other hand he may not, and he certainly never used the word "obedient" in this context. As a result of Mencius' reinterpretation of

Careers for girls: There were a large number of female musicians and dancers in Confucius' time, but this occupation was not open to members of the *Shi* class to which he belonged. Girl Musician playing pipe (Han Dynasty pottery figurine). Capital Museum Beijing. *Photo: Jonathan Price*

Confucius, which was taken up enthusiastically by those who followed him, by far the biggest misconception about Confucius is that he actively supported the suppression of women's rights. Even today many people seem to think that one of the 492 *Analects* reads: "A woman's place is in the kitchen."

Not so—once again he may well have thought this and probably did, but then so did everybody else living at his time and for thousands of years afterwards not only in China but all over the world. In fact he never discussed this question at all: there is only one authenticated saying of Confucius in which he refers to the relationship between men and women. It is from a misreading of this passage that the whole idea of the male chauvinist Confucian seems to have arisen, but in this remark he was clearly referring to servant girls or "dancing girls," that is females who were by definition inferiors by virtue of their employment and not women in general:

Confucius said: "Of all people, girls and servants (*literally 'inferior men'*) are the most difficult to handle. If you are familiar with them, they lose their humility. If you maintain a reserve towards them, they are discontented."

Analects, 17:25

The "girls" he talks about here cannot mean a man's wife or even his "girl-friend" (Mencius said "concubines" should also be "properly obedient") because a man is obviously "familiar" in these relationships—so this is clearly about servants, most probably the beautiful girls who served as dancers and musicians at the courts of the dukes and nobles. They are referred to several times in the *Analects*, and their status was similar to that of servants, though of a superior kind, so they would naturally be quite "difficult to handle"—if you showed them too much familiarity they would start behaving like prima-donnas; if you ignored them and just gave them orders they would not give of their best.

The argument about the exact interpretation of this passage has raged for centuries, but many modern Chinese scholars have pointed out that in the original manuscripts of the *Analects* the word translated above as "girls" is accompanied by the "erotic" sub-character and therefore cannot refer to women in general and certainly not to a wife.

It is possible to argue that his comment was mildly sexist but that is all. We have to remember that he said this around 500 BC, and it is quite possible to imagine a restaurant manager of today making a similar remark about waitresses. Yet it is this relatively innocuous remark about "management"—one of many that he made—that led to the whole corpus of misogynistic "Confucianism" compiled by his later "followers." Like the face of Helen of Troy, this is the *Analect* that launched a million words.

The reason why he never talked about the status of women in general and referred to his ideal person as a "superior *man*" was simply because this was how society worked at his time. Women had no decision-making power, either within the family or in society as a whole. Ode 169 in the *Book of Songs* summarizes very succinctly

A woman's role – in the temple: this painting on white silk from the Warring States Period – very close to Confucius' own time - shows a female priestess conjuring spirits: in front of her is a dragon and above her head a rising phoenix. This is the earliest Chinese painting ever discovered, and was found in a tomb near Changsha, Hunan Province – formerly part of the ancient State of Chu. *Qilu Press*

the whole attitude of the male-dominated society at this time towards women, which continued for well over 2,000 years, but it is clear that this was not a uniquely Chinese attitude and the same thing applied in Europe until very recent times:

Sons shall be born to him: they will be put to sleep
on couches;
They will be clothed in robes, they will have
sceptres to play with;
Their cry will be loud.
They will be hereafter resplendent with red knee-
covers,
The future princes of the land.

Book of Songs, 189, Si Gan

This poem uses colorful images to convey the idea of the privileged existence of boy children, who of course played with sceptres and not dolls. They were allowed to be "loud" ("boys will be boys") while girls were expected to be quiet and demure. It is only in extremely recent times that this gender-typing in childhood has been criticized, and even today this vivid poem strikes a chord—boys still play with toy guns and little girls with Barbie Dolls except in the most "advanced" families.

Daughters shall be born to him:
They will be put to sleep on the ground;

They will have tiles to play with,
It will be theirs neither to do wrong nor to do
good.
Only about the spirits and the food will they have
to think,
And to cause no sorrow to their parents.

Book of Songs, 189, Si Gan

Little girls in other words play with "tiles" to build "dolls' houses," but the most significant passage is: "It will be theirs neither to do wrong nor to do good." This refers to the women the small girls would become: they would not be able to make any moral decisions about right or wrong because they were forbidden from making any decisions at all—everything was decided on their behalf by men.

The ode ends up by saying: "Only about the spirits and the food will they have to think …" which is certainly another way of saying "a woman's place is in the kitchen" (or in a temple to commune with the "spirits"—women could be "earth-mothers" as well as housewives but that was about it). There were of course many highly accomplished female musicians at this period, but as already pointed out they were technically speaking servants and were simply told what to play— all the music-masters were men. Nobody is denying that women were considered subservient to men during Confucius' time, nor that he himself probably thought the same; but this did not form part of his philosophy, which is all about making the right choices. It was considered a waste of time to give moral instruction to girls since they could not choose for themselves how to behave, and Confucius was simply following the conventions of his day by confining his tuition to boys and men.

Today the world is very different. We now have women running schools, businesses, and even countries, activities which certainly involve decision-making and moral choices, so it obviously makes sense nowadays to apply Confucius' ideas equally to men and women, even though he himself used the term *junzi*, which is a male compound noun, to describe his ideal person.

This is not an original term—the word is used many times in the *Book of Songs* and literally means the "king's son" or the "ideal prince." Confucius, however, was obviously not giving advice exclusively to the sons of princes, so he must have been using the term *junzi*

"The Wedding Night"
Bronze figurines known as 'The Lovers' on the lid of a Western Zhou Period vessel. Shandong Museum.
Photo: Jonathan Price

metaphorically, in the sense that we can all be "princes" if we behave in a princely way, and nowadays princesses too.

Junzi was first translated as "gentleman," and although this gives some sense of Confucius' meaning—the "true gentleman" as opposed to somebody who simply calls himself one—the word has a class connotation which he definitely did not intend since his classes were open to everybody. Nowadays *junzi* is usually rendered as "superior man," but that brings us back to the "men only" situation of Confucius' own day—why can't we have "superior women" as well?

If we therefore translate *junzi* as "superior person," the whole of Confucius' philosophy applies immediately to anybody of either sex without any difficulty whatsoever, and there is nothing in anything he said to prevent our doing this. Surely, he would approve? Although he can hardly be represented as a proto-feminist, neither was he a chauvinist despite all that has been said or written about him, if anything he was simply a "*person*-ist." After all, as will be remembered, he never played with toy swords as a child, but ritual utensils, which is something

Dancer (pottery figurine – Han Dynasty). Henan Museum.
Photo: Jonathan Price

for which his mother's family, who encouraged him in this, would be applauded in our own enlightened times.

For the moment, however, it is back to the fifth century BC, when gender issues were a thing of the future. As Confucius and his bride looked at each other across the tables at the wedding feast, they must have both have been wondering what they were getting themselves into. If indeed they only stayed with each other for four years, they obviously had nothing whatsoever in common from the first, and the bride was probably wondering how she had ended up with this swarthy young man who always seemed to have a half-smile on his face, as if life were some kind of great joke that she did not understand. If it was true that Confucius was "nine-and-a-half feet tall," as Sima Qian claimed, she was probably wondering how she was going to survive the wedding night apart from anything else, but this is obviously one of the Grand Historian's quirky little details that he invented himself.

For his part, Confucius was probably wondering what he and his wife were going to say to each other for the next fifty years, if they were both lucky enough to live that long. Since Confucius was brought up in a cultured family, it is very likely that his wife's family the Qis, although from the same *shi* class, were what we would now call "loud-mouthed and vulgar," and his wife's lack of refinement began to grate on him very quickly.

Perhaps even now, as the wedding feast grew more uproarious, the bride's relatives were already well into their cups and disgracing themselves:

When the guests have drunk too much,
They shout out and brawl.
They disorder the dishes;
They keep dancing in a fantastic manner …
With their caps on one side, and like to fall off,
They keep dancing they will not stop.
Book of Songs, 220, Bin Zhi Chu Yan

This is what Confucius later said about people without culture or refinement:

"What can be done with people who stuff their faces with food all day, without exercising their minds? They could at least play [board] games or chess. It would be better than nothing."
Analects, 17:22

What indeed, Confucius must have thought morosely as he sipped from his cup of millet-spirit, was he letting himself in for?

Taking Care of Business

As soon as the wedding feast was over, perhaps even before the tables had been cleared away and the courtyard swept, it would have been time for Confucius and his wife to travel to their new home on the estate of the Ji family.

His first job was to be as "Steward in Charge of Grain" and he would certainly have been provided with a house close to his work—somewhere near Lord Ji's grain warehouse. Perhaps the couple had already started seeing less than eye-to-eye on many things. Their new house, with a view across muddy fields and with a pig-pen attached on one side, would hardly have been the dream house which Confucius' young wife had nurtured in her imagination since girlhood. Confucius himself, with his usual cheerful acceptance of whatever life chose to throw at him, would have opined that it is good neighbors, not a good view, which is the more important thing:

Confucius said: "As for a neighborhood, it is its humaneness that makes it beautiful. If you choose to live in a place that lacks humaneness, how can you grow in wisdom?"

Analects, 4:1

This cheerfulness would have infuriated his wife even more, although there was nothing she could do about it; she had to stand by her man. This was not, as explained

Pottery model of house from Han Dynasty. The houses in Confucius' time – a little earlier – would have been very similar. *Qilu Press*

Confucius in charge of Lord Ji's grain warehouse.
Ming Dynasty Painting. *Qilu Press*

in the previous chapter, because her husband was a particularly extreme example of male chauvinist piggery, but simply because that was how things were at the time. In fact things are still like that in most of China—except in "advanced" cities like Shanghai and Guangzhou the woman normally follows the man wherever his job takes him. Like her descendants thousands of years later, all Confucius' wife could do was try and upset her husband's habitual bonhomie by clattering plates and making as much noise as she could while he was trying to read.

Confucius' job was probably less of a chore than trying to live in reasonable harmony with his wife. After his years at Lord Ji's school he was considered to be formally qualified in mathematics and writing, so he was now required to keep the grain records, recording the amount gathered each year, and keeping a tally of the baskets of grain which were stored in the warehouses. Most of the grain was not grown on Lord Ji's estate itself but was collected from local farmers as a form of tax—under the feudal system which operated at the time the farmers were obliged to donate a portion of each harvest to their feudal lord. After storage, the grain was distributed as payment in kind to all the officials who worked for Lord Ji, like Confucius himself, while some of it was retained for the Ji family's own use. Confucius' starting salary was a hundred bushels of grain a year, and he would then have had to "pay" his own employees out of his own grain allowance.

"Grain" at this time meant millet seeds, which were ground to flour and used to make bread and noodles, the staple diet in this part of China then as now. Thick noodles—or "pasta"—very similar to the dishes served today have been discovered almost perfectly preserved from Neolithic times, so by Confucius' day making noodles would have been one of the most common uses of millet grain. We incidentally have Confucius himself to thank for our detailed knowledge of the ancient Chinese diet—descriptions of food, crops, and farming practices abound in the *Book of Songs*, which Confucius is supposed to have edited for posterity:

In the ninth month, they prepare the vegetable
gardens for their stacks,
And in the tenth they convey the sheaves to them;
The millets, both the early sown and the late,
With other grain, the hemp, the pulse, and the
wheat.
"O my husbandmen,
Our harvest is all collected."

Book of Songs, 154, Qi Yue

Although grain was used for the payment-in-kind of salaries and also on occasion as barter, for many other sales and purchases money was used, so Confucius as an accountant and manager would certainly have handled cash. Chinese currency even at this period used a very advanced system which was not adopted in Western countries until the nineteenth century AD: token

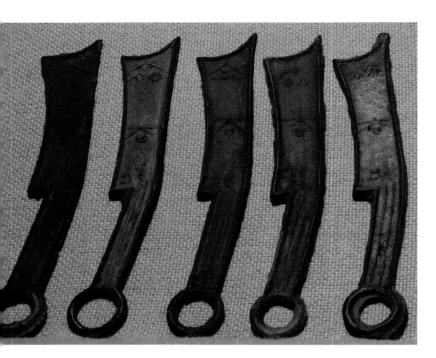

Ancient Chinese money from Spring and Autumn Period.
Above: Bronze 'Knife money'.
Below: Bronze coins in various denominations. Shandong
Museum. *Photos: Jonathan Price*

money. This means that the coins had little value in themselves but were simply symbols. All Ancient Greek and Roman money and indeed all Western coins until very recent times were actually worth their own weight in gold, silver, or bronze, and it was not until Western merchants first encountered paper money in China that the idea of token money became universally adopted.

Many coins from Confucius's day have survived, and the main denominations seem to have been the "knife" (*tao*) and the "wall" (*yuan*). The original ancient currency of China was in the form of "knife money"—small knives made of precious metal which were at first worth their own weight, like Western coinage from the same period. When the system of token coinage was adopted this was first in the form of "token knives" made of less valuable material, and then round bronze coins of different token value, for example with an engraved design of a single knife and the inscription *Yi Tao*—"one knife." A smaller-value coin bore the design of a city wall (*yuan*) and this name is still used for Chinese currency today.

With such a familiar accounting system in use even at this period it is easy to visualize the sort of work

Confucius was required to do, balancing columns of figures and double-checking the number of grain baskets stored in the warehouse. It can also be imagined that he must have found this sort of job tedious at times, and would have often dreamed of doing something more challenging and scholarly. For the moment, however, he was stuck with it, and he did not complain.

We have all met people doing a job they consider "beneath them," and who as a result make no effort to do it well, but Confucius' attitude to life was the exact opposite. Instead of feeling bitter and resentful and always feeling he was cut out for better things, he always treated every task as if it were the most important thing in the world, and urged everybody else to do the same:

"Go out of your home every day and behave to everybody as if you were receiving an important guest, employ your people as if you were assisting at a great ceremony. Try and live without stirring up resentments."

Analects, 12:2

Certainly work-wise he seems to have been a great success, and the Grand Historian records: "His accounts were clear and his measures were always correct."

So successful in fact that after a couple of years tediously accounting for sacks of grain and cheerfully "going out of his house every day" he was promoted and received a welcome increase in salary: he now got 150 bushels of grain a year. His new job was "Steward in Charge of Livestock." The "livestock" Confucius was to supervise did not include horses—the breeding of horses was an altogether grander thing—but only cattle, and he was now to be responsible for keeping records of all the animals, and supervising the breeding program.

The sturdy cattle in Confucius' herds would have been used only as draught animals, to pull plows or carts, or sometimes to be sacrificed in very grand ceremonies, for at this time neither milk nor beef were part of the Chinese diet. As an official, albeit a lowly one, Confucius would not have had to shovel out manure or feed the animals—all the stories which feature him doing this are complete misunderstandings of his position, which was as a "manager," similar to his previous position. Although not required to do any manual work, however, he probably had to "get his hands dirty" to a certain extent, helping to hold down a struggling bull while it was having its hoofs seen to for example or being present at the birth of the calves.

Later in his life, Confucius' various practical skills were hailed by his admirers as evidence of "divine sagehood", as if the gods had endowed him at birth with

Confucius in charge of livestock on Lord Ji's estate.
Ming Dynasty Painting. *Qilu Press*

a proficiency in accounting and the ability to mend his own fences.

> **A high minister asked Zigong: "May we not say your master is a sage? How various are his many abilities!"**

Analects, 9:6:1

His disciple Zigong, anticipating the later "deification" of his Master, claimed that he had been "endowed by heaven" with myriad abilities, but Confucius himself would have none of this—it always infuriated him when people treated him as some sort of divinity:

> **The Master, hearing about this, said, "What does the minister know about me? When I was young I was in a lowly position so I acquired many ordinary skills. Does a 'sage' need all sorts of abilities like this? No of course he doesn't!"**

Analects, 9:6:3

Although his mundane position as "livestock manager" still did not require him to use any of the other skills or subjects he had studied at school, such as literature or music, he seems once again to have cheerfully accepted his lot. The many paintings and descriptions of Confucius' life at this period all depict him as happily performing his lowly tasks to the best of his ability, and there is no reason to think this was not the case, since by all accounts he once more did a very

good job and Sima Qian writes in his *Records of the Grand Historian*: "His herds were plump and grew in number."

When he first started he would of course have known nothing whatsoever about efficient cattle-breeding, or any of the other myriad skills and techniques which he had to employ to achieve his goal, which was increasing and improving Lord Ji's herd. So instead of setting himself up as an omniscient boss who issues directives from on high, he knew that he had to learn—and quickly. What he did was ask the experts, the cowherds and stockmen who, although socially inferior to him, had long experience in their jobs. In Confucius' opinion the truly wise person—the really good manager—is always:

> **"… unashamed to ask questions to his inferiors."**

Analects, 5:15

So he would have asked his men what grain they recommended for fattening up the herd; how to treat the diseases to which cattle are prone; which animals should be used for breeding; and countless other questions before he himself, as the steward in charge, made the decisions.

This idea, that the power to succeed depends on knowledge, has been taken up by modern business-management gurus in America such as the late Peter Drucker, who has been called "the father of modern management." Drucker not only coined the phrase "knowledge is power" but said he got the idea from Confucius, and urged managers to read the *Analects*. Echoing many of Confucius' ideas, Drucker urged his audiences of

Farmers ploughing with oxen. Detail from Ming Dynasty Painting illustrating Confucius' life. *Qilu Press*

businessmen in countless lectures and presentations to heed the advice of the ancient "management expert." In Drucker's words: "My greatest strength as a consultant is to be ignorant and ask a few questions."

"He was unashamed to ask questions to his inferiors. Therefore he got the name 'Man of Wisdom.'"

Analects, 5:15

Peter Drucker: "Knowledge has to be improved, challenged, and increased constantly, or it vanishes."

"Study as if you have not reached your goal—as if you were afraid of losing what you have."

Analects, 8:17

Confucius himself, as he trudged across the stockyard on a cold winter's morning to take down the details of a newly-born calf, would have been very surprised if one of the gods had told him that his ideas on management would be finally hailed as the way-to-go, but not until another 2,500 years had passed. Then again, perhaps he would not have been so surprised; few people in his own time took any notice of his ideas about anything.

Sima Qian's sentence "his herds were plump" has been cited down the centuries as evidence of Confucius' sage-like ability to achieve success in any field as if by magic. This is nonsense—there was nothing magical about it at all, he was simply a *good manager*—and one aspect of good management which Confucius frequently stressed was the importance of employing specialists. The successful manager, Confucius said:

"… does not seek for all abilities in one man."

Analects, 18:10

According to Confucius the manager's job is to manage—to keep the enterprise moving in the right direction—and then leave the nuts and bolts of the job to a team of expert professionals who should work with as little supervision as possible. This is another aspect of

"Confucian Management Philosophy" which Peter Drucker and his followers stressed as particularly important for the running of an efficient modern company. Later in life Confucius himself often got extremely annoyed when people began calling him a "sage" and expected him to be an omniscient guru about absolutely everything, when his whole aim was to teach people how to learn things for themselves—and put this knowledge to the best use. A student called Fan Chi came to him one day and asked Confucius to teach him all about agriculture.

Confucius said, "Why don't you ask an old farmer? He would know more about it than me."
Fan Chi then said that he would like to learn about gardening.
Confucius said, "Why don't you ask an old gardener?" Fan Chi left.

Analects, 13:4

Confucius then shook his head and told his students: "That was an extremely stupid man."

Apart from the importance of employing specialists, Confucius had many other very good pieces of general advice for managers. He used the term *junzi*—or "ideal prince"—when speaking about administrators, but since the duty of a prince is to "manage" a state, the translation "superior manager" gives a very good idea of what he was talking about:

Confucius said: "The Superior Manager does not promote a man because of his words, and does not disregard the words because of the man."

Analects, 15:23

What he means here is that managers should be completely impartial and think only of the success of their enterprise. Accordingly they must not be susceptible to flattery or necessarily believe employees' assessments of themselves when considering them for promotion, but instead look at the results they have achieved. Conversely, a manager might dislike someone personally but they still might be high achievers with a lot to offer.

Of course a manager not only has to hire staff but sometimes fire them. Confucius maintained that this should be avoided if at all possible:

"The Superior Manager doesn't fire any high-level people unless there is a really good reason."

Analects, 18:10

Instead, he insisted, *train* them—use the human resources you have got, and run your department by encouragement not fear. What makes staff give of their best is the hope of promotion, not fear of getting laid off:

"… promote the able and teach those who are less able, and they will all work positively for you."

Analects, 2:20

It will come as a surprise to many people, especially those Chinese people brought up on the Thoughts of Chairman Mao, that Confucius actually hired and fired people as we do today, and it is probably even more surprising that he appeared to have delicate scruples about doing both. According to Mao—and this idea was repeated endlessly in newspapers and in speeches throughout the period of the Cultural Revolution of the 1960s and 70s—Confucius was an exploiter of slaves. If this had been the case, however, he would not have needed a comprehensive set of management principles to get maximum efficiency from his workers—all he would have needed was a whip. In fact slavery in China had been all but abolished by Confucius' time and had been replaced by the Zhou feudal system which operated by a complex arrangement of mutual obligation and certainly not by bondage or enslavement; there is no reference to slaves either in the *Analects* or even in the *Book of Songs*, which was written much earlier.

Confucius supervising the livestock breeding programme. Ming Dynasty Painting. *Qilu Press*

Confucius in management role while his farm workers toil happily. Ming Dynasty Painting. *Qilu Press*

This meant that a manager like Confucius could not *force* his staff to work hard any more than a manager of today—they were not his slaves and if discontented could look for other work. Of course many people would have been forced economically to stay in their jobs; this also applies today and is sometimes called "wage slavery," but it is not the same as real slavery. Many modern managers would doubtless be happy to be able to flog their staff into increased productivity but they are unable to do this, and neither was Confucius. Instead they would be wise to listen to his advice and become good managers themselves.

There are many other qualities which characterize a good manager according to Confucius, and a very important one is a willingness to admit mistakes and just get on with the job. Lousy managers will always try and hide their mistakes in order to maintain their position:

"The inferior person always glosses over his errors."

Analects, 19:8

Good managers should also be above office politics and immune to it:

Confucius said: "Superior managers are easy to serve but difficult to please. If you try to please

them by devious means, they will not be happy."

Analects, 13:25

"Devious means" would include for example the common "back-stabbing" technique of withholding crucial information just before a meeting so that rivals will make complete fools of themselves in front of the senior partner. Superior or "Confucian" managers see through this ploy immediately. They also have particular qualities of leadership which inspire their staff to give of their best not because they are ordered to do so but because their manager has confidence in their abilities.

"Superior managers are easy to work for, and in their employment of people, they give them work according to their ability. Inferior managers are difficult to work for, but easy to please. Even if you have used devious means to please them, they will still be happy. And in their employment of people, they try to squeeze everything out of them that they can."

Analects, 13:25

Thus ideal managers are "difficult to please" because they *expect* their team to achieve their goals. Their members of staff know that they can only expect praise if they surpass their goals, and so strive to achieve this. These "Confucian" managers are "easy to work for" because they just let their team members get on with their jobs without nagging them to work faster or piling more and more work upon them.

Above all, the Confucian manager leads by example, and sets very high standards which the employees themselves follow:

Confucius said: "If your own behavior is exemplary, things will go well without your giving orders. But if your own way of behaving isn't straightened out, even if you give orders, no one will follow them."

Analects, 13:6

When facing a deadline, the Confucian manager does not take three-hour lunches and then return to ask why the job has not been finished. Confucian managers work through lunch themselves and everybody else does the same without being asked until the job is finished. Although this seems like extremely obvious advice we have all encountered managers whose job description seems to consist of two things: having lunch and issuing instructions (normally before lunch) so it is advice that is certainly worth restating.

A manager also faces the problem of exactly how to treat employees. Should a manager be relaxed and casual—the "all-mates-together" approach—or maintain a certain aloofness so that authority can be exercised when necessary? Confucius himself preferred the relaxed approach, but a manager who is too "easy-going" can have a negative effect on efficiency, as one of his former students, Zhonggong (then working as a government official), once pointed out to him:

Zhonggong asked about Zisang Bozi's suitability for office.

Confucius said, "He will do. He is easy-going."

Zhonggong said, "If you are strict with yourself in your attention to business, but relaxed about small matters, you will be seen as a good administrator. But if you are as easy on yourself as you are with others, wouldn't that be going too far?"

Confucius said, "You are right."

Analects, 6:2

What Zhonggong meant was that if a manager—or government official—is too relaxed then everybody in the team relaxes as well and this has to be a bad thing, so Confucius had to agree with him. In a later saying he revised his ideas. Ideal managers should exercise a relaxed and friendly approach when dealing one-on-one with members of their team, but should nevertheless preserve a certain dignity and aloofness in order to maintain their authority:

"From a distance, he appears severe; when approached he is affable and friendly; when he speaks his language is firm and decisive."

Analects, 19:9

At the same time ideal managers should not be authoritarian; while maintaining the dignity of their position they should also be flexible and willing to take advice from those under them:

Confucius said: "The Superior Manager is firm but does not expect blind fidelity."

Analects, 15:37

The *Analects* read like transcripts of interviews (which is what they purport to be—verbatim reports by his students) and it is this which still makes them seem so alive even after so many centuries. In a modern interview with a management guru there is always the final question: If you could sum up in one word the most important quality of a good manager, what would it be? Confucius rose to the occasion even with this, and came up with not one but five words:

"Courtesy, generosity, honesty, persistence, and kindness. If you are courteous, you will not be disrespected. If you are generous, you will gain everything. If you are honest, people will rely on

you. If you are persistent you will get results. If you are kind, you can employ people."

Analects, 17:6

As a manager he was unquestionably a success, and yet he must often have thought … was this *it*? Was this going to be his whole life, producing better and better cows? Like any other young person, Kong Qiu, who was still in his early twenties, would certainly have been ambitious, dreaming of "better things" as he made the rounds of the cowsheds every day. He was never resentful or bitter, however, because of the way the divining sticks had fallen.

He knew that in some way or other his time would come.

'Superior Managers are easy to work for.' Confucius listening to an employee. Detail from Ming Dynasty painting. *Qilu Press*

Family Life

Confucius was now twenty-two and it was two years since he had married and started work. On the work front he was certainly doing well. He was already as much of a success in his new job as a livestock breeder as he had been as an accountant and all his staff members were happy and contented. Whatever lofty ambitions he may have nursed deep inside himself, for the moment he was still just an obscure steward on a country estate, and he continued cheerfully "going out of his house every day as if receiving an important guest," treating his own employees well, and keeping a cheerful face on things.

His situation at home may not have been so happy. The clock on his marriage was ticking and had only two more years to run, so that by now there must have been severe strains. We know nothing of the reasons for the break-up, but it is likely that Confucius' wife considered she had married a no-hoper who came home each day with cow manure on his boots and was making no effort to better his lot. Instead of using his spare time to cultivate useful social contacts, he spent every evening reading!

During this period of increasing strain in their marriage, there was at least one happy event for the ill-matched couple to celebrate: the birth of their son. The name they gave the baby boy, Kong Li, is the subject of another of the charming stories about Confucius' life which may or may not be true—this one probably is, at least in part.

At this time *li* meant "carp"—a fish which was considered a delicacy and was served minced with spices at banquets:

> He entertains and feasts his friends
> With roast turtle and minced carp.
> *Book of Songs*, 177: Liu Yue

Rich noblemen had their own carp ponds and the dish was always served as part of a major feast—for example to celebrate the birth of a son. Confucius, as a humble steward, would not have had access to carp unless he poached one from Lord Ji's pond (a decidedly un-Confucian act) or tried his luck in one of the nearby lakes (which he would not have had the time to do). In the event, according to legend, he was presented with a succulent carp from one of the nobles' ponds, and named his son Li in acknowledgement of this great "honor." So far, so believable—"Carp" is a very unusual name and quirky names seem to have been a family tradition as Confucius himself was of course named Kong Qiu—"Sacred Hill."

According to the earliest biographies the nobleman who presented the carp to Confucius was no less than the Duke of Lu himself, but at this point the legend ceases to be credible. Modern biographers have always found it difficult to explain how the Duke of Lu—supreme leader of the whole state—happened to hear

Confucius giving thanks for the gift of the carp while his wife and servant look on. Ming Dynasty Painting. *Qilu Press*

Confucius presented with a carp to celebrate the birth of his son. Ming Dynasty Painting. *Qilu Press*

about the birth of a son to an unknown junior steward on another nobleman's estate, and then why he immediately got into his travelling carriage for what must have been at least a day's journey at the time, just in order to present the proud father with a fish?

The whole story is reminiscent of many other religious myths, and seems to have been concocted during the later period when Confucius was gradually being turned into a god—the Adoration of the Magi immediately comes to mind. Was the Duke of Lu perhaps guided by a star? Whereas the infant Jesus received gold, frankincense, and myrrh, Confucius only received a fish. Surely there is something wrong here?

Obviously if this gift had been presented by his employer Lord Ji, and not the Duke, then the whole thing makes sense. As a bottom-level steward, Confucius would have qualified for a carp from Lord Ji's pond. The chief steward of the household might have got a silver knife at the birth of his own son if he was lucky; the more senior retainers would have got more valuable gifts, and so on up the hierarchy. It is even perfectly possible to imagine Lord Ji himself riding over to present this gift; feudal lords liked to ride around their estates and do this sort of thing, it made them feel powerful. We can also imagine Confucius bowing his head and thanking Lord Ji for the wonderful gift, adding (with his tongue possibly slightly in his cheek) that he would name his

son Carp in view of the great honor.

Whether this was a good-natured joke on Confucius' part, or simply a case of crawling to the boss we do not know, but certainly the baby, Kong Li was nicknamed *Bo Yu* ("little fish"), a name which stuck with him for the rest of his life whether he liked it or not.

Now that Confucius was a proud parent, we might expect some useful words of wisdom on the subject of rearing children to appear in the *Analects*, but unfortunately his various pronouncements about family life are very ordinary. While his ideas about management have been enthusiastically adopted in our own time and the *Analects* describing his teaching read like a master-class on educational method, the passages about "filial duty" all seem like second-hand wisdom, the sort of thing anybody might be expected to say:

Confucius said: "…at home serve your father and elder brothers, selflessly carry out your duties to the dead, and don't get into trouble with alcohol. Which of these do I attain to?"

Analects, 9:16

If Confucius meant that he had adhered to all three precepts in his own life, in the first case this was not strictly true—we know for certain that he was taken away from his father when he was only two years old. He probably did not feel obliged to reveal the intimate details of his childhood to his audience, but nevertheless his was a second-hand family. In the end it probably boils down to this: while he was a very successful manager and is arguably the greatest teacher who ever

Filial Piety: a son making obeisance to his father during the Qing Dynasty, when "Confucian Values" were still very much alive. Tableau in Shanghai Jiading Museum. *Photo: Jonathan Price*

lived, he was even by his own admission a dismal failure as a parent, and his own father was even worse.

Confucius did manage to do a little better than Kong Shuliang, who threw his own baby out of his house when he was two and then promptly died. Confucius either threw himself out or was thrown out (we do not know which) when his own son was the same age but he did make some effort to return home periodically to check on the boy's progress. Unfortunately Bo Yu inherited neither his father's intellectual ability nor his appetite for hard work, and Confucius' students were amazed to discover when they finally met Carp that the only thing Confucius ever appeared to have said to him as a boy was "have you done your homework?"

Chen Kang asked Bo Yu: "Have you heard anything from your father different than we disciples have?"

Bo Yu replied, "Not yet. Once, when my father was standing by himself, I passed by the hall quickly, and he said, 'Have you learned anything from the *Book of Songs* yet?' I said, 'Not yet.' So I went and studied the *Book of Songs*. On another day, the same scene occurred, and he asked me, 'Have you learned anything from the *Book of Rites* yet?' I said, 'Not yet.' He said, 'If you don't learn proper rules of behavior you will have no structure.' So I went and studied the *Rites*. I have only heard these two things."

Analects, 16:13

Confucius gave his son another lecture about not studying hard enough a little later. Bo Yu had still not read the first two parts of his father's favorite book the *Book of Songs*:

The Master said to his son Bo Yu, "Do you give yourself to the *Zhou Odes* and the *Odes of Shao*?

Posthumous Piety: Confucius held that a father's wishes for his family should be strictly adhered to even after he was dead. For thousands of years, one room in every traditional Chinese house was always reserved for the family altar, which honoured the 'ancestors'. This altar is in the side hall of the Confucius Temple, Qufu. *Photo: Jonathan Price*

The man who has not studied the *Odes of Zhou* and the *Odes of Shao* is like somebody who stands with his face right against a wall. Is he not so?"

Analects, 17:10

Clearly Confucius' luckless son was a bitter disappointment to him. He once made the rather bitter remark:

"Everyone calls his son his son, whether he has talents or has not talents."

Analects, 11:8

Bo Yu must have disappointed him in other ways which we will never know, for surely his father would have forgiven him for merely "having no talents" even though the boy evidently combined this with chronic laziness. Perhaps Bo Yu sided with his mother and made no secret of his dislike of his father. This is plausible because there is no evidence that they ever had any contact after Bo Yu became an adult. In the *Analects*, apart from the two entries describing his laziness as a

student, which seem to have been a result of Confucius' students meeting him independently of his father, the only other time Bo Yu is mentioned is when Confucius arrived late for his funeral—he died four years before his father at the early age of forty-six.

In fact, despite his extremely conventional pronouncements about family values, Confucius behaved in his own life as if he were living in some kind of futuristic society in which the conventional hierarchy still exists but beyond this is a higher level, a community of minds and souls, in which parents and children "choose" each other. Interestingly Mahatma Gandhi thousands of years later (whose philosophy was remarkably similar to that of Confucius) also more or less disowned his own family and lived with his "disciples." Confucius himself later claimed that his real son was not Bo Yu but Yan Hui, his most talented and unquestionably his favorite student. When Yan Hui also died young shortly before he himself died, Confucius was prostrate with grief, and insisted on being given the right to bury him as his own son. In the event his other students moved against him and Yan Hui was buried as the son of his family even though he shared Confucius' idea and regarded his Master as his real father.

This then was the strange lifestyle of the man who is considered the embodiment of conventional family values, yet who spent a good part of his life wandering

"Personally cleaning his mother's chamber pot". An illustration of one of the '24 Examples of Filial Piety' by Guo Ju-jing. *Painting by Bo Jingzhen*

around the countryside with his students, whom he appeared to regard as his true family. None the less he had a lot to say about these "family values," which he called *hsiao*—usually translated into English as "filial piety" but which really meant loving and respecting your parents as individuals not just as authority figures; and caring for them because you love them not simply as a duty:

> **Confucius said: "Nowadays being a good son means being able to feed your parents, but everyone does this for even horses and dogs. Without respect, what's the difference?"**
>
> *Analects*, 2:7
>
> **You should not understand 'filial' to mean merely doing physical tasks for your parents, or setting food and wine before them... what is important is the expression you show in your face.**
>
> *Analects*, 2:8

In other words, if your parents ask you to wash the dishes, do it with a smile on your face. This is good advice but none the less somewhat obvious, not much above the level of an advice column in a teenage magazine. Here is some more:

> **Confucius said: "While your parents are alive, it is better not to travel far away. If you do travel, you should have a precise destination."**
>
> *Analects*, 4:19

What he meant by "not travel far away" is "not go out of touch so you are unreachable" since in his day if people were separated by only a relatively short distance, communication was almost impossible. Nowadays mobile phones and email make the actual distance irrelevant, but a "precise destination" is still important. Our parents will always worry about us, so it is our basic duty as loving and caring sons or daughters to let them know exactly where we are when we travel. Again, this is advice-column stuff, but many teenagers today still ignore this advice so perhaps it is worth having.

Next we come to the always thorny problem of whether we should always do what our parents tell us to do. Confucius saw it as practical that parents should ultimately have the last word within the family, otherwise this basic social unit would not work. This is not the same as blind obedience, and in fact he was very much in favor of discussing things and even arguing strongly with your parents, with the proviso that in the end they will make the final decision:

Confucius said: "When you serve your mother and father it is quite all right to try to correct them once in a while. But if you see that they are not going to listen to you, keep your respect for them and don't distance yourself from them. Work without complaining."

Analects, 4:18

When asked to define what he meant by this aspect of *hsiao* or "filial piety" and whether it meant merely respect or obligatory obedience, Confucius said:

"It means 'not diverging' from your parents …"

Analects, 2:5

Significantly he does not use the phrase "always obeying" but "not diverging," which conveys the idea of the family moving in one direction as a team, so that while there is room for discussion and even argument, in the end the parents have to steer the ship.

Confucius said: "When your father is alive, observe his will. When your father is dead observe his former actions. If, for three years you do not change from the ways of your father, you can be called a 'real son.'"

Analects, 1:11

Again, although the three-year period Confucius talks about refers to the official period of mourning in his time, the basic idea can still have some relevance today. For example in the case of a son or daughter taking over a family business on the death of their father, they would be well advised not to change everything immediately but continue in the same direction for a period—and three years is as good a yardstick as any for this.

It can be accepted then that many of Confucius' remarks about *hsiao*, his concept of love and caring behavior within families, and of the ultimate duty of children to respect the decisions of their parents, have some limited if rather obvious relevance to our lives today. It must be remembered, however, that he was not really talking about parents and *children*, but was primarily speaking about adult sons and daughters, who were also supposed to abide by the decisions of their parents until three years after the father's death. Obviously this has little relevance to anybody over the age of eighteen in most Western countries today, although the principle still applies in Asia, especially in

those countries directly influenced by Confucianism like China and Korea. In the end, although discussion is allowed and even advised in Confucius' code of family behavior, *hsiao* for him ultimately meant not only respect but obedience, and although this might be a very good idea in a family of rebellious teenagers, it will not work any more in Western countries for 22-year-olds, and even in China the situation is changing.

He also suggested that because the family is the basic social unit, the love and care flowing between family members can somehow filter upwards and will ultimately produce a more just society—in other words stable and caring families actually help to produce a stable and caring society. He said that we can all start by trying to be good brothers and sisters, mothers or fathers, and if everybody does this then society is already changing for the better:

Confucius said: "Just by being a good son or brother you can have an effect on government without actually being in the government."

Analects, 2:21

It is clear what he meant by this and also that this idea is possibly still relevant to an extent. Just by looking after your little sisters while your mother goes out to work you are, according to Confucius, already changing society because if all families behaved in this caring way, then governments would have to spend less time and money on policing crime and could start turning

Family Values: the feudal warlords of Confucius' time carried the idea of 'family first' to extremes, barricading themselves and their clan members behind massive fortifications guarded day and night by archers. Han Dynasty pottery model in Shanghai Museum. *Photo: Jonathan Price*

towards solving the larger problems. Therefore by looking after your little sisters you are having an effect on government, and in addition by your good example you will influence others to behave in the same way.

Nowadays most people would regard this aspect of Confucius' thinking as naïve, based as it is on the idea that all human beings are innately good and will in the end respond to examples of goodness around them. We have already seen that he also claimed that criminals would be shamed into refraining from wrong-doing if there were enough good people around them, an idea which also seems extremely naïve to us today. Of course we should follow his advice and be good brothers to our little sisters—but whether our next-door neighbors will follow our example is another matter. Perhaps the point is that we should try. Confucius was one of humanity's great optimists and optimism is something we will always need.

In other ways Confucius' idea of "family first—then society" has more negative consequences, since most people are not, as he wanted them to be, innately good but interpret this as "family first and to hell with everybody else." In his own time the savagery inflicted on innocent humanity all around him was mostly carried out by families—the feudal clans—whose individual members were no doubt loving fathers and good brothers within their own households, but became inhuman once they stepped outside the walls of their strongholds.

Another consequence of "family first," when practiced by what Confucius called "inferior people," is nepotism—once described in a wonderful pastiche of Hemingway as "the nephew also rises." This has existed in all societies and at all periods (the Ancient Greek word *nepos* means "nephew" and *nepotismos* already thrived in pre-Periclean Athens), nevertheless it is no coincidence that it remains firmly entrenched today in those Asian countries which once used Confucianism as their state philosophy. The irony is that Confucius himself was firmly against promotion of family members who had no talent, although he was not above a little bit of "family-first" himself:

> **The Duke of Sheh told Confucius: "In my land, there are Just men. If a father steals a sheep, the son will testify against him."**
>
> **Confucius said, "The Just men in my land are different from this. The father conceals the wrongs of his son, and the son conceals the wrongs of his father. This is Rightness!"**
>
> *Analects*, 13:18

This is, of course, a relatively trivial example, but the whole concept gets much more serious if the "wrongs of the father" are directed against the children themselves, who are still obliged by the Confucian concept of "filial piety" to conceal them. In our own time if a child arrives at school covered in bruises and claims that he or she "fell down the stairs" this immediately sets off alarm bells, whereas all Confucius' ideas about filial obedience are directed at a sort of ideal family in which it is inconceivable even to imagine that parents would harm their own children.

Even this possibility was recognized by Confucius' followers of a much later period, and the work *Twenty-Four Examples of Filial Piety* written by the Confucian scholar Guo Jujing during the Yuan Dynasty (fourteenth century AD) contains several stories of young children suffering the most horrific treatment from parents or step-parents but enduring this without protest, and the fact that they say nothing about it is held up as a noble virtue and an example to be followed by children everywhere. Confucius' advice is fine when applied to what might be called "normal" families, but if you hear screaming coming from next door do not reach for the *Analects*—call a social worker.

Young girl (Han Dynasty figurine). Henan Museum. *Photo: Jonathan Price*

Even Confucius' most sensible advice about caring for our parents as they get older was taken to extremes by the later Confucians.

Confucius said: "Your parents' age should not be ignored. Sometimes it will be a source of joy, and sometimes it will be a source of apprehension."

Analects, 4:21

There is nothing wrong with that and we should all follow this advice. However, the fanatical Guo Jujing goes a lot further than this: one of his stories is entitled "Personally Cleaning his Mother's Chamber Pot," while another is called "Tasting his Father's Stool." This story also appeared in some editions entitled "Cutting off pieces of his own flesh to give to his father as Medicine." These examples were directed at adult sons caring for elderly parents and were accompanied by illustrations.

Although Confucius always talked about "sons" when discussing family matters, he did of course also have a daughter. Sadly, apart from one reference in the *Analects*, we know nothing else at all about her, not even her name:

Confucius said of Kung Ye Chang that he was fit for marriage. Even though he was arrested once, he had been innocent; therefore Confucius gave him his daughter in marriage.

Analects, 5:1

It is quite possible that the girl could have inherited her father's intelligence, and the gentle and scholarly instincts of the Yans, her grandmother's family, but would have had no chance to develop or even display these qualities. Disappointed in his son, Confucius in another age such as our own might have discovered in this nameless girl the true daughter of his soul, and spent long and happy hours discussing the *Book of Songs* with her. As it was he had to look outside his own family for the experience of true fatherhood, even for the experience of a true family. Within his own family there seems to have been only coldness, and it was to be with his students that he would experience his greatest joy, and his greatest sorrow. When his own son died he did not weep—at least he is not recorded as having done so—but when Yan Hui, the student he regarded as his real son in the eyes of Heaven, passed away before reaching the age of thirty Confucius broke down completely.

At the very end of his life, Confucius was finally rewarded with a soul-mate within his own family: his little grandson Zisi, Bo Yu's son. Zisi became a teacher just like his grandfather, carrying on Confucius' work and promulgating his ideas. He was also an author,

producing several works which summarized and explained Confucius' ideas and which were collected under the general title *The Book of Zisi*. A bamboo-slip book with this title, bearing his name as the author, was among those discovered in the Guodian Tomb in 1993. Other bamboo manuscripts discovered in the tomb are by authors who identify themselves as from "The School of Zisi," which is how we can be certain that Zisi carried on his grandfather's work as a teacher.

Sadly, Confucius was never able to appreciate how much Zisi had inherited from him since the boy was only about eight years old when he died. The only stories surviving about their relationship portray little Zisi as a dutiful grandson chopping firewood for his grandfather, the embodiment of *hsiao*.

Confucius himself argued vehemently against inherited talents, claiming that everything he had achieved was through hard work and application. Nevertheless his own grandson seems to prove him wrong about this. Confucius' own intellectual ability was obviously inherited from his mother, who is recorded as coming from "a family of scholars." From his father he inherited his stubbornness and courage (and his height), while his own son Bo Yu apparently only inherited the stubbornness. The cleverness obviously skipped a generation unless Confucius' daughter was clever, which sadly we have no way of knowing. Zisi, however, took up the mantle of his grandfather with total assuredness. Perhaps he was inspired even as a small boy when he heard his grandfather talking about things he barely understood, but it is unlikely, and this is clearly a case of "genes will out."

Family is after all crucially important, but not quite in the way that Confucius imagined…

Confucius with his grandson Zisi. *Qilu Press*

The Eternal Student

Confucius said: "I don't worry about being unknown. I worry about my lack of ability."

Analects, 14:30

Confucius had now been "steward in charge of livestock" for several years but there had been no more talk of further promotion. Although he had been given a raise and now received 200 bushels of grain a year, once he had passed the age of twenty-five and began heading into his late twenties Confucius must have started to feel rather depressed about his overall progress in life so far. All he had to show for almost a decade of hard work was an ex-wife, a son who never did his homework, a sweet little daughter he hardly ever saw, and what was looking increasingly like a dead-end job from which he had little hope of escaping.

He was still sure that he could make his mark on the world somehow, although he was never interested in fame for its own sake. Later in his life one of his students asked what one had to do in order to be thought of as

"Riches and honors are what all men desire"—ancient Chinese coins (Spring and Autumn Period). Shandong Museum. *Photo: Jonathan Price*

"distinguished" and "outstanding" in society, as Confucius himself was regarded?

Confucius said, "What do you mean by 'distinguished'?"

Zizhang replied: "I mean to be famous in your town, and famous in your clan."

Confucius said, "That is *fame*, not *distinction*. A distinguished person has an upright character and lives by the highest principles. Famous people can put on a show of goodness, but do otherwise in private, and as long as this doesn't bother them, they can indeed still be 'famous.'"

Analects, 12:20

"Wanting to be famous" has become a modern disease, and the only cure, according to Andy Warhol, is that "In the future everybody will be famous for fifteen minutes." Confucius did not want that kind of fame:

Confucius said: "I don't worry about not having a good position; I worry about the means I use to gain position. I don't worry about being unknown; I seek to be known in the right way."

Analects, 4:14

Confucius eventually achieved this, and has certainly

Wealth equals success? Stamped gold ingots from Warring States Period. Confucius maintained that if to obtain such riches a person abandoned humanitarian principles this was not success but failure. Shanghai Museum.
Photo: Jonathan Price

been famous for a lot longer than fifteen minutes, although in his own lifetime he did not enjoy the usual trappings of fame: great wealth and status. When he was young and unknown he probably wanted—like all of us—to have it all:

Confucius said: "Riches and honors are what all men desire ..."

Analects, 4:5

In other words, riches plus fame equals success, and most people even today believe this, prepared only to dispense with the adulation as long as they can still keep the money. Confucius, however, introduced a third component into the "real success" equation: *ren* (sometimes spelled as *jen*). This means humanity or good behavior to others, which he said was the number one ingredient in *human* success, so that ambitious people in any field should shun the other two—riches and fame—if they have to abandon their humanity in order to achieve them:

Confucius said: "If riches and honors cannot be

attained in accordance with the Way of Humanity they should not be kept. Poverty and low status are what all people hate, but if they cannot be avoided while staying in accordance with the Way of Humanity, you should not avoid them."

Analects, 4:5

Many very successful people have risen to the top by destroying other people or sometimes whole companies, and then go on to donate large amounts of tax-free dollars to charity in order to re-establish themselves as "good people"—the *junzi* Confucius describes. This will not do, Confucius insisted. The Superior Person *never* departs from right behavior:

"If so-called 'Superior People' depart from decent behavior, how can they be worthy of that name? A Superior Person never abandons decent behavior for even the time of a single meal."

Analects, 4:5

How many of those who head the Fortune 500 can truly put their hands on their hearts and say they have never abandoned "decent behavior"? It was the same 2,500 years ago. Confucius looked at his own society and shook his head in despair, but he could equally well have been talking about that same society two and a half thousand years later:

"These mean creatures! When they don't have

something, they make themselves miserable in getting it. Once they get it, they fret about losing it. Once they are worried about losing it, there is nothing they won't do."

Analects, 17:15

Confucius did not disapprove of worldly success in itself but only the means by which many people achieve it. He was especially contemptuous of those who continue to make themselves richer (especially government officials) when the whole of the society around them is corrupt:

"If the Way prevails in a state, you can work hard for the government and take your salary, it is fine; but if the Way doesn't prevail in a state and you still work for the government to get a salary, then this is shameful."

Analects, 14:1

He never in fact condemned the making of money as such (something his later interpreters claimed he did), but simply deplored its elevation into the main purpose of existence. In fact he once made a joke about everybody's secret dream (including his own) of becoming a millionaire overnight:

Confucius said: "If the attainment of wealth was guaranteed in its seeking, even if I were to become a stable-groom with a whip in hand to get it, I

A row of dancing girls according to strict Zhou ritual: life-size model of Spring and Autumn Period dancers in the City of the Six Arts Qufu. *Photo: Jonathan Price*

would do so. But since its attainment cannot be guaranteed, I will go with that which I love."

Analects, 7:12

In other words, if somebody told him it was a hundred percent certain he could earn a million by shovelling horse manure he would shovel it, but since no such sure-fire road to riches exists, he would stick to what he loved doing—which at the time he made this remark was being a teacher.

While he was still a steward, however, to become a teacher was not Confucius' number one ambition, and his secret dreams were centered round the seemingly impossible idea of becoming a government officer. Failing this, perhaps he could make it as a tutor in one of the noble houses, but whatever it was he ended up doing he certainly did not intend to stay in charge of Lord Ji's cattle all his life and to this end he spent much of his free time studying.

"If you already have a job, you should devote your spare time to studying."

Analects, 19:13

This idea, that learning should never stop, is another of the key concepts from the *Analects* that Peter Drucker seized upon as particularly relevant to the rapidly changing world of today: "Knowledge has power. It controls access to opportunity and advancement." Agreeing totally with his unlikely disciple from thousands of years into the future, Confucius concentrated his new career-oriented course of self-study on the massive work entitled the *Li Ji* or *Book of Rites*, convinced that this could be his passport out of the warehouse.

The title of this book (one of the five "ancient classics") is often translated as the *Book of Propriety* ("appropriateness"), since it not only describes ceremonies for use on various occasions but also general rules of correct behavior in many different social situations. Confucius could see that an encyclopedic knowledge of these rules could be a marketable commodity, for the nobility especially needed to know the exact forms of ritual and etiquette in order to avoid major embarrassment when entertaining distinguished visitors or when visiting other states, and somebody needed to advise them about this.

Some of the rituals which Confucius studied are of only quaint historical interest to us today, for example "The Ceremony of Hatting." In this coming-of-age ceremony, the young man would be crowned successively with three different kinds of hat, representing childhood, youth and adulthood, and would then be paraded through the streets wearing a black cap and robe to symbolize his acceptance as a grown-up member of society. Similar rituals still exist today of course, like the Christian confirmation and the Jewish *bar mitzvah*: only the hats are different.

Other ceremonial specified in the *Book of Rites* included rules for sporting events in the section entitled *Xiang Sheli* ("Procedure at a District Archery Contest"), while in the chapter headed *Pinli* ("Interstate Missions") the exact numbers of dancers to be used when greeting a visiting dignitary was laid down precisely. A visiting duke—the head of one of the states—would therefore have had more dancers greeting him than a mere lord; nowadays we call this "protocol" and a similar type of ritual is still observed today: a visiting president always gets a much grander reception at an airport than a foreign minister.

Other rules outlined the appropriate way to behave in public especially on formal occasions, so there were other sections in the book covering this such as *Yanli* ("The Banquet") and *Yousi Che* ("The Assistant Clears Away"). These "rules of propriety" extended down to the smallest details of dress or the correct way to say goodbye to somebody according to their social status—the type of behavioral code we would now call

Confucius attending an archery contest. *Qilu Press*

Confucius as a model of ritual politeness: "Bowing to the emissaries of Lu". Life-size model in the City of the Six Arts, Qufu. *Photo: Jonathan Price*

"etiquette." Confucius himself was renowned as a model of old-fashioned courtesy and proper etiquette in this respect:

> **When he was sending complimentary inquiries to anyone in another state, he bowed twice as he escorted the messenger away.**
>
> *Analects*, 10:15
>
> **When he got up into the carriage, he would stand straight, holding the straps. Once inside the carriage, he did not look about, talk rapidly or point around with his hands.**
>
> *Analects*, 10:26
>
> **When he was standing, he did not occupy the middle of the gateway; when he passed in or out, he did not tread upon the threshold.**
>
> *Analects*, 10:4

Almost all of these customs involved respect—for example standing in the middle of the gateway (which Confucius never did) meant drawing attention to yourself as if you were more important than your host or other visitors, while treading on the threshold literally raised you up above other people (totally unacceptable) since the threshold set across the doorway extended at least a foot above the floor. Examples of raised thresholds may still be seen in many old Chinese houses,

including the "Confucius Mansion" in Qufu, which was built many centuries after his death but still retained the style of the old houses.

One aspect of the ritual of Confucius' time which is difficult for us to understand today is the religious element. Religious ritual was not confined to temples or only used on grand state occasions; instead the heads of each individual family, even the humblest, were required to conduct ceremonies in their own back yards, for example the slaughtering of a sheep after the harvest. As a result everybody needed to know the basics of ritual since the ceremonies were so much a part of their everyday lives. Even the most important rituals which were held in the Grand Temple of Lu—which was on the slopes of the sacred Mount Tai—would be conducted not by a priest but by the Duke of Lu. There was no "separation of church and state" as there is in most places nowadays.

Even ceremonies of welcome contained a religious element, and the exact number of bulls which should be sacrificed upon a distinguished guest's arrival varied

Raised threshold in gateway to ancient Chinese mansion, Qufu. It was impolite to actually step on the threshold as one entered the house. *Photo: Jonathan Price*

according to his status. Sacrificing one bull too few when welcoming a head of state was an insult, while slaughtering two bulls too many for a mere minister indicated that the host state supported the visitor's ambitions to take power by force in his own state.

This is very similar to the protocol of "airport welcomes" today, but generally speaking this aspect of Confucius' thinking has much less relevance to the modern world than his views on say, education or management. Presentations entitled "Confucian Management for Modern Business" or "Teaching the Confucius Way" play to packed houses, whereas a lecture entitled "Confucius' Guide to Table Manners in the Fifth Century BC" would attract a much smaller audience of historians or specialists. Nevertheless, to understand Confucius truly it is important to understand what he meant by "ritual" and "propriety" since he talked about these subjects so often, and indeed in his own day he was more celebrated as a "Master of Ritual" than anything else.

Confucius said: "The linen cap is prescribed by

the rules of propriety, but nowadays they use a [cheaper] silk one. It is economical, and I will go along with the consensus."

Analects, 9:3

He is talking here about the type of headwear to be worn when attending religious ceremonies. Although unimportant in itself, this passage from the *Analects* does show that Confucius was not a believer in tradition for its own sake, since here he is recommending breaking with it. Somewhat unfairly, Confucius was considered by many of his contemporaries to be an old fuddy-duddy conservative, who was always ranting on about the importance of observing ancient ceremonials just because they were ancient.

"The rules of ceremony prescribe the bowing below the hall, but now the practice is to bow only after ascending it. That is arrogant. I continue to bow below the hall, though I oppose the common practice."

Analects, 9:3

This time he is saying that failure to make a bow before entering the main hall is arrogant because it does not show respect to the owner of the house, so he prefers the old way. Again, from our own perspective in the modern age this seems a relatively trivial piece of etiquette, but Confucius interpreted the "arrogant" ways of the feudal lords and their followers as one of the reasons why society was disintegrating.

More seriously, he held that ritual (or protocol) was the glue which held society together, and once it was neglected the whole delicate structure would come unstuck and the result would be anarchy: a free-for-all in which each powerful family struggled for power without respect for the established order, inevitably causing untold suffering and unnecessary loss of life among the ordinary people who are inevitably caught up in such conflicts. Confucius lived through several military coups so he knew what he was talking about.

An example of this was when he criticized his own sponsor, Lord Ji, for whom he was still working at the time:

Confucius, speaking about the head of the Ji family said, "He has eight rows of dancers in his court. If he does this, what will he not do?"

Analects, 3:1

What he meant was that having eight rows of dancers was, according to the *Book of Rites*, a privilege reserved for a head of state—in other words the Duke of Lu could have eight ranks of dancing-girls but not Lord Ji—and by breaking protocol in this way he was signalling that he had eyes on taking power himself. Even as a humble steward Confucius would still have been invited to official feasts at the Ji mansion, where he would have observed his lord and master sitting on a throne-like chair as eight rows of beautiful dancing girls whirled brightly-colored sashes in front of him to the rhythm of the drums and zithers. He would have seen the satisfied glint in Lord Ji's eyes too, and the arrogant smile which showed all too plainly his hunger for power. Confucius was right—eventually Lord Ji did stage a coup, forcing the rightful Duke of Lu and also Confucius himself into exile.

Although all this seems very remote to us in our more laid-back times, ritual does still exist—for instance in matters of table etiquette which vary so much from country to country that it is very easy to make a major

Traditional Ritual: sacrificing bulls - re-enactment at Qufu.
Qilu Press

Life-size model of ritual dancing-girls from the Spring and Autumn Period in the City of the Six Arts, Qufu. *Photo: Jonathan Price*

gaffe without realising it. To take one example, in Sweden and also in China it is considered extremely rude to start drinking at a formal dinner party before the host has proposed the first toast. Business people can lose a contract in either of these countries simply by the act of raising a wineglass to their lips, so there is a clear need for somebody to advise them before they get on the plane. There are indeed people whom companies can hire to do this—etiquette advisors—so ritual still matters even today. In Confucius' world it was overwhelmingly important.

It was for this very reason that Confucius concentrated so much of his time and energy on making himself a master of ritual, since a position as one of the "etiquette advisors" that rulers and noblemen employed was the most distinguished and highly paid appointment that he could realistically hope to attain. There was still a problem, however: he had no formal qualification. Nobody could call themselves a *Zi*—or "Master"—of Ritual simply because they knew the *Book of Rites* from cover-to-cover, they also had to do a course of study at the Grand Temple in Luoyang, the ancient capital of the old Zhou Empire, which was a considerable distance away from Lu to the west, and Confucius had absolutely no hope of getting there.

Although the Zhou Dynasty no longer exercised any political control over its former provinces, Luoyang in the central state of Zhou was still considered the religious and cultural capital, and its Grand Temple would regularly issue proclamations about one ritual or another in the same way that the Vatican still does today from Rome. The successful ritual advisors, many of whom "freelanced" by travelling from state to state and receiving high fees for their services, had all "graduated" in Luoyang. If Confucius was to stand any chance of breaking into this highly competitive job market, somehow he had to get to the capital—but how?

Although very ambitious, he was still determined to stick to his principles and achieve success through honesty and hard work and not "devious means." A well-placed bribe in the right quarter (which would have meant a portion of his grain allowance) could have helped him a little further up the ladder, but for Confucius this was always out of the question. His principles of upright behavior, which he said we should never abandon "even for the space of a single meal" in order to advance our careers, were summarized by his grandson Zisi in the *Book of Zisi*. Zisi called these the "Five Principles of Confucius" (*Wu Xing*) and listed them as: Humanity; Appropriate Behavior; Observance of Ritual; Wisdom and Knowledge; and Sagacity in Decisions.

In real life, unfortunately, these five qualities are not enough; they should never be abandoned but they will only take you so far. Unfortunately there is also the Sixth Principle, which has always applied and always will, and which of us can say it has not operated in our own lives? Confucius was no exception, and so here it is, the Sixth Principle of the Successful Person:

It's not *what* you know, it's *who* you know …

Universal Truth: All cultures

Many people cultivate this as principle number one, but it does not work like that. If you make friends with people because you think they can help your career you are using them and in the end they will use you. True friends, however, will always help you if they can, and this sixth principle does not really violate any of the others.

Confucius did in fact have at least one true friend in high places, although he had never asked him for any help. At this critical point in his life, when he was despairing of ever making any further progress, this friend unexpectedly came to his aid and kick-started his career. The legend of Confucius was about to be born, not because angels had sung at his sagely birth or because he was "descended from kings"—but because he had the gift of friendship.

Confucius was about to get lucky …

Below left: The Grand Temple of Ancient Zhou. Model in the the City of the Six Arts, Qufu. *Photo: Jonathan Price*

Below right: The "Five Principles of Confucius" (*Wu Xing*) on an early stone stele inscription. *Qilu Press*

The Road to Camelot

The friend who came to Confucius' aid at this critical juncture in his life (he knew that if he was still a steward by the time he reached thirty he would probably stay in this position for ever) was Nangong Jingshu—his old school friend and the younger son of Lord Meng. They must have kept up their friendship in the intervening years, since Nangong suddenly pops up again in the recorded history of Confucius' life at this point as his main benefactor and supporter. Like Confucius, Nangong Jingshu was fascinated by ritual and they may even have previously visited the Grand Temple of Lu on Mount Tai together to observe ceremonial at first hand.

What is certain is that one day Nangong Jingshu turned up at Confucius' office next to the cattle sheds and announced to his friend that he had persuaded his father, Lord Meng, to finance a trip for him to Luoyang, the ancient Zhou capital, to study the latest thinking on ritual. Jingshu had convinced his father that somebody in their family needed to do this, and none of his other brothers were interested. Lord Meng had ambitions of attaining supreme power, and had accepted his younger son's argument that unless he knew the latest ritual rules he could make a major gaffe in public and lose face.

At first Confucius would have been bitterly envious—this was something he had always dreamed of doing—a trip to Luoyang was at this time the equivalent of a pilgrimage to Rome in Medieval Europe or to Athens in Ancient Greece. So Nangong Jingshu was going there—well good luck to him. Confucius would have told himself that the rich and noble always have everything handed to them on a plate and there was nothing he could do about it, so he forced a smile and congratulated his friend on his good fortune. Then Nangong Jingshu dropped an unexpected bombshell: "You don't understand brother—*you* are coming with me!"

At first Confucius would have hardly been able to believe his ears, and even when he realized it was true would have imagined that he would be part of the large

Ox-drawn traveling wagon (Warring States Period). Museum of Chariots, Linzi. *Photo: Jonathan Price*

Frontier post: Confucius would have passed guard towers like this as he passed from one state to another on his journey to Luoyang. Han Dynasty pottery model in Capital Museum Beijing. *Photo: Jonathan Price*

retinue of senior family members, scholars, stewards, and servants which would inevitably have to accompany a lord's son on any official visit to the capital. Jingshu had much better news than that, however—they would be travelling entirely by themselves! Just a couple of servants and a driver—he had even managed to get his father to provide them with a travelling carriage!

This would have been almost unheard of at the time because a nobleman's son would have been expected to arrive with a large entourage, yet it is corroborated in several independent sources, including the Daoist manuscripts which also describe Confucius' visit to Luoyang, that the two of them arrived unaccompanied just like a couple of students. Somehow Jingshu had brought it off. He seems to have been a very independent character, and as the younger son he was under less pressure to obey his father's wishes than his brother, who had also been at school with Confucius. Nangong Jingshu felt he could do more or less what he liked, and he certainly used his position to help his socially inferior friend Kong Qiu many times throughout his life.

Confucius' reaction to this unexpected good news is not recorded. But throwing his silken cap in the air, letting out a whoop of joy, and punching a hole in a basket of cattle feed in front of his astonished assistants would no doubt have been the least of it …

They set off early one spring morning, their covered ox-cart trundling noisily along the rutted dirt road which led out of Lu to the west, while they both lay back on cushions inside the wagon and chatted happily about any subject that caught their fancy, just as they used to do at school.

The exact year of this momentous journey is unknown; a good guess would be 524 BC, when both Confucius and Nangong Jingshu were about twenty-seven years old. It must have taken place a year or two before 521, for in this year all contact was lost between the old Zhou capital of Luoyang and Confucius' home state of Lu, when the former center of the Zhou Empire was engulfed in bloody clan feuding which lasted for many generations.

As the two friends lazily enjoyed this first part of their journey, following the winding track westward which eventually led down into the valley of the Yellow River, they had no idea that they were to be among the last visitors to the ancient Zhou city while it still retained some vestiges of its former glory. The end of Camelot was coming, sooner than anybody knew.

Once they reached the river the going was easier, and they were able to proceed at a brisker pace along the dusty road which hugged the eastern slopes of the valley. Soon they left Lu and passed into the state of Song, which was the original home of Confucius' father's family. The border crossings between states, marked by towers and mud-brick walls, would have been easy for the two travellers, as Nangong Jingshu's

father, Lord Meng, would have obtained travel documents for them: rolled silk scrolls stamped with the official seal of the Duke of Lu. Officially speaking, the Duke of Lu was still the representative of the King of Zhou in his own state; it was only on a *de facto* basis that the states were independent, so that technically speaking Confucius and his friend were not travelling to another country but simply between provinces in one empire.

The journey would have taken the best part of a fortnight by ox-wagon, so each night they probably slept inside it and enjoyed barbeque suppers under the stars. Although ostensibly a trip with a serious purpose, it was for both of them also a glorious holiday and a welcome break from account books and responsibility—Nangong Jingshu appears in various records as having been in charge of the financial affairs of his father's estate.

We can imagine them pulled up for the night, their servants lighting a fire and busying themselves with the cooking while their master and his companion lay back lazily on the ground and tried to pick out the patterns in the constellations.

> There is the Milky Way in heaven,
> Which looks down on us in light;
> In the north is the Ladle,
> Raising its handle in the west.
> And the three stars together are the Weaving
> Sisters.

Book of Songs, 203: Da Dong

For Confucius the whole trip must have seemed like a magical journey into the *Book of Songs* itself, the book that had meant so much to him from childhood onwards, and especially when they finally reached the actual border of Zhou itself—the "center of the world." Although Confucius understood that this was not the actual site of the "golden age"—he knew that the Zhou had fled to Luoyang from their original capital in 771 BC—nevertheless his first sight of the state of Zhou must have held an almost mystical significance for him:

> The plain of Zhou looked beautiful and rich,
> With its violets and sowthistles sweet as
> dumplings.
> Oh! Great now is Zhou!
> We ascend the high hills,
> Both those that are long and narrow, and the lofty
> mountains …

Book of Songs, 237: Mian   *Book of Songs*, 296:
                                             Ban

Eventually they reached the great bend in the river where it turns westwards and winds its way towards the city of Luoyang itself, but they still had two or three days of bumpy riding ahead before they would reach the capital. Already there were indications that this was no

The Yellow River near Zhengzhou, Henan (ancient state of Zhou) – part of the route taken by Confucius on his journey to Luoyang.
Photo courtesy Yellow River Geology Park Zhengzhou.

The Yellow River (*Huang He*) - the northern frontier of the ancient Zhou state. *Photo courtesy Yellow River Geology-Park Zhengzhou.*

idyllic paradise, and the situation here might indeed be even worse than back home in Lu. Barren fields left unploughed and unsown were a tell-tale sign—by now they should be green with the new season's grain crop. Echoes of the *Book of Songs* were everywhere:

The grass is no longer green;
And I do see in this country,
All going to confusion.
The wealth of former days
Was not like our present condition.
The distress of the present,
Did not previously reach this degree.

Book of Songs, 265: Zhou Wen

Confucius was later to criticize rulers and feudal lords for causing this very problem—taking farmers off the fields to serve in their armies at critical times in the agricultural year. Already he had gone beyond "ritual studies" in his mind and was starting to think about how these unnecessary ills could be prevented—what could be *done* about it. No crops resulted in a shortage of food, a critical shortage meant famine, and these calamities were not caused by the gods but men. No matter how many sacrifices were made to Houji, the god of millet, no crops would come up if nobody bothered to plant the millet seed in the first place.

As their ox-cart finally trundled into Luoyang, and jolted along the stone-paved arteries of the ancient Zhou capital, they would have been struck by even more evidence of the "decline of civilization." The great temples and public buildings still towered above the narrow streets, their undulating roofs supporting golden serpents and dragons. Scholars and government officials still thronged the pavements in embroidered robes trimmed with scarlet, the nobility and the wealthy were still carried through the streets on litters, their heads held high, the collars trimmed with fur, and yet over all this hung an all-pervading atmosphere of decay. The scholars' robes were plain and neatly tailored, but their boots were splashed with mud. The rich looked well-fed but their faces were proud and arrogant, not even acknowledging the existence of the ordinary people who scraped a living in the streets.

It was the end of Camelot, and all that was left was the dream. As Confucius peered out from the back of the wagon, receiving only sullen stares from the grimy-faced poor who hated him because he rode in a carriage while he was ignored by the rich because his carriage was not grand enough, the poignant poems from the *Book of Songs* that he knew so well would have echoed inside his head:

If we could go back to the old Zhou, and see those officers of the old capital,
With their fox-furs so yellow, with their hats of Tai leaves and small black caps!
If we could go back to the old Zhou, and see those ladies of the noble Houses
With their hair so thick and straight, and each one fit to be called a Princess!
Alas! I do not see them now,
And my heart grieves with indissoluble sorrow.

Book of Songs, 225: Du Ren Shi

Model of the ancient Zhou capital in the City of the Six Arts, Qufu. *Photo: Jonathan Price*

Nevertheless this was still the capital, and both Nangong Jingshu and Confucius were looking forward to enjoying their stay: visiting temples during the daytime and savouring the renowned Luoyang cuisine in the evening—not to mention the renowned Luoyang beauties. At this time, as today, the further west you go in China the spicier is the cooking, as the Central Asiatic influence becomes more pronounced. The modern cuisine of Shandong, the area where Confucius lived, is bland compared to the cuisines of areas further west, where China meets Central Asia and the resulting synthesis is gastronomic heaven— and even today all Chinese agree that the further west you go the more beautiful the girls become. For the two "eternal students" this was going to be the holiday of a lifetime, and it was all being paid for by Lord Meng.

For the first few days the visitors would have attended to the main business of their trip, visiting the Grand Temple, where Confucius no doubt asked endless questions and made copious notes. He wanted to know *everything*, from the minutest detail about each ceremony to the ceremonies' broader relevance in society as a whole. This habit of endless research he continued all his life, and many people were amazed that even after he had achieved legendary status as an omniscient sage he still behaved as if he had so much to learn:

When Confucius entered the Grand Temple, he asked about everything. Someone said, "Who said Confucius is a master of ritual? He enters the Grand Temple and asks questions about everything!"

Confucius, hearing this, said: "This is the ritual."

Analects, 3:15

Confucius and Nangong would also have found time to look at the many lesser temples scattered all over the city—just like a couple of tourists. There was music too, especially in the temples:

There are the bird musicians; there are the blind musicians;
In the court of the temple of Zhou.
There are the music frames with their face-boards and posts,
With the drums, large and small, suspended from them.

Book of Songs, 280: You Gu

Confucius was always entranced by any opportunity to hear new styles of music, and although Luoyang was on its last legs politically it was still the cultural capital. Traditional ceremonies, fine art, and classical concerts: what more could he ask for? The smelly cattle sheds must have seemed a world away:

Confucius said: "… the finale of the Guanju was magnificent. How it filled my ears!"

Analects, 8:15

He was of course a practising musician as well as an avid listener, and he probably also took the opportunity to join in with some of the temple choirs, no doubt to the acute embarrassment of Nangong Jingshu:

When Confucius was singing with someone, and he found out that they sang well, he would make them start over again, and he would sing the harmony.

Analects, 7:32

Despite all these cultural attractions, however, sooner or later they would both have become aware of the buzz in the air about the exciting new school of philosophy called Daoism. Confucius appears to have known nothing about this before he went to Zhou, and when he heard that the Daoists railed against the decline of civilization and preached a new *Way* forward, he would have been acutely interested, for he was beginning to think along the same lines himself. Something had to be *done* in his opinion, before it was too late.

Perhaps, he thought, these Daoists could show him the *Way* to do this, and he looked forward to being able to talk to some of them. He got this opportunity by chance, one day when he had business at the Great Library of Zhou in the center of Luoyang, which was the ancient Chinese equivalent of the Library of Congress or the Bodleian Library, where scholars and authors were required to "deposit" their works, much as they are today.

If he imagined, however, that the Daoists shared his ideas about the importance of human values as a way of halting civilization's downward slide, he was in for a rude shock …

The Classical Music of Zhou: Above: Member of the Huaxia Ancient Music Ensemble in Henan Museum performing on a reproduction of the ancient Stone Flute. Below: Musical Bells from Spring and Autumn Period (Shandong Museum) *Photos: Jonathan Price*

~Two Ways of Being~

According to the Daoist writer Zhuangzi, Confucius originally met the Daoists by chance, when he was visiting the Great Library of Luoyang: Confucius went to deposit some writings in the library and was told: "The officer in charge of this Repository was one Lao Tze, who has given up his office, and is living in his own house. As you, Master, wish to deposit these writings here, why not go to him and obtain his help?"

Book of Zhuangzi, 13:7

The sources for our knowledge of Confucius' encounter with the Daoists in the Zhou capital are more extensive than usual, for we have not only the Confucian texts themselves but a number of Daoist writings which record the same event, but of course from their own perspective. The principal of these is the *Book of Zhuangzi*—Zhuangzi being the writer who said that "Confucius is a dream" and suggested that he himself might be a butterfly dreaming he was a man.

Although Zhuangzi was to a large extent writing anti-Confucian fiction, the Confucian version of their Master's encounter with the Daoists is in fact the less reliable. The traditional idea, and the subject of so many paintings, is that Confucius "studied ritual under Lao Tze" but this is impossible for two reasons. First of all most scholars now agree that Lao Tze almost certainly did not exist but was a name invented by the Daoists as the author of their primary text the *Dao Dejing* (*Way of Being*). Not only is this text clearly written by many different hands, even the name Lao Tze is itself allegorical, meaning something like the "Ancient Master." There is also no contemporary reference to anybody of that name outside the Daoist texts themselves, in contrast to Confucius whose name is mentioned in a variety of independent sources. Nobody has ever suggested that Confucius did not exist or that the *Analects* were delivered by a committee, whereas over Lao Tze's familiar head hangs a big question mark

Apart from this, even if there had been somebody of this name preaching Daoism in Luoyang at this time, ritual would have been the last thing he would have

Confucius talking to Lao Tze in Luoyang. Ming Dynasty painting. *Qilu Press*

lectured about, since the Daoists despised all forms of ritual and ceremony and in fact held that the petty customs of humankind in all their forms were utterly irrelevant to the true meaning of existence. A "Daoist ritual teacher" is therefore a contradiction in terms, in the same way that a "Confucian monk" would be.

So Confucius could not have "studied ritual" with the Daoists, but he certainly met them and apparently disputed with them if the Daoist texts are to be believed, although Zhuangzi portrays him as a kind of cartoon country bumpkin who always comes off looking simple-minded and often downright stupid when in the presence of the all-wise and all-knowing Lao Tze. However, if we temper the picture of Confucius so that he is more in line with the man we know him to have been from the *Analects*, Zhuangzi still seems to be describing something which actually happened. When he describes other events in Confucius' life which also

Lao Tze, credited as the author of the *Daodejing* ('Way of Being'), was traditionally held to have been the keeper of records at the Great Library in Luoyang. *Qilu Press*

Butterfly Dreamer: Zhuangzi provides the most detailed record of Confucius' visit to Luoyang - although we don't know how much of it he dreamed up himself. *Painting by Bo Jingzhen*

appear in the *Analects* (for example the "Madman of Chu" who shouted at him in *Analects*, 18:5) the background details are the same and it is only the character of Confucius himself which is changed in order to make him look like a buffoon; probably therefore his description of Confucius' first encounter with Daoism is also fairly reliable except in this respect.

According to Zhuangzi's account (*Book of Zhuangzi, 21:4*) Confucius went to Lao Tze's house as instructed, and discovered the Sage in a state of total immobility "letting his dishevelled hair get dry, motionless, as if there were not another man in the world." Confucius waited for several minutes, clearing his throat, and finally the Sage turned to him and apologized: "I am sorry—I was enjoying myself in thinking about the commencement of things." Zhuangzi then has Confucius making a rather lame joke: "For a few moments there I thought you were a tree trunk!" which Lao Tze ignored and immediately asked him what he

wanted. (Whether this is in any way authentic or Zhuangzi made it all up we do not know but it is entertaining and very realistic-sounding.)

Confucius explained that he wished to deposit in the library some versions of the great classics which he had edited in his spare time—he continued this kind of scholarly work throughout his life. As we know, Confucius considered that the *Book of Songs* could be used as a textbook for right behavior, so he started to explain how he had arranged and annotated the texts with this in mind:

Confucius said: "The 300 verses of the Book of Songs can be summed up in a single phrase: 'Don't think in an evil way.'"

Analects, 2:2

He started to elaborate on this but after a few minutes Lao Tze waved his hands impatiently for him to stop.

"This is too vague; let me hear the substance of them in brief."

Confucius said, "The substance of them is occupied with Benevolence and Righteousness."

The other said, "Let me ask whether you consider Benevolence and Righteousness to constitute the nature of man?"

Cartoon character? In the *Book of Zhuangzi* Confucius is portrayed as a simple-minded buffoon who is constantly humiliated by the all-wise Lao Tze. *Illustration to 'Book of Zhuangzi' by Bo Jingzhen*

The traditional image of Lao Tze. Over the centuries the appearance of the Daoist sage has been standardized, even though there is no concrete evidence he actually existed. *Painting by Bo Jingzhen*

Zhuangzi (369 - 286 B.C.). One of the greatest writers of all time, he was nevertheless writing anti-Confucian and pro-Daoist propaganda, and his portrayal of Confucius has to be taken with lashings of salt.

"I do," was Confucius' answer. "If the superior man be not benevolent, he will not fulfil his character; if he be not righteous, he might as well not have been born. Benevolence and Righteousness are truly the nature of man."

Book of Zhuangzi, 13:7

This is of course a succinct summary of Confucius' general principles, and he would no doubt have expected at least guarded approval, and hopefully immediate acceptance of his own version of the *Book of Songs* into the library (at this point he still imagined that the Daoist "Way" was essentially similar to his own). Instead, to his astonishment, Lao Tze told him in no uncertain terms that he was a simpleton:

Lao Tan continued, "Let me ask you what you mean by Benevolence?"

Confucius said, "To be in one's inmost heart in kindly sympathy with all things; to love all men."

Lao Tan exclaimed, "Ah! You show your inferiority by such words! 'To love all men!' is not that vague and extravagant?"

"To—allow no selfish thoughts—"

"Unselfishness! That *is* selfishness!"

Book of Zhuangzi, 13:7

By this time Confucius' would have been losing the thread. What was the man talking about? He pressed the Daoist sage to be more specific. If trying to be unselfish was selfish, and trying to love all men was too woolly, what exactly was this "Way" he was talking about? What was he suggesting we *do*?

"Nothing! The Way is always "not-doing." Yet there is nothing it doesn't do!"

Dao Dejing, 37

Zhuangzi records that as Lao Tze started to explain his philosophy Confucius' mouth dropped open and he was speechless. Knowing Confucius this is probably true, but not as Zhuangzi suggests because he was speechless with awe but because it was becoming clear that as far as he was concerned the Daoist sage was talking complete nonsense.

If you wish to be guided by the Way, the Sage proceeded to tell Confucius, do not think of rightness and love and all these other meaningless concepts:

"Think of Heaven and Earth, which certainly pursue their invariable course; think of the sun and moon, which surely maintain their brightness; think of the stars in the zodiac, which preserve their order and courses …"

Book of Zhuangzi, 13:7

Now it was Confucius' turn to interrupt. Why should he think of heaven and earth and the sun and stars? What can they tell him?

"**Confucius and Nangong Jingshu consulting Lao Tze**" (their travelling wagon can be seen on left). This Ming Dynasty painting shows the conventional 'Confucian' version of the event, with the younger sage 'learning ritual' from Master Lao. In Zhaungzi's account (which is probably more reliable) Nangong did not accompany Confucius to see Lao Tze and the meeting was confrontational. *Qilu Press*

Confucius said, "Does Heaven speak? Yet the four seasons continue to change, and all things are continually born. Does Heaven speak?"

Analects, 17:19

The Daoist sage continued without bothering to reply. "Think of birds and beasts, which do not fail to collect together in their flocks and herds; and think of the trees, which do not fail to stand up in their places …"

Book of Zhuangzi, 13:7

All these things are part of the great Way, the Sage told the increasingly infuriated Confucius. It is only humankind which has lost the Way. Therefore true sages are not concerned with rightness or wrongness, rather they seek to escape from the world altogether.

"Escape from the world altogether"? Confucius sighed and said:

"**I can't form associations with the birds and beasts. So if I don't associate with people, then who will I associate with?**"

Analects, 18:6

With the truth of the great oneness, the Sage continued serenely, all other associations are vain. The sage abides

Confucius 'humiliated' by Lao Tze – in Zhuangzi's version of their encounter.
Illustration to the 'Book of Zhuangzi' by Bo Jingzhen

Lao Tze is often depicted 'communing with nature', an integral part of the Daoist philosophy. *Painting by Bo Jingzhen*

By holding to the ancient Way, you can manage present existence
And know the primordial beginning.
This is called the very beginning thread of the Way.

Dao Dejing, 14

In Zhuangzi's version of this first meeting between Confucius and the Daoists, Confucius is bowled over by this mystic philosophy and falls to his feet in awe and reverence:

Confucius said, "Master, your virtue is equal to that of Heaven and Earth!"

Book of Zhuangzi, 21:14

This is part of the "Daoist propaganda" element, however, Confucius never showed any sign of being the least bit sympathetic to their ideas at any time in his life, and although many people around him "followed the Dao" and withdrew from society completely by going to live in the forests and mountains, he was never tempted to do this himself. In another propaganda section of his book Zhuangzi has Confucius actually doing this later in his life: abandoning his students and retiring to live on acorns—but this is pure fiction:

The Daoist said: "The perfect man does not seek to be heard of; so how is it that you delight in doing so?"

Confucius said, "Excellent advice!" Thereupon he took leave of his associates, forsook his disciples, retired to the neighborhood of a great marsh, wore skins and hair cloth, and ate acorns and chestnuts.

Book of Zhuangzi, 20:1

In reality Confucius "forsook" neither his students nor his beliefs, and his first encounter with Daoism in Luoyang marked the beginning of a battle between two

with the One, in a condition of *wu-wei* ("actively doing absolutely nothing"). "Actively doing absolutely nothing!" This must have caused Confucius to sigh and shake his head again. He did not need to hear this: it was a complete waste of time. Finally he had grasped what the man was talking about—or at least he thought he had. The Daoist "Way" was not, as he had imagined, a "way" which could be followed at all:

The Way that can be followed is not the eternal Way.
The name that can be named is not the eternal name.

Dao Dejing, 1

In fact they seemed to mean by the term "*Dao*" (which means "way" in the sense of "road" or "path") not a way to be followed but the actual force which guides the universe, perhaps even the universe itself:

Existing continuously, it cannot be named and it returns to nothingness.

Thus, it is called the formless form, the image of nothing.

The 'primordial beginning' - weirdly shaped columns of gas and dust in the Eagle Nebula, 65000 light years away from Earth, which have been dubbed 'the 'Pillars of Creation'. Millions of years from now these clouds will give birth to new stars and new worlds. The Daoist 'Way' can be interpreted as the moving spirit of the universe itself. Hubble Telescope visible-light photo. *Courtesy NASA/ STScL*

diametrically opposed philosophies which was to last for many centuries. Whether he actually spoke to "Lao Tze" or to a Daoist with another name is irrelevant—he certainly spoke to some of them, and it seemed to him that his most fundamental ideas were being challenged:

Get rid of "holiness" and abandon "wisdom" and the people will benefit a hundredfold. Get rid of "humaneness" and abandon "rightness" and the people will return to filial piety and compassion.

Dao Dejing, 19

Whereas Confucius emphasized the importance of knowledge, the Daoists held that studying was a waste of time; while his whole life was spent debating and discussing things, the Daoists said that this was pointless:

Get rid of "learning" and there will be no anxiety.

Dao Dejing, 20

One who knows does not speak. One who speaks does not know.

Dao Dejing, 56

The good do not debate. Debaters are not good.

Anti-Confucian propagandist: Zhuangzi described Confucius renouncing his beliefs and becoming a Daoist, but all these stories are pure fiction.

The one who really knows is not broadly learned,
the extensively learned do not really know.

Dao Dejing, 81

It is easy to see how hearing this sort of thing would have been to Confucius like showing a red rag to a bull, and his meetings with the Daoists in Luoyang would have sharpened his belief in his own fundamentally different "Way" rather than influencing his thinking in any way—there is not a single trace of Daoist ideas about nature or the "prime mover of all things" anywhere in the *Analects*. The only thing he took from them in fact was their name, appropriating the word *Dao* to mean "The Way of Humanity" or "The Way of Confucius."

However, although "The Way of Confucius" finally won out in China, Daoism as a religion is still popular and there are an estimated 12 million Daoists worldwide today. As a philosophy its appeal remains phenomenal— the "Way of Being" has been translated into more languages than any other book apart from the Bible.

Although the rivalry between Confucianism and Daoism in China eventually became so intense that

Stylized representation of the three major Chinese religions / philosophies existing in harmony. Confucianism (left), Daoism (centre) and Buddhism (right). *Qilu Press*

everybody had to declare themselves supporters of one or the other, in the first century or so after Confucius' death many people apparently found no difficulty in embracing both philosophies. In the Guodian tomb, together with the bamboo-slips inscribed with Confucian manuscripts, archaeologists also found the earliest extant copy of the *Way of Being*. The tomb seems to be that of a tutor to family of the Duke of Chu, one of the "Warring States" to the south of Lu in the second half of the fourth century BC, who apparently included both

Confucius and Lao Tze in his curriculum. It seems that the era of fierce partisanship started much later, when the supporters of each school were making a bid for political power.

Today, now all the dust has settled, the two philosophies seem not so much incompatible as complementary, since they are talking about totally different things. Daoism never really speaks about social relations while Confucianism has nothing to say about the origin of the universe. Business people, teachers, students, and of course political leaders would do well to keep the *Analects* to hand for constant reference, while the *Way of Being* is a useful tool for understanding quantum physics and makes a delightful companion volume to Stephen Hawking's *A Brief History of Time*:

> All things in the cosmos arise from being. Being arises from non-being. The Way is so vast that it seems to be the ancestor of the myriad things. It is the child of I-don't-know-who, and prior to the primeval Lord-on-high. Mystery within mystery, the door to all marvels.

Dao Dejing

The two ways are in the end not incompatible, and we need them both. As we probe ever deeper into the "the mystery within mystery" and the ultimate secrets of the universe which is the Way of the Dao, we nevertheless still need that other Way, the Way of Confucius, or we may well end up destroying ourselves through our arrogance. Both ways are the gift of time from the fifth century BC, that amazing century which also gave us Socrates, Plato, and Gautama Buddha.

Two Ways: One Universe.

The Way is so vast that it seems to be the ancestor of the myriad things.
The so-called 'Mountains of Creation' in the constellation Cassiopeia, where vast clouds of gas and dust are giving birth to new stars.
Spitzer Space Telescope infrared photo. *Courtesy NASA/ JPL-Caltech*

The Classes Begin

My steeds advanced without stopping;
The way from Zhou was winding and tedious.
Did I not have the wish to return?

Book of Songs, 162: ?? Si Mu

As their carriage rattled and creaked down the winding road away from Zhou and towards the broad plain of the Yellow River, Confucius must almost have wished they could turn back again. After a few blissful weeks of doing what he knew he was born to do—researching ancient wisdom and disputing philosophy with the best of them—it was back to business as usual: breeding cattle. When was it ever going to end?

Nangong Jingshu would have told him not to worry. They had successfully achieved the main purpose of their trip, which was to study Ritual at the Grand Temple of Zhou. Confucius could now put the word "Zi" ("Master") after his name: "Kong Zi"—it sounded impressive already—and Nangong promised to try and find Confucius some tutoring work after they got back to Lu. "Master" Confucius would have nodded gratefully, but without out much hope that this would happen.

Apart from the vague possibility that his studies in Luoyang might kick-start a new career, the main result of his stay in the capital was that it firmed up his growing sense of having a mission to fulfil.

Confucius said: "… at thirty I stood firm."

Analects, 2:4

He was nearing thirty now. All around him he could see more and more evidence of society's deterioration:

Confucius said: "Men of high office who are narrow-minded; propriety without respect and funerals without grief: how can I bear to look at such things?"

Analects, 3:26

In the face of all this uncaring behavior, Confucius believed it was time that right-minded people should start to "stand firm" and re-establish human values. Somebody had to show them the way to do this, and after his less-than-fruitful exchange with the Daoists, he realized that their Way was not going to help. Let the Daoists retreat into the forest if that is what they wanted

Confucius' first teaching job: tutoring the sons of Lord Meng. *Qilu Press*

Confucius' most illustrious student: Duke Jing of Qi – the contemporary equivalent of royalty. Detail from Ming Dynasty painting. *Qilu Press*

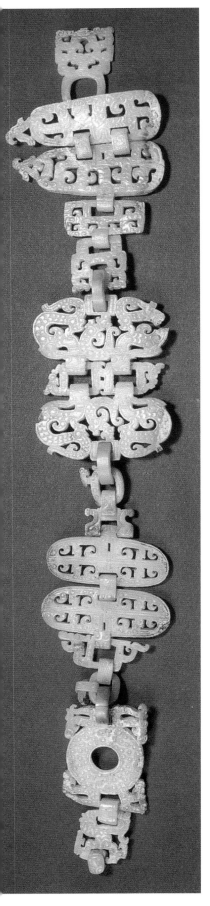

Traditional Ritual: Jade pendant from Warring States Period, as worn by the Dukes on ceremonial and state occasions. *Qilu Press*

to do, but somebody was going to have to come up with another Way that was really going to make a difference to the whole of society, and since nobody else seemed to be bothered, he would have to do it himself. From now on, he was a man with a mission.

Burning with his new-found zeal to change the world, Confucius nevertheless had to go straight back to work in his office near the cattle byres as soon as he returned from Zhou. Not, however, for very long, as Nangong Jingshu kept his promise and very quickly reappeared with more good news—he had found him work as a Ritual tutor to his own brothers, one of whom was Meng Yi, who had been two years ahead of Confucius and Nangong at school, and was his father's heir. It seems probable that Nangong was (like Confucius) the son of one of his father's concubines or junior wives, and this probably explains why he spent his life indulging his hobbies and interests—one of which was promoting his friend's career— rather than grooming himself for leadership, as there was little chance he would ever become "Lord Meng" himself.

Confucius now had to be given time off from his job in order to go and live in the Meng mansion and take up his tutorial duties. Although Lord Ji would have been reluctant to lose his excellent manager even temporarily, he eventually

agreed since it was in his interest to keep on friendly terms with Lord Meng, and he even agreed to Confucius' being given leave-of-absence with pay.

At this time there were three powerful feudal families in the state of Lu, the Ji, Meng, and Shu clans. Although the head of each clan had dreams of usurping power and making members of his own family the Dukes of Lu in perpetuity, none of them was really powerful enough to achieve this on his own, and if there was to be a coup it would have to be by two of the clans acting together. The Ji and Meng families therefore maintained friendly relations while they bided their time for the right moment to seize power jointly, and Confucius' career was a beneficiary of this. Almost overnight Confucius became a teacher, and discovered his true vocation.

The first classes with Lord Meng's sons were a great success. With his new qualifications as Master of Ritual he was employed to teach only this subject, but no doubt enlivened his lessons with readings from the *Book of Songs* and colorful examples from history and everyday life; we know all about his lively teaching methods from the later recollections of his students in the *Analects*. Also from the *Analects* we know that Confucius never gave "lectures" as such, but instead encouraged lively discussions about each topic which were usually based on a passage from one of the classic texts, and in this case he would have used the *Book of Rites* together with the notes he had made himself during his research in Luoyang. His classes were so lively and interesting that his two students gave glowing reports to their powerful father and Confucius' career really began to take off.

Nangong Jingshu immediately set about finding more noble students for the 29-year-old Master of Ritual. If he played this right, he assured Confucius, he would never have to go back to cattle-breeding again.

After Confucius returned from Zhou to Lu, his pupils gradually became more numerous.

Sima Qian, *Records of the Grand Historian*

Even more prestigious tutorial assignments followed, and Confucius soon found himself in the capital of Lu, Chungdu, instructing the family of Duke Zhao himself. Then came the luckiest break of all, the big break that everybody dreams about but more often than not never comes.

By chance, while Confucius was in the capital of Lu tutoring the Duke's family, the extremely powerful Duke Jing, ruler of the state of Qi just to the north, arrived on a state visit. Qi was much larger than Lu and threateningly powerful: it was no secret that Duke Jing wanted to annexe his tiny neighbor into his own dukedom. At this time each state was nominally obliged to provide a fixed number of war chariots to the King of Zhou in the event of war, and although the practice was in abeyance, the states were still classified by this method. Thus Qi was known as a "state of a thousand chariots" while Lu rated only a few hundred. This power imbalance meant that the Dukes of Lu had to be very careful in their relations with the Dukes of Qi and fell over themselves to be subservient and obliging to their powerful neighbor in every way except actually giving away any territory.

Thus it was that when Duke Jing announced that the

A farmer and his son – Han Dynasty figurines. Confucius' revolutionary educational system was open to all, and many of his most famous students were originally the sons of poor farmers. Shanghai Museum. *Photo: Jonathan Price*

main purpose of his visit to Lu was to study the latest thinking on ritual and ceremonial procedure, Duke Zhao told him that he had the very man for the job right here in his court. Kong Zi he told Duke Jing, had only recently returned from intensive study at the Grand Temple of Zhou itself, and although a mere *shi* or humble scholar he was extremely respectful to his superiors and had already distinguished himself as a tutor to the rich and famous all over the state of Lu. Duke Jing was delighted. He sometimes had to visit even more powerful states like Chu to the south, and for these diplomatic excursions a thorough knowledge of up-to-date ceremonial rules was essential. He had originally intended visiting Luoyang himself but according to reports the whole of Zhou was now engulfed in civil war. If this man had been Zhou-trained he sounded perfect.

Confucius was hastily fitted out in a new set of suitable robes and a silk cap, and was ordered to present himself to the mighty Duke Jing. The lessons took place in Duke Zhao's own ancestral temple, and the young teacher and his illustrious student hit it off almost immediately. His early schooling with the nobility now really paid off and Confucius was able to behave with exactly the right combination of respect and professional confidence as if to the manner born:

> **He advanced rapidly to his position, holding up his robe in his arms like wings, and on occupying his place, his manner still showed respectful uneasiness.**
>
> *Analects*, 10:4

There is quite a long section in the *Analects* describing his manner when in the presence of rulers and his "respectful uneasiness" is mentioned several times—it was not proper to appear too relaxed. At the start of each of his lessons with Duke Jing he would also have made sure he appeared suitably overawed and honored:

> **When he was passing the place of the prince, his countenance appeared to change, his legs to bend under him, and his words came as if he hardly had breath to utter them.**
>
> *Analects*, 10:4

Nevertheless he was not *so* overawed that he appeared servile, and this was clearly one of the secrets of his success with the mighty—while showing rulers due respect he still remained confident and authoritative in his role as teacher or advisor:

> **When a ruler was present, his manner was grave and respectful, but self-possessed… when he was in the prince's ancestral temple, or in the court, he**

Confucius' famous 'scholar-wagon', donated by Nangong Jingshu. Ming Dynasty Painting. *Qilu Press*

classical Chinese compositions—and the duke, who was only about ten years older than Confucius himself, often requested him to play on the *guqin*—the Chinese zither—a skill at which Confucius had been adept since childhood. It had been his young mother who had first encouraged him in this, and he must have often wished she could see him now: her little boy in whom she had invested so many hopes, singing along with the Duke of Qi!

This was of course the first time that Confucius had ever been on anything like intimate terms with an actual ruler, and he must have been tempted to open up discussions about his other burning passion—the "Way" to create a just society. Perhaps he made a few tentative beginnings (while maintaining of course the utmost respect) since it was in fact to Duke Jing that Confucius later made most of his famous pronouncements about ruling and politics, but at this time he was still inexperienced and feeling his way cautiously in the halls of power.

spoke minutely and eloquently on every point, but cautiously.

Analects, 10:2/10:1

He would of course have been required to stand the whole time while in Duke Jing's presence, so he was careful to maintain the correct posture:

He moved his left or right arm, as their position required, but kept the skirts of his robe before and behind evenly adjusted.

Analects, 10:3

All in all, Duke Jing was delighted with his new tutor, and after the day's ritual practice they relaxed with music—they had discovered a shared passion for

Certainly he did not put a foot wrong at this stage, and when the tutoring sessions came to an end Duke Jing was so effusive in his praise of Confucius that he invited him to come and stay at his court in Linzi—the capital of Qi—at any time, where he would introduce him to his renowned musicians and treat him to music that seemed to come from heaven itself. Duke Jing was almost as proud of his musicians as he was of his chariots. When they said goodbye to each other Confucius would

Confucius' first classes. Life-size tableau in the City of the Six Arts, Qufu. *Photo: Jonathan Price*

naturally have been obliged to bow low and address his student as "Your most illustrious and heavenly majesty," but then perhaps Duke Jing, with the faintest inclination of his head, uttered the words "Great Master."

It was from this time onward that Kong Qiu, having been the tutor of a ruler, was known as Kong Fu Zi, in other words not merely "Master Kong" but "Grand Master Kong." A glittering career as the tutor to the great now opened up before him, and there seemed no question that he would ever have to go back to the cowsheds.

Since he played a leading part in setting up and financing Confucius' school, it was probably Nangong Jingshu who initially negotiated with the Ji family about this. However it was arranged, Lord Ji was somehow persuaded to allow Confucius to teach full time but still retain his grain allowance salary. Confucius was summoned to an audience with his feudal lord, thanked him effusively for his generosity, and then dropped an unexpected bombshell by insisting on certain conditions. What he was asking for was so astounding that Lord Ji must have been rendered speechless for several seconds. This was one of the pivotal moments in human history.

He would be happy to continue tutoring the sons of the nobility, Confucius told his feudal lord, but he also wanted to open his classes to everybody, regardless of rank.

"Everybody?" Lord Ji managed at last. "You mean 'everybody' in the sense of artisans or, shopkeepers?"

"Yes."

"Even 'everybody' in the sense of *farm laborers*?"

"Yes."

Another long moment of silence. "And you expect *me* to pay for this—"education of the lower classes"?"

"No." Confucius explained his plan. He would tutor any members of the nobility that Lord Ji passed his way in return for his salary, but other students would have to pay him. There would be a sliding scale; he would for example accept a single dried sausage from the poorest students but those from better-off families would be expected to contribute more. The whole thing would be on an *ad hoc* basis:

Confucius said: "From the one who brings a bundle of dried meat (the poorest person) upwards, I will never deny a person my instruction."

Analects, 7:7

He believed strongly about this:

Confucius said: "In teaching people, there should be no discrimination."

Analects, 15:39

Zilu, lifelong follower of Confucius, as a young man. Jiading Confucius Temple Shanghai. *Photo: Jonathan Price*

Another long moment of silence, and then, amazingly, Lord Ji finally agreed to Confucius' proposal. This was the moment that set in motion the educational revolution which changed the world—at least the Eastern part of it—the Western world would wait another two and a half millenia before it finally adopted the same principle of universal education in exactly the same way. Confucius was certainly the first "professional" teacher in China, and perhaps in the world, who opened his classes to everybody regardless of rank or their ability to pay.

With this financial backing in place—Confucius' own living expenses would still be covered by his grain allowance and he would probably also be able to support needy students from this as well—Nangong Jingshu quickly got the project rolling. He donated his own covered travelling wagon, together with a team of oxen and drivers, and Confucius had the exclusive use of

this vehicle for the rest of his life. The wagon, which has become immortalized in the hundreds of paintings depicting Confucius' life as a travelling teacher, may even have been the same one they used for their trip to Zhou.

Later on, Confucius was to acknowledge how important all this early support had been to him:

"Since Lord Ji granted me a stipend of one thousand bushels, friends got closer to me; since Nangong Jingshu transported me in his carriage, my ideas spread wider; without these two benefactors, my way would have lapsed."

Liu Xiang (Shuo Yuan), *The Realm of Sayings*

This saying, which was quoted in a book which appeared much later during the Han Dynasty, is considered authentic since the details are so specific. Although, as Confucius points out, Nangong's wagon allowed him to travel around "spreading his word," it also gave him a certain status in society—which was essential if he was to recruit the type of student who saw his courses as a passport to employment in government or with one of the powerful families. He did in fact attract many such students, and a large number of "Confucius School" graduates went on to successful careers in administration. In this respect his classes performed a similar function to the "academy for gentlemen" which he himself had attended, with the significant difference that even the talented sons of farmers could now join his own school.

Zilu's poor childhood. Painting from the collection of the Kong Family illustrating Guo Jujing's '24 Examples of Filial Piety'. *Qilu Press*

Stylised representation of Confucius' students. Detail from Ming Dynasty Painting.

Zilu (foreground) listening to Confucius teaching. Tableau in the City of the Six Arts, Qufu. *Photo: Jonathan Price*

When he says in the same passage that "friends got closer to me" owing to Lord Ji's generosity, Confucius probably meant the core group of students who became like his family and stayed with him for many years; they were only able to do this because his allowance of "a thousand bushels" of millet a year enabled him to provide for them as well as himself.

Several members of this core group were indeed among his first batch of students, the principal of whom was Zilu, often referred to by Confucius by his nickname "Yu." Sima Qian says in the *Records* that Zilu was nine years younger than his teacher, so he was in his early twenties when he first enrolled as Confucius' student.

The young man was from a poor family and was one of the first to take advantage of Confucius' revolutionary new equal-opportunity classes, which gave him a chance in life that he would never otherwise have had. He did in fact go on to work as a steward for the Ji family, just as Confucius himself had done, but he was so grateful that even after he started work he returned to the classes in his spare time and then joined his Master during his long exile. Zilu used his salary from the Ji to support his parents, who were very poor farmers, and he was included in the book which was mentioned in an earlier chapter, the *Er Shi Si Xiao* (*Twenty-Four Examples of Filial Piety*) written by Guo Jujing during the Yuan Dynasty.

The faithful followers like Zilu, who formed a kind of inner family, are often called the "disciples," since it was estimated by Sima Qian that over the course of his whole career Confucius taught more than 3,000 ordinary

"students," in the sense of people who simply enrolled for short-time courses. This is a not unreasonable estimate since a modern teacher might well handle many more pupils than this over a lifetime's career. Confucius' number one student of all time, Yan Hui, was not even born when he first opened his classes.

Zilu was probably Confucius' most enthusiastic student of all, however, and every time the Master asked a question he was always the first to answer, often rushing out his words without thinking. Confucius often made fun of him for this:

Confucius said: "Yu is the kind of man who could settle a lawsuit after hearing a single sentence. He never sleeps before giving his ruling."

Analects, 12:12

He also had tunnel vision, and could only ever grasp one thing at a time:

When Zilu heard a teaching and had not yet put it into practice, he would be apprehensive about hearing something new in the meantime.

Analects, 5:14

Zilu is described in another of the *Analects* as "looking bold and soldierly," but Confucius considered he was bold to the point of rashness, and always rushed into things without thinking:

Confucius said: "Nobody ever listens to me, so I shall take a raft and cross the ocean. I'm sure Yu will go with me." Zilu was very happy to hear this. Confucius said, "Yu likes daring more than I, but he lacks discretion."

Analects, 5:7

These rebukes are always full of gentle humor, and Confucius was obviously very fond of his excitable and impetuous student, who not only had ambitions of becoming a steward, but dreamed of military glory.

Zilu said, "If you were in command of a major army, who would you choose to assist you?"

Confucius said, "I would not select the kind of man who likes to wrestle with tigers barehanded or cross rivers without a boat, dying without a second thought. It must be someone who proceeds with caution, adjusts his plans accordingly, and sees them through to their completion."

Analects, 7:11

Although all this was an affectionate joke, Confucius is also supposed to have said: "Yu, there—he will not die a natural death." (*Analects,* 11:12) Sadly he was right about this, and his disciple's rash boldness killed him in the end. Many years later, only a year or two before Confucius himself died, Zilu was killed in a military coup in the neighboring state of Wei, while bravely trying to defend its ruler.

It would have been a sad moment for his old teacher. Excitable, impetuous, and often absent-minded, Zilu had always been his most exasperating student, but nevertheless one of the most likeable. Always in such a hurry, he would not even spend time to dress himself properly:

Confucius said: "Standing in tattered work clothes among gentlemen clothed in fine furs without any embarrassment; it is Yu!"

Analects, 9:27

Or he would leave his possessions strewn about the place without even realizing he had mislaid them:

Confucius said, "What is the lute of Yu doing at my door?"

Analects, 11:15

This vivid little picture—Confucius has obviously just tripped over the lute—seems to suggest that he had some sort of school-house at least in the early days, and that the students themselves lived there. The complete absence of any reference to Confucius' wife, son, or daughter in any of the *Analects* describing his teaching also reinforces the idea that

Confucius' student Ranyu ("Qiu"). *Photo: Jonathan Price*

by now he was separated from them. We know nothing of any of this for certain, but when he became ill in old age he told Zilu who was at that time still alive, "I don't want a pompous funeral, I want to die in the hands of my disciples," which suggests that even at the end of his life he was still living with his student family rather than his actual family. He got his wish, and did die in the hands of his weeping students, although by this time poor Zilu had gone to the gods himself.

Not all of the students from his early group stayed with him, however, and one or two, after showing early promise, were expelled by the Master from the inner circle for conduct unbecoming a Confucian gentleman. One of these appears in the translated versions of the *Analects* under a bewildering assortment of names, sometimes as Ranyu but elsewhere as "Zan Yu," "Ran Qiu," or "Yen Qiu," but most often as plain "Qiu," which is how Confucius referred to him in class. Like Zilu, Qiu started in Confucius' first batch of students. At first Confucius was very patient with him since he lacked confidence, unlike his fellow-student Zilu who had too much of it.

Confucius said, "Qiu has a tendency to give up easily, so I push him. Yu rushes at everything too fast so I restrain him."

Analects, 11.22

Yen Qiu said: "It is not that I don't enjoy your Way, but my strength is not enough."

Confucius said, "Those whose strength is not enough give up half way. You are now limiting yourself."

Analects, 6:12

After Qiu had successfully completed his course Confucius recommended him to the Ji family for a post as a steward.

"What do you think of Qiu?"

Confucius said, "Qiu is talented. What difficulty would he have in handling administration work?"

Analects, 6:8

This was not exactly a glowing reference but it got Qiu the position, which was in fact doing his old job as steward in charge of grain, a post which had now been expanded to include the supervision of the collection of "tithes," the portion of each farmer's millet harvest that he had to pay to his feudal lord. The feudal lords were in turn obliged to turn over a proportion of their total grain stock to the Duke of Lu, who was supposed to use this to distribute to the poor in times of need. This was the Zhou "social welfare" system that Confucius had always so much admired—when it worked.

Model son: Min Ziqian as a child pleading with his father to forgive his stepmother for her horrible cruelties towards him. Illustration of one of the "24 Examples of Filial Piety" by Guo Jujing. *Qilu Press*

progressively more impotent, and would soon become, like his own nominal overlord the King of Zhou, a mere figurehead with no real power. From now on they would keep all the grain taxes for themselves, and Confucius expected Qiu, as his student, to object to this since he had taught them:

"The Perfected Man helps the distressed, but does not add to the wealth of the rich."

Analects, 6:4

Qiu ignored this teaching, and instead threw himself enthusiastically into the task of extorting even bigger grain tithes from the farmers on behalf of his millionaire master:

Even though the head of the Ji family was "wealthier than the Duke of Zhou," Qiu collected taxes for him, and made him richer. **Confucius said, "He is no disciple of mine. My students, you can beat the drum and attack him if you want."**

Analects, 11:17

Many of the students who started with Confucius in his "first term" were much more worthy, even though few of them were brilliant—the most outstanding of his students were to belong to the "Class of 497" which was a long way into the future (at this time we have only reached 521 BC). One of these worthies was Min Ziqian, who like Zilu came from an extremely poor family and was another of Confucius' "scholarship boys" who went on to a successful civil service career. Min Ziqian, like Zilu, became legendary as an example of devotion to his parents, and features as another of Guo Jujing's *Twenty-Four Examples of Filial Piety*. He became so celebrated for this that in several Chinese cities there are streets named after him, although the stories of his piety were probably invented long after his time and derive originally from a single one of the

Now, however, both Lord Ji and Lord Meng had decided that they no longer needed to give up any part of their grain stock to Duke Zhao, who was becoming

Analects:

The Master said, "Filial indeed is Min Ziqian! Other people say nothing of him different from the report of his parents and brothers."

Analects, 11:4

According to the legend of Min Ziqian's childhood, he was extremely cruelly treated by his evil stepmother, who forced him to work in freezing winter weather protected only by a few rushes under his thin clothes. While poor little Min chopped wood outside and was so cold his fingers almost froze solid, his stepbrothers lazed about wearing many layers of cotton padding under their fur coats. Being a good son Min never complained or said anything about it, and even when his father finally discovered what had been going on and threatened to throw his wife out, the boy pleaded for her to be forgiven, saying, "If she goes, then my stepbrothers will not have a mother!"

Like many of the apocryphal stories about Confucius and his disciples, this one is so like a fairy-tale that it probably has no foundation, but it does illustrate how the Confucian idea of filial piety can be easily abused. Min Ziqian was obliged as a good little Confucian son to go on enduring this horrific treatment, if necessary without saying anything until he finally died from hypothermia; in the story it is only by chance that his father discovered what was happening. There must have been thousands of other children who were not so lucky. Of course this story like all fairy-tales has a happy ending—shamed by the boy's example the stepmother mends her ways and becomes a model parent—but this again is a Confucian concept based on his somewhat over-optimistic view of human nature.

Whether or not this story about his childhood was true,

Min Ziqian was certainly renowned for his noble behavior as an adult:

Min Ziqian was distinguished for his virtuous principles and practice.

Analects, 11:3

Unlike his classmate Qiu, Min Ziqian refused an offer of very high office with the same employer, Lord Ji,

Zao Wo. Photo: Jonathan Price

when offered the governorship of a small city the feudal baron had taken by force:

The head of the Ji family sent to Min Ziqian to ask him to govern Pi for them. Min Ziqian said, "Please decline for me politely. If they pursue me further, I shall have to go live on the banks of the Wen River."

Analects, 6:9

As a student, Min Ziqian was noted for being quiet and reserved, and he spoke very little during Confucius' classes, although when he did it was invariably to express the perfect Confucian point of view:

The men of Lu were rebuilding the Main Treasury. Min Ziqian said: "Why don't we keep its old style? Why do we have to change it completely?" Confucius said, "This fellow doesn't say much, but when he does, he is right on the mark."

Analects, 11:14

Like Confucius himself, Min did not object to change, but he also loved tradition and objected to change for its own sake. Bulldozing ancient buildings rather than restoring the exterior and modernizing them inside would be a modern equivalent of this, and many would agree with the sentiments of Confucius and his student.

Every teacher will have some hopeless students, and Confucius was no exception. In his first classes, the award for dumbest student of the year went to Zai Yu, and Confucius gave up on him:

Zai Yu slept during the daytime. Confucius said, "Rotten wood cannot be carved; dirty earth cannot be used for cement: why bother scolding him?"

Analects, 5:10

Confucius encouraged his students to ask intelligent questions, and Zilu was always up for this, asking for example "Does the Superior Man esteem bravery?" to which Confucius replied that a "superior man" is always brave but a brave man is not always superior. However another student, Zai Wo, was notorious for asking the most unbelievably stupid questions which completely exasperated his teacher:

Zai Wo asked: "If you tell a humane man that there is a human being at the bottom of a well, will he climb into it?" Confucius: "He would not be such a fool!"

Analects, 6:26

Despite his obtuseness, Confucius was still able to make something out of his exasperating student and Zai Wo is recorded in historical annals as having later worked as a senior official for Duke Jing of Qi, who was himself of course among the first and most illustrious alumni of the Confucius Academy. This may even have been a case of jobs for the boys, since Confucius remained on very good terms with Duke Jing almost all his life, and it is probably no coincidence that so many of Confucius' former students went on to work for the Ji family, with whom their teacher also had very good connections.

Many of the students in Confucius' first classes seem to have come from extremely poor backgrounds, so he was really putting his ideas of social equality into practice as he said he would, and this is indeed one of the main qualities of a "Confucian," as he always insisted. Fine words are not enough:

"Act before you speak and then speak according to your actions."

Analects, 2:13

Probably most of the students could contribute a little bit more than a "piece of dried sausage" towards the cost of their tuition, but with so many from humble backgrounds Confucius would have had to rely mainly on his grain stipend from Lord Ji to keep going. One of the very poorest of all his earliest pupils was Yan You, the father of Yan Hui who was to become many years

later his best and brightest student. Without the opportunity that Confucius gave to them, both father and son would have spent their lives laboring in the fields, and in this way, although on a very small scale, his new school was truly a social revolution.

Yan Hui tragically died before his promise could be realized, but the principle nevertheless remains: there are young people like him in every village, and it is only universal education that can give them a chance to realize their full potential.

This principle remains Confucius' greatest legacy.

Students at Confucius' class. Life-size models in the City of the Six Arts, Qufu. *Photo: Jonathan Price*

The School of Confucius

Apart from making a small donation, the only other qualification that Confucius required from somebody who wanted to study with him was that they should genuinely want to learn.

Confucius said: "If a student is not eager, I won't teach him."

Analects, 7:8

His brighter students sometimes complained that he was wasting his time trying to teach people who although "eager" enough, were not really up to it, and he should start to be more selective. Confucius did not agree:

Confucius said, "Take people the way they come to you ... why be so strict?

Analects, 7:29

"The Superior Man venerates the worthy but accepts everyone… why should I push others away?"

Analects 19:3

Nevertheless he only wanted active students who were prepared to think for themselves:

Confucius said, "If a student doesn't continually question: "What is it? What does it mean?" I don't know what I can do for him."

Analects, 15:16

There are so many detailed references to his teaching in the *Analects*, not only recollections by his students but comments by Confucius himself on his methods, that as

Probable site of Confucius original school and residence, Qufu. *Qilu Press*

we read it seems as if we are travelling back in time and attending his classes ourselves. Some aspects of his teaching are very familiar, for example he used "textbooks," basically three of them: the *Book of Songs*, the *Book of Rites*, and the *Book of History*:

> **Topics which the Teacher regularly discussed were the *Book of Songs*, the *Book of History*, and the maintenance of propriety in the *Book of Rites*.**
>
> *Analects*, 7:18

One big difference to modern teachine, however, was his inclusion of music as another basic subject. He always ended up the day with group singing and dancing, accompanying his students on his *guqin*, and he also encouraged them to play their own instruments—it will be recollected that Zilu left his lute outside Confucius' door where his Master could easily trip over it. In this he was echoing the curriculum of his own school on Lord Ji's estate; it was considered at this time that high culture in the form of musical accomplishment was the final polish in the educational process, without which a gentleman could not call himself truly refined:

> **The Master said, "It is by the *Book of Songs* that the mind is aroused. It is by the *Book of Rites* that the character is established. It is from Music that the finish is received."**
>
> *Analects*, 8:8

The crucial difference was that many of Confucius' students were not "gentlemen" by birth, but he was training them in the accomplishments previously reserved for those born to greatness. Even if they were the sons of farmers, once they had completed Confucius' course they could go on to work in royal or lordly households and they would know how to behave, could even if necessary acquit themselves without embarrassment on the lute or zither, and although not "high-born" they would seem to be so. It is not difficult to see how attractive his courses must have seemed at the time, and why he was so immediately successful— not only the poorest people but rich farmers and merchants fell over themselves to enrol their sons with him. Graduation from Confucius' school appeared to be a passport to careers these families had formerly only dreamed about.

Confucius' main "textbook" was of course his favorite book, the *Book of Songs*, which he used as a jumping-off point for class discussions of many issues:

> **The Master said, "My students, why do you not study the *Book of Songs*? The Odes serve to stimulate the mind. They teach the art of**

Confucius relaxing with his students. Ming Dynasty Painting. *Qilu Press*

Confucius and his students discussing the classics. Ming Dynasty Painting. *Qilu Press*

> **sociability. They show how to regulate feelings of resentment. From them you learn the more immediate duty of serving one's father, and the remoter one of serving one's prince. From them we become largely acquainted with the names of birds, beasts, and plants."**
>
> *Analects*, 17:9

Certainly the *Book of Songs* could be used in this way as textbook of botany, agronomy, and many other practical subjects:

> We remove the insects that eat the heart and the leaf,
> And those that eat the roots and the joints.
> So they shall not hurt the young plants of our fields.
>
> *Book of Songs*, 212: Da Tian

Confucius was not very interested in teaching mere facts, however, and preferred those poems which helped students to—as he put it—"stimulate their minds." Almost any of the Odes could be used for this purpose, even those which were at first sight simply descriptive,

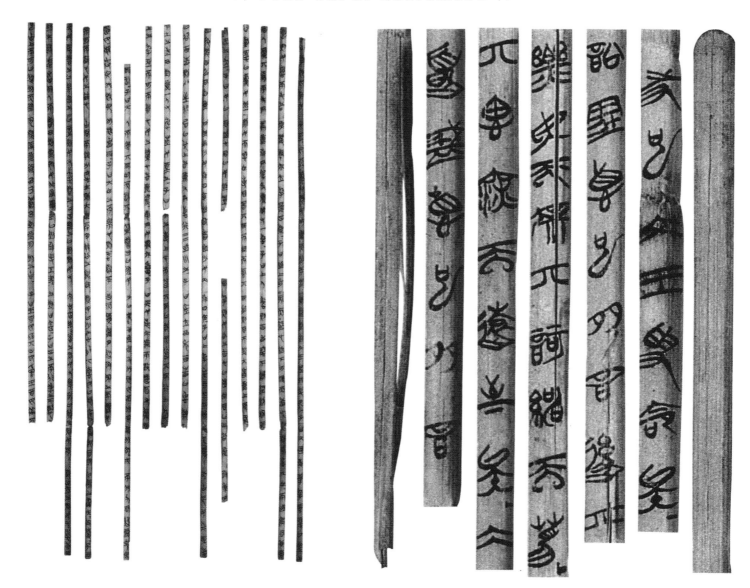

Bamboo-slip manuscript entitled 'Confucius on Poetry' thought to have been originally written by his student Hsia ('Zixia'). The book describes how Confucius used 'The Book of Songs' in his teaching. From the Shanghai Museum Bamboo-Slip collection. *Photo courtesy Shanghai Museum*

and this is one of the lessons that teachers anywhere can gain from him—it is not important which textbooks you use, what matters is how you use them.

There are several passages in the *Analects* which are almost like recordings of one of Confucius' classes, in which we can hear him using his technique of reading poems from the *Book of Songs*, and then starting a class discussion. One day his class looked at some poems which describe a beautiful lady of the old Zhou Empire:

She appears like a goddess!
Her black hair in masses like clouds,
No false locks does she descend to.

Her skin was like congealed ointment;
Her teeth were like melon seeds;

What dimples, as she artfully smiled !
How lovely her eyes, with the black and white so well defined!
Ah ! Such a woman as this! The beauty of the country!

Book of Songs, 47: Jun Zi Xie Lao *Book of Songs*, 57: Shuo Ren

"What does this mean," his student Hsia asked?
"That the ladies of old were naturally beautiful without the aid of adornment?"

Confucius said, "Yes—in the same way that the best paintings use a plain background, there is no need for finicky decorations."

Hsia said, "Then rituals and ceremonies are a secondary thing? First there must be natural goodness?"

Confucius said, "Ah, Hsia, you uplift me. Now we can really begin to discuss the *Book of Songs!*"

Analects, 3:8

Hsia was another of Confucius' students who went on to a very successful career, and he is recorded in *Analects*

13:7 as having become the governor of Qufu, the small city which is considered to be Confucius' "home town" and where he based his school. He also became a writer under the name Zi Xia (Master Hsia), and fragments of his work on bamboo-slips, which later were incorporated into the *Analects*, have been discovered in tombs. Although very talented Hsia unfortunately also had a massive ego, and in his writings, parts of which were copied verbatim into the *Analects*, he attributed many of his Master's most famous sayings to himself:

> One student, upset, said: "Everyone has brothers, I alone have none."
>
> Master Hsia said, "If the Superior Man is reverent and courteous to everyone, everything within the four seas will be his brother."
>
> *Analects*, 12:5

This is quintessential Confucius and obviously Hsia is quoting his Master to somebody else, but by leaving out the conventional preface "*Confucius said …*" he leaves us to understand that the words of wisdom are his own. Sima Qian in the *Records of the Grand Historian* tells us that Hsia later went blind as a punishment for his hubris, and when he asked another of Confucius' disciples, Zengzi, what he had done to deserve this cruel fate, Hsia was told: "You tried to make people think you are comparable to our Master—*that* is your sin!"

As they discussed the poems in the *Book of Songs* each day Confucius would not laboriously explain the meaning, instead he would give his students some sort of lead and then expect them to arrive at conclusions themselves:

> Zigong said, "As the *Book of Songs* says: 'Like cutting and filing, grinding and polishing.'"
>
> Confucius said, "Ah! Now I can begin to discuss the *Book of Songs* with Si. I give him a hint and he gets the whole point!"
>
> *Analects*, 1:15

Here, his student had understood that a poem in the *Book of Songs* was referring to how we should continually "grind and polish" our behavior—never stop making adjustments and improving ourselves, and Confucius was very happy that Zigong had "got the point" himself without any prompting.

As a teacher, Confucius believed that if he served up portions of knowledge piecemeal—"spoon-feeding" students—they would neither remember nor understand anything. Instead:

> Confucius said: "If a student is not struggling with the truth, I won't reveal it to him. If I lift up one corner and he can't come back with the other three, I won't do it again."
>
> *Analects*, 7:8

He also encouraged students to disagree with him and not simply sit passively at the feet of their master. He once joked about this, referring to Yan Hui, who usually made highly intelligent remarks in his class but on that particular day had just said: "I agree"; "Exactly;" "I couldn't agree more":

> Confucius said: "Hui is being no help to me. He simply delights in everything I say!"
>
> *Analects*, 11:4

He also said that students should not accept what teachers say as gospel just because they are teachers, especially if they are promoting values which the student thinks are wrong:

> Confucius said: "It is better to follow your conscience than passively follow your teacher."
>
> *Analects*, 15:36

Zilu in particular set himself up as his master's conscience in this respect, several times urging Confucius not to embark on a course of action which would be seen to compromise his principles, and in most

Confucius teaching. Life-size model in the City of the Six Arts, Qufu. *Photo: Jonathan Price*

cases the Master followed the advice of his student (except in the case of his visit to the infamous concubine Nanzi, as we saw earlier).

Although Confucius' classes were lively and interesting he also expected everybody to put in the hours studying each text exhaustively—he always said it was impossible for students to have new and interesting ideas unless they really knew their subject: this was why he was particularly pleased with Zigong for coming up with an apt quotation to illustrate his point. To this end he was strict with his students if he thought they were not working hard enough:

> **Yuan Zang was waiting for the Master in a sprawled-out position … Confucius whacked him on the shins with his staff.**
>
> *Analects*, 14:43

However, although he required all his students to study hard, Confucius insisted that this in itself was not enough; they had to *think* about what they were reading:

> **Confucius said: "To study and not think is a waste of time. To think and not study is dangerous."**
>
> *Analects*, 2:15

In particular he insisted that simply reciting texts without thinking about what they meant was a complete waste of time, and he once castigated Zilu for doing this:

> **"Not harming, not coveting, How can he do wrong?**
>
> **"Not harming, not coveting, How can he do wrong. Not …"**
>
> **Zilu continuously chanted this. Confucius said, "With just this, how can you attain excellence?"**
>
> *Analects*, 9:27

Even if you could recite all 300 poems in the *Book of Songs* off by heart, Confucius continued, what would be the use if you could not apply any of it in real life? Knowledge in itself he told his students again and again is pointless unless you can *use* it, and thus study is not an end in itself, but the key to our becoming responsible and humane individuals. In particular we can learn from history and from great literature about how other people have made right or wrong choices in order to avoid making the same mistakes ourselves, and he once outlined to the indefatigable Zilu (who was his most enthusiastic student but by no means his hardest-working) the six ways in which high ideals can be thwarted by lack of study and knowledge of the past:

> **If you love humaneness, but don't like to study,**

Portrait of Confucius in joking mood. Ming Dynasty Painting. *Qilu Press*

then you will be foiled by ignorance.

> **If you love wisdom, but don't like to study, then you will be foiled by aimlessness.**
>
> **If you love sincerity, but don't like to study, then you will be foiled by unforeseen consequences.**
>
> **If you love honesty, but don't like to study, you will be foiled by your own rudeness.**
>
> **If you love boldness, but don't like to study, you will be foiled by your own lack of control.**
>
> **If you love firmness, but don't like to study, you will be foiled by your own arrogance.**
>
> *Analects*, 17:8

Despite being very strict on occasion, Confucius' general classroom manner was apparently relaxed—but not too relaxed—and once again this is a lesson from the Confucius Master Class for Advanced Teachers. Totally casual teachers may get their students' approval but not good enough results.

> **The Master was mild yet strict, authoritative yet not mean, courteous, yet relaxed.**
>
> *Analects*, 7:38

He often made jokes, as when he told Zilu that if in command of an army he would certainly not choose Rambo to assist him—he actually said "a man who wrestles tigers barehanded" but the idea is the same—and no doubt sent a ripple of laughter around the class, especially as he was having a dig at Zilu himself who admired such mindless heroism.

Another example of Confucius' deadpan humor is when a student very pompously claimed in front of the class that he:

> **"… always contemplated something three times before acting upon it."**
>
> **When Confucius heard this, he said, "Twice is enough."**
>
> *Analects*, 5:20

The effect of this would have depended very much on the way he said it, no doubt with a glint of amusement in his eyes directed at his other students yet remaining totally straight-faced. Amazingly, this expression appears in many of the portraits of Confucius, which although painted long afterwards nevertheless capture his ever-present good humor.

Summing up his advice for would-be teachers, Confucius emphasized yet again that nobody, and especially teachers, should ever stop learning:

> **Confucius said: "Reviewing what you have learned and learning anew, you are fit to be a teacher."**
>
> *Analects*, 2:11

Above all, in Confucius' opinion, great teachers should pass on everything they have learned without reserve. Many teachers, especially at university level, only impart so much of what they know to their students, afraid somehow that they will be themselves surpassed, or that their really significant ideas should be reserved for publication (from which they will of course be able to earn additional money). This, according to Confucius, is wrong. The best teachers hold nothing back, and especially they do not teach one thing and then do exactly the opposite in private:

> **Confucius said to his disciples: "My boys, do you think I conceal things from you? There is nothing I conceal from you. There is nothing that I do that is not right out in front of you. That is the way I am."**
>
> *Analects*, 7:24

"Reviewing what he had learned and learning anew," Confucius continued teaching happily and successfully for four years. The first "graduates" found jobs, while more and more students applied each year to join the classes. While by no means rich, he was comfortably off and still received Lord Ji's allowance in addition to his students' fees. Not only this, his school was becoming well known all over the state of Lu. His friend and business partner Nangong Jingshu, who had helped him set up the school, apparently enrolled himself as a student in order to attract other pupils from the nobility—although he is not quoted in the *Analects* his name was found among a list of students on the bamboo-slip manuscripts discovered in the Guodian tomb.

Confucius himself still nurtured ambitions of becoming a government officer as well as a teacher, and the fact that he was now respected and admired by the most powerful men in the state, including Duke Zhao, must have encouraged him to believe that this might now be possible. Unfortunately he could also see clearly that the very government he hoped to serve might collapse at any moment, and the state of Lu could easily split up into a patchwork of small areas controlled by the clan warlords.

The most ominous sign of coming trouble was when Lord Ji announced that he would conduct a religious ceremony at the Grand Temple of Lu, on Mount Tai. Only the Duke of Lu himself was permitted to do this according to the ritual tradition outlined in the *Book of Rites*, so Lord Ji was arrogantly declaring himself to be the real power in the land:

> **The Ji family went to make a sacrifice at Mount Tai. Confucius said to Ranyu: "Can't you save them from this?" Yu responded: "I can't."**
>
> *Analects*, 3:6

Ranyu (Qiu) was the former student who had been expelled for milking taxes on behalf of his master. By this time he was higher up the ladder in the Ji household than Confucius himself had once been but there seems to have been a reconciliation between Master and former pupil, if only because Qiu was very useful as an "insider" who could try and influence his powerful employer. Even Qiu, however, was unable to control his lord and master—nobody could. The inevitable result, which Confucius clearly could see coming, would be civil war. Even in our own day a military coup is often foreshadowed by the aspirant for power driving about in a motorcade as if he were already the president—which is very similar to what Lord Ji was doing in Confucius' state of Lu by sacrificing bulls at Mount Tai.

Confucius' forebodings proved right. One day in 571 BC, by which time Confucius was thirty-four years old, his class was interrupted by some alarming news: Lord Ji was staging a coup. There were soldiers on the march everywhere, part of the capital was on fire, and there were rumors that Duke Zhao had been killed in the fighting. Confucius cancelled that day's classes until he could find out what was happening.

As it turned out, they were to remain cancelled for the next seven years.

Insider: former student Ranyu now worked for the Ji family and could keep Confucius posted about what was happening in the halls of power. Figurine in the Jiading Confucius Temple, Shanghai. *Photo: Jonathan Price*

The Thousand Chariots

With several of his students now in the pay of Lord Ji, it did not take Confucius long to find out what had happened. Ji Ping Zi—Lord Ji—who was also of course Confucius' own sponsor and paymaster, had shortly before this managed to get himself appointed the prime minister of the whole state, ostensibly the number two to Duke Zhao but in reality the power behind the throne. Once in this commanding position Ji Ping Zi had set about stripping the Duke of all real power, issuing decrees which allowed his own family and the almost equally powerful Meng clan officially to collect state taxes themselves. In a last futile bid to reassert his authority, the Duke had the previous day dismissed Lord Ji and then had him arrested.

This had been the excuse the powerful families had been waiting for. The whole Ji clan mobilized, calling on the farmers and peasants who worked their lands to honor their feudal obligations and immediately report to barracks. The armies of all three feudal clans—the Ji the Meng and the Shu—then marched on the capital with the twin objectives of releasing Lord Ji and getting rid of the Duke, who could now be conveniently "killed during the fighting" instead of being assassinated, something the barons had held back on doing as this would have risked intervention from the other states.

Unfortunately for both families, the coup did not go according to plan. Although they succeeded in rescuing Lord Ji, by the time the smoke cleared and the bodies began to be carted from the streets it became clear to the rebel barons that Duke Zhao had escaped. Their original plan, to install a puppet Duke acceptable to all three families would not now work. To usurp official power while the rightful Duke still lived would give the other states the perfect excuse to invade Lu themselves "on behalf of the King of Zhou," and although there was still a risk of this happening, the barons decided to cut their losses and allow Duke Zhao to be the nominal ruler *in absentia*. In reality they would now be able to carve up the state of Lu for themselves, and if Duke Zhao ever showed his face inside its borders he was a dead man—they had now heard that he had ridden north and had been given asylum by Duke Jing of Qi, to whom Confucius had once acted as tutor.

Confucius was now faced with the first really big

Battles for power in the Spring and Autumn Period: Model of chariot and infantry engagement in Museum of Chariots, Linzi. *Photo: Jonathan Price*

The Great Wall of Qi: untouched and forgotten for two millennia, this section still stands almost intact on a lonely mountaintop near Chanqing, Shandong. Below the battlements can be seen the sentries' living quarters.
Photos: Jonathan Price

decision of his life. Although many historians later claimed he was a big fan of the *Yi Ji* or *Book of Divination*—the manual which was used in conjunction with the casting of milfoil sticks to predict the future—he believed not in fate but in personal choice. If he had cast the sticks on the day he heard about the half-successful coup the *Book of Divination* would have predicted that he was about to hit the jackpot.

The clan leaders were now effectively dukes in everything but name: one of them was Confucius' sponsor and lifelong employer, while another—Lord Meng—was the father of his best friend Nangong Jingshu. A glittering future, with the possibility of not only political power but of earning some really serious money had now opened in front of the 34-year-old master of ritual.

The only thing which now stood between him and this assured and secure future was his conscience. He had always taught his students that to serve a usurper was wrong, even if the rewards were very tempting, because this would only invite others to take power by force in their turn. To illustrate this he always used the example of two heroes of antiquity, Boyi and Suqi, who were ministers and scholars under the last of the Shang Emperors, the dynasty which had preceded the Zhou. When Wen of the Zhou clan had usurped power in 1027 BC and started a new dynasty, the two heroes had chosen exile:

Confucius said: "… Boyi and Suqi died of starvation at the foot of Shou Yang mountain, and the people praise them up till this day!"

Analects, 16:12

Now he himself was faced with the same choice, to abandon his principles or emulate his heroes by going into exile and facing starvation as they had done—Lord Ji would hardly be likely to continue paying his annual salary if he absconded. The temptations to stay were undeniable, but at the same time the principles he had tried to dun into his students' heads now echoed in his own:

"Riches and honors are what all men desire. But if they cannot be attained in accordance with the Way they should not be kept."

Analects, 4:5

"The Superior Man cares about virtue; the inferior man cares about material things and seeks favors."

Analects, 4:11

"The Superior Man is aware of Rightness, the inferior man is aware of advantage."

Analects, 4:16

"The Superior Man is concerned about following the Way, and is not concerned about avoiding poverty."

Analects, 15:31

In the end there was no choice. If he stayed, his teaching would no longer mean anything, he would be living a lie and no longer "practicing what he preached"—and so he decided to leave, even though his students and former students, sure that he would soon be offered a government post, begged him to stay:

Zilu said, "Not to take office is not right!"

Analects, 18:7

Confucius was adamant. He did not expect his students to follow him—he wanted them to stay to try to maintain some standards of decency in the increasingly deteriorating situation, but he himself had to go and he told his students not to worry about him. He did not intend to starve to death in the mountains like his ancient heroes, but would follow Duke Zhao to the state of Qi, taking up the long-standing invitation from Duke Jing to visit his court. Tearfully, he said goodbye to all these young men to whom he had given so much hope, and performed the rituals of farewell.

When Confucius was leaving Lu, he said, "I will set out by-and-by"—this was the way in which to leave the state of his parents.

Book of Mencius, Book 7, Part 2, Chapter 17

So it was that Confucius set out by ox-cart one autumn morning in the year 517 BC for the journey north to Qi. Nangong Jingshu had generously told Confucius that he could continue using the travelling wagon—it was his as long as he wanted. Sad like the students to see his friend go and with his hopes about the school apparently dashed, Nangong himself was in an invidious position. Circumscribed by the demands of filial piety (Confucius did not invent this, it was the prevailing ethos of the time) he was obliged to support his father even if he disagreed with him, and so the two friends said farewell and hoped to meet again in happier times.

It was about two days' journey to the northern frontier of Lu, where Confucius would have had to pass through

the gates in the Great Wall of Qi. This wall, which was built several hundred years before the better-known Great Wall of China and still stands today, ran right across the southern frontier of the ancient state of Qi from the Yellow River to the Yellow Sea, clinging for most of its way to the summits of mountains. The construction of the wall took 400 years from 685 to 281 BC, and by Confucius' day must have been at least halfway completed. The section stretching across the valley which marked the route from Lu to Qi would certainly have been in place, and this is the only surviving building which we may be sure Confucius' eyes looked upon.

There is no better way to get a feel for those ancient times than to stand on its lonely and crumbling battlements. When we stand on its windswept ramparts, or crawl into the shadows of the barrack rooms (which still exist) it is easy to imagine the sentries in their helmets and leather armour, perhaps playing ancient Chinese chess in their off-duty moments, or pacing the battlements while they were on duty, bows at the ready and waiting constantly for any sign of an attack.

It is perhaps a grim and forbidding picture, but this was the world of Confucius and if we can imagine ourselves into it, it helps us to understand why this was a world he wanted to change. To understand why he wanted a world without walls, there is no better way than to stand on one of the walls that existed at his time.

Once past the wall, it was a fairly easy journey along the broad valley on the western flanks of the sacred mountain, Mount Tai, and then into the state of Qi proper. Much of the state was made up of completely flat land, extending all the way from the mountains to the Yellow River, and on these parched plains exercised the "thousand chariots" of Duke Jing, sending up clouds of dust as they galloped in perfect unison, formidable phalanxes of military might.

Duke Jing of Qi invites Confucius to hear the *Shao* music at his court. Ming Dynasty Painting. *Qilu Press*

Once onto the plain Confucius would have been delayed while he was questioned by outriders about his business in Qi, but the next day a much greater number of chariots would have ridden to meet him—informing him that he was the honored guest of the Duke himself and they would now have the honor of escorting him to the capital, Linzi. If only his mother could have seen him now …

His old student Duke Jing gave him if not a royal welcome at least one that was considerably above that which should have been accorded to somebody of Confucius' relatively low social status as a mere *shi*:

Duke Jing of Qi, with reference to the manner in which he should treat Confucius, said: "I cannot treat him as the Duke of Lu treats the chief of the Ji family. I will treat him as though he ranked between the head of the Ji and the head of the Meng."

Analects, 18:3

Confucius, now considered superior in status to Lord Meng himself, would hardly have complained. He was given his own apartments in the Duke's palace and was treated as Jing's personal advisor, although this position was never made official. Duke Jing was delighted that his old tutor was now an ornament to his own court, and shortly after his arrival honored the promise he had

made five years before by inviting Confucius to a performance by his renowned orchestra. These were the musicians, Confucius remembered, that Duke Jing had claimed played the music of heaven. The Duke had not been boasting—Confucius was so bowled over by the sound that his reaction has passed into legend:

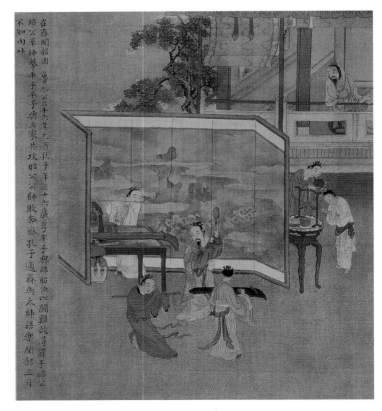

Confucius listening entranced to the *Shao* music in Qi. Ming Dynasty Painting. *Qilu Press*

When Confucius was in Qi, he heard the Shao music … and he exclaimed, "I never knew music could reach this level of excellence!"

Analects, 7:14

So entranced was he by the purity of sound Duke Jing's musicians could produce that he spent most of his time during the first three months of his stay in Linzi in their rehearsal rooms, almost forgetting to eat:

He discoursed with the Chief Music-Master of Qi on the subject of music. He heard the tones of the Shao music, he learned them, and for three months he forgot the taste of meat.

Sima Qian, *Records of the Grand Historian*

While Confucius was received with great enthusiasm by Duke Jing, his fellow exile Duke Zhao of Lu seems to have met with a much cooler reception and there is no record of anything he said or did during the whole of his stay in the state of Qi—he died there still in exile seven years later. Probably he had originally hoped that Duke

Jing would mount an invasion of Lu to restore him to power, but the music-loving potentate ignored his requests.

Duke Jing was in fact a curiously old-fashioned ruler (perhaps this is why he and Confucius always got on so well together) and his army of massed chariots—his pride and joy—was not really suited to the style of warfare of his period, which is probably why he never committed them to battle. In the earlier Zhou era military engagements had been more like ritual combats involving chariots driven by youths of the nobility, but by this time warfare had become a much bloodier affair. Both sides now used mass attacks by infantry as their main weapon, using regiments made up from

Members of the Huaxia Ancient Music Ensemble playing *Shao* music on reproductions of ancient instruments in Henan Museum. From left: Guqin; Shao Flute; Bamboo Flute; Chime stones. *Photos: Jonathan Price*

Life-size model of 4-horse chariot from Spring and Autumn Period, based on the actual remains found at the Linzi chariot-burial site. Museum of Chariots, Linzi.
Photo: Jonathan Price

conscripted farmers and laborers (whose lives were considered disposable) and the winner was the army with the most men left standing at the end of each bloodbath.

This shift in methods of combat was echoed in recent times in the 1914–18 war, when a very similar mass slaughter of infantry replaced the heroic cavalry charges of earlier times, which had also been led by scions of the nobility. In Confucius' day mounted cavalry did not exist since the technology of stirrups had not yet reached China: it was impossible during his time for archers to fire arrows from horseback and in fact it was very difficult to ride a horse at all. Stirrups, which revolutionized not only horse-riding but warfare, were invented in central Asia. Early adoption of the technology took place first in the Middle East and then Greece, before arriving in China several hundred years after Confucius' time.

Duke Jing, who was probably more concerned with the risk of losing his precious horses than his citizens, preferred to use his magnificently accoutred chariots in mock-battles on the plain outside his capital, and Confucius would no doubt have been required to attend these events which took place almost weekly. These events would certainly have been spectacular:

There is his war chariot—
With its beautiful mat of tiger's skin,

His four horses are in very fine condition,
And the six reins are in the hand of the charioteer
Piebald, and bay with black mane, are the insides;
Yellow with black mouth, and black, are the outsides;
Side by side are placed the dragon-figured shields;
Gilt are the buckles for the inner reins.

Book of Songs, 128. Xiao Rong

Living in a dream of the magnificent past like his tutor, even in death Duke Jing wanted to emulate the ancients and had himself buried with hundreds of his chariots and horses. The skeletons of his horses have ended up underneath a freeway—the gold-attired body of the Duke himself was removed centuries ago by grave robbers—but he has nevertheless become immortal, although not for the reason he himself imagined. Duke Jing has become immortal not because he had so many chariots, but because he was one of the very few people who ever listened seriously to Confucius.

The Duke had always deferred to his old tutor's advice on matters of ritual and protocol, now, however, he also asked his advice on the art of good government, and Confucius rose to the occasion in a series of

The Linzi Chariot Burial. The semi-fossilized remains of Duke Jing's chariots and horses are preserved in a special museum underneath the Jinan-Qingdao expressway.
Photo: Jonathan Price

celebrated conversations that in fact lasted over many years. Confucius had no illusions that Qi was the ideal state for an experiment in humane rule, but it was the only one available to him at the time:

Confucius said: "The state of Qi, with one change, could be at the level of Lu. The state of Lu, with one change, could attain to the Way."

Analects, 6:24

His homeland, in other words, was more fertile ground for the creation of a perfect state, if only the endless fighting between the feudal families could be stopped. For the moment, however, there was no chance of going back there, and although the Duke of Qi was an autocrat who beheaded anybody who challenged his authority, he did at least sincerely wish to be a good ruler. In Duke Jing, at last, Confucius had found a willing audience:

Confucius said: "If you would govern a state of a thousand chariots, you must pay strict attention to business, be true to your word, be economical in expenditure and love the people."

Analects, 1:5

We can imagine the Duke nodding sagely as he received this advice. Autocrat though he was, Duke Jing comes across as a rather endearing character, almost childishly eager to hear Confucius' ideas about absolutely everything, even though his tutor was younger than he was himself:

"Once there are so many people, what should be done?"

"Enrich them," said the Master.

"Once they are enriched, what next?"

"Educate them."

Analects, 13:9

Whether the Duke ever acted on any of Confucius' suggestions is not known—he seems to have loved his horses more than his people—but he was certainly enthusiastic about the ideas:

Duke Jing of Qi asked Confucius about government. Confucius replied: "Let the ruler be a ruler, a minister be a minister, a father be a father, and a son be a son."

The Duke said, "Excellent! Indeed, if the ruler is not a ruler, the ministers not ministers, fathers not fathers and sons not sons, even if I had enough revenue, how could I enjoy it?"

Analects, 12:11

In this, the most celebrated of Confucius' remarks about government to the Duke, he is talking about the

A waste of lives: Soldiers in the 'Spring and Autumn' and 'Warring States' periods were mostly ordinary farmers conscripted according to the feudal system. Model in the Museum of Chariots, Linzi. *Photo: Jonathan Price*

importance of roles and hierarchy, duties and responsibilities, without which society will not work properly. He did not mean, as this saying was later interpreted, that "everybody should know their place" since from the evidence of his own life he was obviously a believer in social mobility and of course he enabled many students from poor backgrounds to achieve government positions. Rather, he meant that at any given moment everybody should fulfil the role they have been given in society responsibly and to the best of their ability.

The key to this, in Confucius' view, was specialization. Not only should a "minister be a minister" but "a steward should be a steward," and society should be made up of highly trained individuals doing a specific job and nothing else.

> Confucius was once keeper of stores, and he then said, "My calculations must be all right. That is all I have to care about." He was once in charge of the public fields, and he then said, "The oxen and sheep must be fat and strong, and superior. That is all I have to care about."
>
> *Book of Mencius*, Book 5, Part 2, Chapter 5:4

Many of the ideas that Confucius expounded to

Duke Jing about the running of his state were taken up two and a half millennia later by Peter Drucker, who said that his principles of hierarchy and specialization were directly relevant to the efficient running of large modern companies, which closely resemble in their organizational structure the mini-states of Confucius' own era. The CEO of today, according to Drucker, is the equivalent of the "dukes" of Qi and Lu, who should concentrate on management (the ruler should be a ruler) and leave specific tasks to specialists. As Confucius sat for hours discussing good government with Duke Jing of Qi, neither of them could have had any inkling that the ideas they thrashed out together would 2,000 years later be applied not to the state of Qi, which no longer existed, but companies like General Motors (which was the first organization Drucker advised).

In fact the Chinese economic structure at the time of Confucius was much more modern than might be

"State of a Thousand Chariots". Model of a Spring and Autumn Period army belonging to one of the larger 'warring states'. City of the Six Arts, Qufu. *Photo: Jonathan Price*

imagined, and was already beginning to resemble the highly specialized industrial economies of the present day, so it is in fact no surprise that Confucius' ideas seem equally modern and highly relevant to our own age. In Europe at this time tools and weapons were still forged individually but at this period in China both bronze and iron implements began to be mass produced, that is to say they were cast from molds. This technology of casting from molds, which is universally used in industrial production today, did not appear in Europe until the end of the Middle Ages, 2,000 years after the technique was adopted in China. Several molds from this period have been discovered, together with a large number of artifacts ranging from large tripod urns to small bronze ornaments which were clearly mass-produced using molds since the decorative elements are repeated exactly.

This kind of technology requires a high level of expertise among the workers. The society of the Zhou Dynasty thus evolved into greater and greater specialization—farmers did not have to make their own tools but bought them from the specialists, while the tool-makers knew nothing about farming techniques but confined themselves to their own area of expertise, a situation which closely resembles modern industrial society.

Unfortunately the rulers of Confucius' day were not really keeping up with these changing times. Behaving like Bronze Age warriors in the new Iron Age society, they still treated their vassals as an undefined pool of labor to be used in any way they wanted instead of giving them clearly defined roles as Confucius suggested. Farmers and agricultural workers were frequently conscripted into the army for some petty campaign against a neighboring state, or in Duke Jing's case drafted into construction teams to help with grandiose projects like the Great Wall of Qi. Duke Jing even forced many farmers to take part in his spectacular mock battles during which several of the participants

Mass-production: Spring and Autumn Period technique of making wax moulds for casting bronze objects. Henan Museum. *Photo: Jonathan Price*

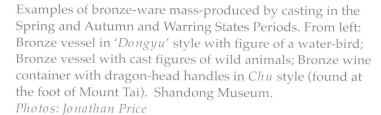

Examples of bronze-ware mass-produced by casting in the Spring and Autumn and Warring States Periods. From left: Bronze vessel in '*Dongyu*' style with figure of a water-bird; Bronze vessel with cast figures of wild animals; Bronze wine container with dragon-head handles in *Chu* style (found at the foot of Mount Tai). Shandong Museum. *Photos: Jonathan Price*

were frequently killed. This was often done during the planting or harvest seasons, and as a result the crops of millet either failed to come up at all or withered and blackened on their stalks and remained un-harvested. The inevitable consequences were hunger or even starvation.

The poets of the *Book of Songs* often railed against their rulers, and the misery they inflicted on their people by removing workers from the fields:

And so we cannot plant our millet and maize;
How shall our parents get food?
O thou distant and azure Heaven!
When shall we get back to our ordinary lot?

Books of Songs, 121. Bao Yu

Confucius had read all these poems, and could see that the same situation prevailed in his own time. What was so original about his interpretation was that he also saw that this misery was in fact completely unnecessary and was simply the result of bad management. The agricultural sector should be *named* as such, and that was *only* what they should do—grow crops and raise animals. That was their *role*; that was their field of expertise. The army was another sector and should therefore be *named* according to its role as the professional military, while construction should be carried out by equally professional and experienced workers. For these reason he also lectured Duke Jing on this subject:

Confucius said: "In a state of a thousand chariots ... you should use the people according to the seasons."

Analects, 1:5

In other words not take them off the fields at harvest-time.

Politically, Confucius has often been accused of being a status-quo man, and certainly he never advocated revolution but rather the more efficient and humane use of the existing social structure. Once again, Peter Drucker found this approach also relevant to modern companies:

"Company cultures are like country cultures. Never try to change one. Try, instead, to work with what you've got."

Peter Drucker

Mencius later claimed that Confucius talked about the duty of a failed leader to resign, but Confucius himself (as recorded in the *Analects*) never said a single word about the possibility of replacing a ruler, concentrating instead on the idea of the ruler "correcting himself":

Above all, a ruler should be trustworthy and honest,

Confucius told his ever-willing listener, Duke Jing:

"If the men in charge can be trusted, then the people cannot do anything but be sincere and honest in return. If you were to govern in this way, the people would come flocking to your kingdom, carrying their babies on their backs."

Analects, 13:4

"After the ruler has the trust of the people, they will toil for him. If he doesn't have their trust, they will regard him as oppressive. Once they trust him, they may criticize him openly. Without this trust, the ruler will think he is being slandered."

Analects, 19:10

"Excellent … excellent." the Duke must have muttered as he heard all this (he is recorded as having said this the first time Confucius gave him advice on governance). Did Master Confucius have any final words on the subject, any sort of motto, as it were, for leaders?

"Yes," Confucius said:

"Lead the people and work hard for them."
"Is there anything else?"
"Never grow weary."

Analects, 13:1

Duke Jing of Qi and Confucius. Ming Dynasty painting.
Qilu Press

Under the Apricot Trees

Confucius' exile was certainly more comfortable than that of his heroes Bo Yi and Shuqi, who had starved to death on the slopes of a mountain 600 years earlier after quitting their own state for similar reasons. He was quartered in the royal palace complex, had access to books and music, and was the respected advisor of the Duke himself. Going into exile could almost be described in his case as a smart career move. In theory he could return to Lu at any time he wanted since, unlike the Duke, he had not been forced to flee for his life but had left voluntarily on a question of principle. On these matters, however, he was very stubborn—he was after all the son of a man who had once held up a gate with his bare hands to let his comrades escape—and unless Duke Zhao were invited back Confucius did not intend to return either.

Unfortunately the feudal families of Lu gave no sign that they were prepared to hand back power to the rightful ruler. The weeks of exile stretched into months, the months into years and, although the time passed pleasantly enough, it began to seem to Confucius as if would never see his homeland again. When not conferring with Duke Jing, attending chariot races, or going on the ducal hunting trips (all these activities were naturally compulsory) he had plenty of time to indulge his main hobby, which was of course music, and enrolled for classes with the Grand Music Master of Qi, Xiang Zi.

Confucius was evidently no Mozart, and although he passionately loved the zither, he achieved his passable and sometimes commendable skill by endless practice rather than by letting the instrument sing for itself. The Music Master's exasperation with his celebrated pupil has passed into the Confucius legend. Any parent who has had to endure the same piece on the piano played over and over again for hours will sympathize with him, especially as Xiang Zi's own pupil was now in his mid-thirties:

Confucius took lessons in zither-playing from the Music Master, Xiang Zi. For ten days, Confucius made no progress. The Music Master, said: "We will try another piece." Confucius said: "Not yet—

Confucius taking *guqin* (zither) lessons with the Grand Music Master of Qi. Ming Dynasty Painting. *Qilu Press*

The Music Master of Qi exasperated with his pupil – Confucius. Ming Dynasty Painting. *Qilu Press*

I have got the melody right, but I have not yet got the rhythm." After a time, the Music Master said: "Now that you have practiced the rhythm, we will proceed." Confucius said: "I have not yet caught the mood." After a while, the Music Master spoke again: "Now that you have practised the mood, we will proceed." Confucius said: "I have not yet ascertained what kind of man composed the music."

Sima Qian, *Records of the Grand Historian*

After each session the Music Master probably retired

Ducal hunting expedition similar to those attended by Confucius in Qi. *Qilu Press*

to his own apartments and screamed. Another incident from the period of Confucius' exile in Qi is related by Mencius, and like the music lesson story seems so much in character that it may well be authentic.

> Duke Jing of Qi, once when he was hunting, called his forester to him by a flag. The forester would not come, and the duke was going to kill him.
>
> *Book of Mencius*, Book 3, Part 2, Chapter 1:2

Confucius was obliged to participate in these hunting expeditions, since being at the Duke's beck-and-call at all times was part of the deal which allowed him to stay rent-free in his palace. The hunting trips took place in the forests which covered the slopes of the mountains to the south of Qi's capital, and the ultimate prize was a full-grown tiger or a rhinoceros, although there is no record that any were killed while Confucius was a guest in Qi. The Duke sat on a tiger skin in his chariot, but that one had been caught by his father, and failing a tiger-sighting (a very rare occurrence) he would settle for a wild boar or deer. The whole operation involved large numbers of people: foresters, beaters, spearmen, and archers, and it was essential for each group to be able to communicate efficiently. This was done by waving colored flags or sometimes hats, the exact movement of each signal meaning something different, rather like the semaphore system of modern times.

On this day Duke Jing wanted to consult his head forester and ordered the signals officer beside him to wave his flag (which was crimson and embroidered with green dragons) in the accepted signal "Come immediately!" For some reason the unfortunate forester was either relieving himself in the woods at the time or failed to understand the signal, and this led to the wild boar they were stalking getting clean away into the trees. Furious, Duke Jing had the poor forester dragged over to him and ordered him beheaded on the spot.

"One moment your majesty …" The Duke's Ritual Advisor stepped hurriedly forward, bowing to everybody. One of the Duke's henchmen had already unsheathed his sword, and was flexing the blade with his wrists, preparatory to severing the forester's head from his body. Like everybody else, including the Duke, he glared angrily at Confucius. Yes—Confucius continued hurriedly—unfortunately the wrong signal had been used. According to the *Book of Rites* a commoner could not be summoned by a flag appropriate to a member of the nobility—as was done just now. So the forester as a mere common man had acted correctly by not responding to the summons, and in fact had he done so he would have shown so much presumption that he would indeed have deserved to lose his head. The Duke rounded angrily on his flag-man, called him an imbecile, and then asked Confucius how the forester should have been summoned?

> "With a skin cap. A common man should be summoned with a plain banner; a scholar who has taken office, with one having dragons embroidered on it; and a Great officer, with one having feathers suspended from the top of the staff."
>
> *Book of Mencius*, Book 5, Part 2, Chapter 7:6

Duke Jing grunted furiously, but accepted as always his old tutor's advice on any matter of protocol, and the trembling forester was spared. The unfortunate flag-officer would no doubt have feared a beheading instead, but apparently nobody was executed that day and Confucius scored a significant victory. At the same time he made many enemies, for all the nobles resented the growing influence of the upstart *scholar-shi* on their lord and master, and secretly began to plot amongst themselves about how to get rid of him.

Mencius in his account of this incident goes into a long rigmarole about his revered Master's correct stance on matters of ritual and how important this is for society, but clearly misses the point—Confucius was simply saving the poor man's life. He knew how to get round the Duke by banging on about protocol, and as we shall see he would use this ploy with Duke Jing on a more momentous occasion a few years later.

Confucius himself remained tight-lipped about why he had intervened, making only this typically dead-pan remark:

> With reference to this incident, Confucius said, "The determined officer never forgets that his end may be in a ditch or a stream; the brave officer never forgets that he may lose his head."
>
> *Book of Mencius*, Book 3, Part 2, Chapter 1:2

One of his most enduring memories of his long stay in Qi would probably have been the smell of horses, and he would even on occasion have had to follow the Duke around the stables while he petted his favorite steeds and simultaneously discussed political philosophy with his ever-humble advisor.

> **There was a fire in the stables. When the Master returned from court, he asked: "Was anybody hurt?" He did not ask about the horses.**
>
> *Analects*, 10:17

This incident, which is quoted in the *Analects* and is almost certainly authentic, might well offend animal lovers of today, but what Confucius meant was that the horse-mad Duke and all his courtiers would have reacted in exactly the opposite way: "'Were any horses hurt?' They did not ask about the people." The people in question—grooms and servants—were of no account and certainly ranked well below the Duke's horses in the social scale of the period, so the saying emphasizes Confucius' never-wavering commitment to the idea that all human beings are equals, regardless of their rank in society. This belief, like his determination to open his classes to all, was extremely unusual at this time.

As the years passed Duke Jing's obsession with his horses increasingly grated on Confucius, and it was also becoming clear that there was little hope of his ideas ever being put into practice in the state of Qi, as he had long suspected. The Duke himself remained happy with his advisor, and still enjoyed their long discussions, even though he rarely acted on any of Confucius' suggestions. For his part Duke Jing hoped that Confucius would make his home permanently in Qi, and to that end eventually offered him a considerable amount of land as a "fiefdom," together with the offer of an official position at his court.

This set off alarm bells among the nobles. Already jealous of the scholar's influence, they considered that

Thoroughbred stallions as used by Duke Jing of Qi to pull his beloved chariots. Life-size model in the Museum of Chariots, Linzi. *Photo: Jonathan Price*

"Yan Ying opposed to bestowing the fief in Qi". Ming Dynasty Painting. *Qilu Press*

offering land was tantamount to elevating him to the aristocracy and this would have been the final straw. Accordingly they sent a delegation to the Duke to protest in the strongest possible terms:

> Duke Jing rejoiced in Confucius, and wished to grant him the fields of Ni Chi as a fief. Then Yan Ying interfered and said: "Scholars are smooth and sophisticated; they are arrogant and conceited. They travel about as advisers in order to enrich themselves; they cannot be used in the ruling of the state … this is not the correct way to lead the common people."
>
> Sima Qian, *Records of the Grand Historian*

For all his good intentions Duke Jing was a consummate politician and above all a survivor (unlike his immediate successor he died in his bed) so he could not risk an open confrontation with his feudal lords, especially after what had happened in Lu a few years earlier. Accordingly he backed down and Confucius was not given any land. The Duke also decided that it was not politic to be seen to be asking his scholar's advice about anything for the time being:

> After that time, Duke Jing continued to receive Confucius, always, to be sure, with great respect, but he no longer questioned him concerning decorum.
>
> Sima Qian, *Records of the Grand Historian*

Confucius was now in a marginalized position and the state of Qi began to feel like a luxurious prison where there was little for him to do but eat, sleep, and play the zither. Before he actually expired with boredom, however, the old Duke of Lu finally expired himself. Duke Zhao had been living in exile in Qi all this time without anybody taking the slightest notice of him. His death created a vacancy for a legitimate ruler to take power in Confucius' home state, and if that happened then Confucius could return home.

In the event Duke Zhao was succeeded by Duke Ding, known to history through the *Spring and Autumn Annals* as "Duke Ding the Settler"—as in "settler of disputes." Duke Ding was from the same family as the previous duke and therefore his accession was perfectly legitimate. Unknown to Confucius, however, he was in fact a puppet of the Ji family, and with a real duke in their pockets, the feudal families could still continue as effective rulers with all the associated tax-milking opportunities, but now with the added advantage of not being seen as usurpers themselves. Confucius, blissfully unaware that nothing had really changed, decided that he could now go back to Lu without compromising his principles as there was once again a legitimate ruler in the capital. The year was 510, and Confucius was now forty-one, which was by his own admission a dangerous age—if he did not make it into the big league soon then he never would:

> **Confucius said: "If a man reaches the age of forty or fifty and has still not been heard from, then he is no one to be in awe of."**
>
> *Analects*, 9:23

He had of course already been "heard from" to some extent, but his real ambitions still centered on involvement in government, and not just as an advisor. After almost seven years of pleasantly luxurious theorizing with the Duke of Qi, he was burning to put his ideas into practice in his own state of Lu, which of course he considered "could achieve the Way in one step." He was increasingly certain that he knew exactly what to do:

> **Confucius said: "At forty, I had no more doubts."**
>
> *Analects*, 2:4

Not only this, he was still full of the almost brash over-confidence which had sustained him over many years of waiting for his moment to arrive:

> **Confucius said: "If any of the rulers were to employ me, I would have control of the situation within twelve months, and would have everything straightened out within three years."**
>
> *Analects*, 13:10

The city wall of Qufu (Ming Dynasty). *Qilu Press*

Full of hope that at last he would be a major player in his home state, Confucius packed his belongings onto his old ox-wagon, and made the ritual gesture of farewell:

> When he was leaving Qi, he strained off with his hand the water in which his rice was being rinsed, took the rice, and went away—this was the way in which to leave a strange state.
>
> *Book of Mencius*, Book 7, Part 2, Chapter 17

It took a couple of days of bumpy journeying before he once again reached the Great Wall of Qi. After showing his travel documents he passed through the gates into the state of Lu and after seven years, he was home. As he passed the small towns on the way to his home town of Qufu, however, he would have immediately noticed a change. Every town and small

Confucius teaching – ancient relief. *Qilu Press*

city was now surrounded with walls and battlements, and there were soldiers everywhere. Even though he held a silk travel warrant bearing the red stamp of the Duke of Qi himself, at each city gate there was a long delay and it was clear to Confucius that these were cities held by minor warlords who did not recognize the central authority of the new Duke of Lu. When he said he would have "everything straightened out in three years" it was this he had been talking about, and he could see that the main priority was to bring an end to the clan feuding.

He eventually reached Qufu without incident, and there was a blissful reunion with many of his old students. Zilu and Ranyu were still working for the Ji family, and Zilu filled in his old master with all the gossip: Ranyu was now in charge of Lord Ji's military supplies as well as collecting the grain taxes, while the commander of the Ji army was Yang Huo—the former chief steward and Confucius' look-alike—who many years before had refused him admission to the students' banquet. Lord Ji himself was now very old but as arrogant as ever and still the real power in Lu. Lord Ji's son, Ji Huang, was weak and indecisive compared to his father, and when the old man died everybody expected the power vacuum to cause more trouble, even perhaps another coup by one of the clan armies.

Confucius must have sighed when he heard all this. The political situation was if anything worse than before, but at least now that he was back he could try and do something about it.

> Again the world fell into decay, and principles faded away. Perverse speaking and oppressive deeds waxed rife again. There were instances of ministers who murdered their governors, and of sons who murdered their fathers.
>
> *Book of Mencius*, Book 3, Part 2, Chapter 9:7

Confucius' old friend Nangong Jingshu was also delighted to see him. Over a celebration meal Confucius announced his intention of seeking a government position with the new Duke, and Nangong promised to have a word in the right quarters—as Lord Meng's son he had access to the Duke's court. He did warn Confucius not to get his hopes up too much. Duke Ding was a Ji family stooge and Confucius was not popular at the Ji mansion after pointedly turning his back on them seven years before.

A few days later Nangong Jingshu returned with the not-unexpected bad news. Preferment was reserved for Ji family bootlickers like his former student Ranyu, and there was no way Confucius was ever going to be

Confucius' students listening raptly to his ideas. Life-size models in the City of the Six Arts, Qufu. *Photo: Jonathan Price*

offered a government position by the present Duke. Lord Ji was also reluctant to support the school any more, which meant they would have to rely on the students' fees so things were going to be tough. Confucius was naturally a little crestfallen, but he soon shrugged off his disappointment and put the word around that his classes would be re-starting very shortly.

This time Confucius managed to enroll several relatively rich students from the outset, for many still saw his tuition as a passport to a successful career which would otherwise be denied them. All three of the feudal families said that they would still happily accept staff from among those who had attended Confucius' courses, and even the Duke made the same promise for state government positions. It was only their teacher, much to his annoyance, who was not welcome in the halls of power. He was a little too high-principled for comfort as far as the barons were concerned, especially as one of his principles was reducing the power of the feudal families.

So the classes began again, with some new students and several of the old ones. Zilu, his first and most loyal student, was now in his thirties. As enthusiastic as ever, he rushed to the school house as soon as his work was finished, and as always he was the first to answer every question. One day, just after they had finished singing together, Confucius asked the students what they would do if they were in a position to do whatever they wanted:

Zilu jumped to reply first, saying: "I would like to be in the position of the charge of a relatively small state which was being threatened by the armies of the surrounding larger states, and suffering from crop failure. If I were in this position, within three years my people would be fearless and know how to take care of themselves."

Confucius laughed at him.

Analects, 11:25

When the other students asked him why he had laughed, Confucius told them it was because Zilu as always was quite confident he could achieve the impossible.

Confucius said: "If your words are not humble, it will be difficult to put them into action."

Analects, 14:20

To govern a state, he continued, you needed a systematic approach and above all humility—to know your limitations:

Confucius said: "Even if you have the position of kingship, it would still take a generation for humaneness to prevail."

Analects, 13:12

The Apricot Altar, Qufu – site of Confucius' open-air classes. *Qilu Press*

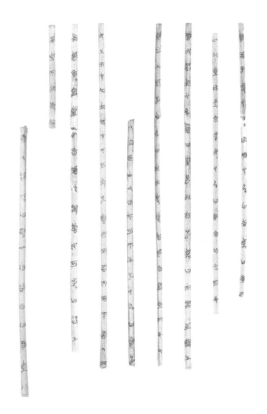

Swim, anyone? Confucius' student Zeng Xi, nicknamed 'Dian' who said his greatest wish was to go swimming in the river and walk home with his friends, singing. Statuette in Jiading Confucius Temple, Shanghai. *Photo: Jonathan Price*

As he sat under the apricot trees with his students, Confucius' own disappointment at being denied a chance to share in governing would probably have melted away—teaching was what he was born to do. It is a mistake to try and elevate him into the position of the world's greatest philosopher or to turn him into a god—he was neither of these things and never claimed to be, but he was certainly the greatest teacher the world has ever known.

"Dian, what about you?" he asked another of the students as they relaxed and played music under the trees.

Dian set his lute down with its strings still ringing, and stood up. "What I would like to do," he said, "is quite different from the others."

The Master said, "What harm can there be? Please speak as the others have."

Dian said, "At the height of spring, all decked

Part of the bamboo-slip manuscript of the 'Book of Zhong-gong' from a 4th Century B.C. tomb, now in the Shanghai Museum Bamboo Slip Archive. The text, which discusses Confucius' theories on criminality and punishment, is almost identical to Analect 13/2. *Photo courtesy Shanghai Museum*

out in spring clothes, I would like to take five or six young men, and six or seven youngsters to go for a swim in the Yi river, enjoying the cool breeze at the Rain Dance Festival, and make our way back home, singing."

Confucius sighed, and said, "Ah, lovely. I am with you, Dian."

Analects, 11:26

The idea of Confucius and his students sitting under the trees with their lutes and zithers is an equally lovely picture and has entered the Chinese subconscious to such an extent that it has become almost a folk memory which can never be eradicated, even though there have been many attempts to do just that. The site of his open-air classes known as the "Apricot Altar" may be visited in Qufu, and this is a sacred place for all Chinese people, not because God walked there, but because a Teacher taught there. A man, not a god, and if you tell him that your greatest ambition is to swim in the river and go home singing and feel the world is a beautiful place, he

will say "How lovely! I am with you!" This is why his students loved him so much and why the memory of him has never died, because he sang the music of the here-and-now, not of heaven.

Another very welcome addition to the roster of Confucius' students in the years after he returned from Qi was Zhonggong (also known as Chung Kung). Not only was Zhonggong from a relatively well-to-do family, so that his fees certainly helped while Confucius' school was in straitened circumstances, he was also very serious about his studies and was soon welcomed into the inner circle. He later became a prolific writer and many passages in the *Analects* are based on his recollections of what his Master said, which he compiled into a work known as the *Book of Zhonggong*, which also contains commentary and interpretation. A copy of this work was discovered among the bamboo-slip books now in the

Confucius and two of his 'disciples' including Zilu (centre). Detail from Ming Dynasty Painting. *Qilu Press*

Shanghai Museum, which can reliably be dated to about a century after Confucius and must therefore have been copied from Zhonggong's original.

It was to Zhonggong that Confucius first declared his celebrated "Golden Rule." The rule appears in the same wording twice in the *Analects*, addressed to different students, and is also referred to in other passages, so Confucius was obviously fond of reiterating the idea and it can even be regarded as the central pillar of Confucianism, around which everything else revolves:

> **Zhonggong asked about the meaning of humaneness.**
>
> **The Master said: "What you don't want done to yourself, don't do to others."**
>
> **Zhonggong said, "Although I am not so smart, I will apply myself to this teaching."**
>
> *Analects*, 12:2

The same idea was of course repeated by Jesus in the Sermon on the Mount:

> Therefore all things whatsoever ye would that men should do to you, do ye even so to them: for this is the law and the prophets.
>
> Matthew 7:12

The Christian version, often rendered as "Do unto others as you would have them do unto you" (the same idea also appears in the sacred books of many religions) is, however, slightly different to its ancient Chinese equivalent. Confucius deliberately uses a negative admonition: *don't do* anything to anybody else that you would not like to be done to you—and as a result it is far more difficult for Confucians than it is for Christians to simply pat themselves on the back for *doing* good works. "I gave at the office" does not cut it with Confucius. Instead the Confucian conscience operates in reverse, by means of a little voice inside us which says *don't do it*, as every day and even every hour we make choices about how we should behave.

Apart from these general ethical principles, Zhonggong was especially interested in politics and law: in the ancient copy of the *Book of Zhonggong* acquired by the Shanghai Museum he deals almost exclusively with Confucius' remarks on these subjects. In the Shanghai manuscript Zhonggong also appears as a staunch supporter of Confucius' idea that the ancient Zhou style of government should be a model for their own times, so it was not

The character *Ren* –'humanity' – the keystone of Confucius' philosophy, on an ancient stone inscription now in the Henan Museum. *Photo: Jonathan Price.*

surprising that his teacher felt that he had found a young man after his own heart. Still frustrated at being denied any chance of a government position, Confucius was nonetheless still eager to discuss political and legal topics and Zhonggong provided an eager and willing sounding-board (the following conversation appears in identical wording in both the *Analects* and on Bamboo Strip 7 of the Shanghai manuscript of the *Book of Zhonggong*):

Zhonggong asked about government.

Confucius said, "First organize your administration; then grant pardon to all the petty offenses and then put virtuous and able men into positions of responsibility."

Analects, 13:2

Zhonggong had a keenly analytical mind and immediately saw a flaw in this argument. Interestingly the following comment was removed from the final version of the *Analects* when this work was compiled nearly 400 years later:

Zhonggong asked, "I am not so wise ... but if you grant pardon to all the petty offenses, how can the populace be intimidated?"

Shanghai Museum Bamboo-Strips 9–10

In other words without any sort of threat of punishment how can criminals be deterred from wrongdoing? This is a valid argument—if the president of the United States declared an amnesty for all petty criminals what would happen? Would this be a license for would-be criminals to rob their local convenience store?

It is clear that this ancient text was the record of a *discussion* on a topic that is still with us. Confucius did not set out to provide answers, but to stimulate us into asking the right questions and to come up with answers which are relevant to our own situation. Compared to other great thinkers he is thus closest to Socrates, who was also above all a great teacher. Over the centuries attempts were made to turn Confucius into the Chinese equivalent of Moses and Buddha rolled into one, but this simply does not work. It is impossible, for example, to imagine Moses coming down from Mount Sinai and *discussing* the Ten Commandments with the Israelites but Confucius did this sort of thing all the time.

The recently discovered text which includes Zhonggong actually disagreeing with Confucius dates from several hundred years earlier than the official text of the *Analects*. In the later version this disagreement was removed—otherwise the texts are almost identical. Why was this cut out? It must have been because by the time the *Analects* were finally compiled, the anonymous editors wanted to present Confucius not as a teacher but

a quasi-god, who simply pronounced things and was always right. Confucius' true philosophy—if it can be called that—is completely different to this in its original form—there are no commandments.

Confucius said: "The human being realizes the Way. The Way doesn't realize the human being."

Analects, 5:28

In other words, we make our own rules. We have to accept the basic principle which is humanity in all our dealings with other people (Confucius called this *Ren* or humanity, usually translated as "humaneness") but the way this principle is realized is up to us. He maintained that nobody in fact can ever achieve perfect humaneness—including himself, but we all have continually to try to score higher marks on the humanity scale, on a daily basis.

Confucius said: "Is it possible to devote oneself to virtue for one whole day? I have not seen anyone who has lacked the strength to do so. Perhaps there has been such a case, but I have never seen it."

Analects, 4:6

Everybody is therefore capable of improvement, and according to Confucius all human beings except the mentally impaired must know there is room for such improvement and have the strength to achieve it if they want. It is all down to us.

Confucius said: "Only the most wise and the most foolish do not change."

Analects, 17:3

He himself, as he repeatedly said, did not fall into the category of "most wise." He allowed the possibility that there might be such people—the so-called sages who were all-wise and perfect in their behavior from birth—but he told his students again and again that he himself was not one of these and was simply a man trying to change himself and the society around him for the better.

Confucius said: "I have not yet been able to meet a sage ... I dare not claim to be a sage or a humane man. But I strive for these without being disappointed, and I teach without becoming weary. This is what can be said of me."

Analects, 7:26 / *Analects*, 7:34

~Coup!~

With old Lord Ji now practically on his deathbed, the other feudal barons and their army commanders were jockeying for power. Individual nobles set themselves up in small walled cities and ignored the waning authority of Duke Ding, who was still in the sway of the Ji family. Much more ominously, army commanders who were not of noble birth also started behaving like feudal barons themselves and no longer showed obeisance to their former masters from the Ji, Meng, and Shu clans.

> The House of Ji, for its part, usurped the prerogatives of the ducal house. Subordinate vassals had gained the power of the state. Thus, in the state of Lu, from the highest dignitaries down, every one was grasping of power, and all had departed from the true way.
>
> Sima Qian, *Records of the Grand Historian*

The most dangerous of the quasi-barons was Yang Huo, Lord Ji's chief steward, who was now also in command of Lord Ji's private army of conscripts. Yang Huo was openly flaunting his power, and frequently disregarded orders from his masters in order to demonstrate that his soldiers' loyalty was to him alone and not to the Ji family itself. Traditionally held to have been so similar in appearance to Confucius that they could have been twins, Yang Huo was the darker face of Janus. Both men came from the *shi* class, both were very ambitious and wanted a seat in the halls of power, but there the similarity ended. Confucius did not want any sort of authority if he had to

abandon his principles to attain it, whereas Yang Huo did not care how many dead bodies he stepped across on his road to power. He also knew that a large number of others would follow him along this road, for there were many who had been taxed almost out of existence by the rapacious and greedy noble families, and they had now had enough. Confucius could see what was happening but there was little he could do except talk about it to his students:

> **Confucius said: "A man who enjoys boldness and hates poverty will be rebellious. If a man lacks humaneness and his dissatisfaction reaches an extreme, he will rebel."**
>
> *Analects*, 8:10

Denied any influence, Confucius concentrated on his teaching, which was growing more and more successful, and also seemingly took part-time work as an archivist for the state government.

Therefore Confucius accepted no office. He lived in retirement, and arranged the odes, the records, the rites, and music. And his pupils grew ever greater in number, while from all sides, from far distant

Confucius editing the classics. Ming Dynasty Painting. *Qilu Press*

Bronze sword from Spring and Autumn Period. Capital Museum Beijing. *Photo: Jonathan Price*

regions, disciples flocked to him.

Sima Qian, *Records of the Grand Historian*

According to tradition Confucius at this period edited not only the *Spring and Autumn Annals*—the official records of the state of Lu which were updated every spring and autumn—but also started compiling definitive editions of the "five classics"—the *Book of Songs*, the *Book of History*, the *Book of Rites*, the *Book of Divination*, and the *Book of Music*. Together with the *Annals* these works (which have all survived except for the *Book of Music* which has been lost) are known as the "six Confucian classics," and even today passages from the books are quoted as being "by Confucius." Unfortunately there is no real evidence that he actually carried out this literary work and the whole thing may be yet another myth. The first mention of his work as an archivist was by Mencius well over a hundred years after Confucius died:

Confucius was afraid, and made the "Spring and Autumn Annals." On this account Confucius said, "Yes! It is the 'Spring and Autumn' which will make men know me!"

Book of Mencius, Book 3, Part 2, Chapter 9:8

As usual Mencius, however incisive his understanding may have been of his Master's ideas, is not very good on Confucius' motives and character. In this passage he seems to imply that Confucius was desperate to be famous for *something*, and, having been denied a political career, at this stage decided to become a renowned writer. Considering the many remarks Confucius made about the pointlessness of fame for its own sake this does not seem likely.

Sima Qian in his *Records* took up the hint given by Mencius and added all the other classics to Confucius' oeuvre, so that his literary activity passed into the official biographical legend. However much we might want to accept this story, it still remains very strange that there is absolutely no mention of his editing of the classics either in the *Analects* or in the bamboo-slip manuscripts discovered recently. Indeed the Guodian tomb and Shanghai manuscripts include several anthologies of extracts from the *Book of Rites*, purportedly compiled by several of Confucius' students such as Zhonggong and Zengzi, but without any mention that Confucius himself had any hand in editing the original text. Nevertheless it

ZIXIA ('Hsia'). Prominent disciple of Confucius who later became a celebrated writer. *Qilu Press*

would be nice to imagine him doing this, especially as Sima Qian describes how he sang each of his selected poems from the *Book of Songs*, accompanying himself on the zither in order to get the meter right:

In olden times, there were over 3,000 songs. Confucius, for his part, eliminated the repetitions, and included those songs which were of value for morals and justice … all the 305 pieces he chose Confucius accompanied with the strings, and he sang them in order to attain agreement with the music.

Sima Qian, *Records of the Grand Historian*

There is one hint in the *Analects* that Confucius may actually have had a literary career of sorts, although it is not clear whether he meant as an interpreter or practitioner:

Confucius said: "In literature, perhaps I am equal to others."

Analects, 7:33

Certainly many of those who attended his classes were very keen to become writers, and even though claims that Confucius was an author himself are very dubious, several of his top students went on to write major works which not only recorded his sayings but interpreted and expanded his ideas. One of these was Zixia, who at the period when Confucius is supposed to have edited the classics (509–505 BC) had just joined his classes and was only known as "Xia" or "Hsia," and not yet "Zixia" or "Master Xia" which is how he styled himself on the bamboo manuscripts. His teacher gave him some valuable advice which he did not entirely heed:

Confucius said to Hsia: "Be a noble scholar; don't be a petty scholar."

Analects, 6:13

Confucius said: "The ancient scholars studied for their own improvement. Modern scholars study to impress others."

Analects, 14:24

It was of course Hsia who in his writings omitted the words "Confucius said …" thereby claiming credit for the ideas himself, and he was not the only former student who did this. Confucius' ideas as we shall see in a later chapter suffered greatly from constant re-interpretation by petty and vainglorious scholars over many centuries. Perhaps the complete absence of Confucius' name on the texts of the classics does after all indicate that he did have a hand in their editing. Unlike

Ji Kangzi is mentioned many times not only in the *Analects* but also in the manuscripts of works by Confucius' disciples found in 4th Century B.C. tombs. This manuscript is entitled "Ji Kang Zi asking questions to Confucius". The three characters of his name can be seen at the top of the right hand slip, reading downwards. From the Shanghai Museum Bamboo-Slip collection. *Photo courtesy Shanghai Museum.*

his student-writers he was not a "petty scholar" and would have wanted simply to preserve these great books and not impose his own personality upon them "to impress others."

So let us imagine him one spring morning in the year 505 BC, busily occupied with the pleasant task of adjusting the syntax of one of the poems in the *Book of Songs* while strumming the rhythm on his zither.

With the spring days the warmth begins,
And the oriole utters its song.
The young women take their deep baskets,
And go along the small paths,
Looking for the tender leaves of the mulberry trees.

Book of Songs, 154, Qi Yue

"Master!" It was Zilu, looking very worried. Confucius looked up, the strings of his *guqin* still ringing. Zilu quickly explained that what everybody had long feared had finally happened—the steward Yang Huo had staged a successful coup, the three families had been powerless to resist him, and the Duke was a prisoner in his own house.

So began the four-year dictatorship of Yang Huo in Lu. He had timed his moment well. Earlier that year old Lord Ji, Ji Pingzi, had finally died, and his son Ji Huan, who succeeded him as head of the family, was not out of the same mold. Now almost fifty, Ji Huan had lived most of his life as prince-in-waiting, and according to Sima Qian he was fonder of pleasure than power and had a weakness for the ladies. Certainly he was no match for his family's ruthless and scheming former steward, and when he made a feeble attempt to bring the Ji army back under family control Yang Huo took him prisoner and forced him to swear a humiliating public oath of allegiance to himself.

The other feudal families proved equally impotent. Old Lord Meng, Nangong Jingshu's father, was himself in his twilight years, and the other family, the Shu, had never been a major player. Yang Huo controlled enough loyal soldiers to crush all resistance, and set about forming a government of equally loyal ministers. The former prime minister had been Ji Huan but he had naturally been fired, as had all the Duke's ministers who belonged to the noble families. Duke Ding was kept under virtual house arrest "for his own protection" while Yang Huo wanted nobody in his government of a higher social status than himself. Among those he invited to serve in his new government was Confucius.

Many messengers arrived at the school-house inviting the renowned scholar–teacher to the capital, but Confucius, although obliged by the rules of ritual to receive these emissaries, never-theless dismissed them with a variety of excuses, usually that he was too ill to travel. This time he was not obliged to go into exile as he did not see that he was compromising his principles by staying—on the last occasion it was his own sponsor who had driven out the duke. So he stayed in Qufu, teaching and continuing with his literary labors and trying to ignore the repeated requests to join the government.

Ju Pei [one of Yang Huo's right-hand men] wanted to see Confucius, but Confucius excused himself on the grounds of illness. When his messenger went to the door, the master picked up his lute and began to sing so that Pei could hear him.

Analects, 17:20

Confucius was pointedly demonstrating by his

Might is right: Soldiers from the Spring and Autumn Period in action. Model in Museum of Chariots, Linzi. *Photo: Jonathan Price*

singing that he was not ill at all, sending a clear message back to Yang Huo: please leave me alone. When his students asked him why he did not simply send back a message of refusal, he gave them a lesson in survival:

> **Confucius said: "When the government is just, you may speak boldly and act boldly; when you have an unjust government, you may act boldly, but be careful of what you say."**
>
> *Analects*, 14:4

Yang Huo did not give up, however. He could not understand why Confucius, as a *shi* like himself, did not leap at the chance of power now the nobles had been put in their place, especially as he had made no secret of his desire for high office. Yang Huo saw Confucius as a potential jewel in his own crown, since he was the former advisor to the Duke of Qi and was now a highly

reluctant sage would then be obliged to pay a call on him at his own house in order to express his thanks. Confucius deliberately chose a time when he knew Huo was out to pay this call, but the dictator was too clever for him and contrived to meet him "by chance" on the road:

> **Huo said to Confucius, "Come, let me speak with you." He then asked, "Can he be called benevolent who keeps his jewel in his bosom, and leaves his country to confusion? No!**
>
> **"Can he be called wise, who is anxious to be engaged in public employment, and yet is constantly losing the opportunity of being so? Of course he can't!**
>
> **"The days and months are passing away; my friend, the years do not wait for us."**

Spring blossoms in the 'Analects Garden' Qufu, near the site of Confucius' school. *Qilu Press*

respected teacher and scholar. He sent word through the students that even the job of prime minister could be on offer. Confucius was certainly tempted, but Zilu in particular continually urged him not even to think about it.

Finally Yang Huo hit upon a clever plan to force the reluctant teacher to come and see him. He had a very large roasted suckling-pig delivered to the school-house with his compliments, and by the rules of etiquette, which Yang Huo knew Confucius would never flout, the

> **Confucius said, "Right; I will go into office."**
>
> *Analects*, 17:1

Amazingly he had agreed to serve the dictator! In the event he changed his mind and did not accept office at this point, but evidently his burning ambition to make a difference in the way his state was governed was almost so strong that he was prepared to fool himself that there was nothing wrong in his serving the "Protector." Confucius would have told himself that Yang Huo had not actually deposed the Duke of Lu, so he would not be

The Dictator Yan Huo (left) speaking with Confucius on the road. Ming Dynasty Painting. *Qilu Press*

serving a usurper. He would also have told himself that Yang Huo had successfully curbed the power of the feudal families, which had always been his own top priority. And yet … and yet … nothing could alter the fact that his double had taken power by force, and that power was real. The soldiers stationed around the ducal palace were not really there to protect Duke Ding; they were there to keep him prisoner.

So, ultimately, he refused the dazzling offer. Once again this whole incident shows us Confucius as a fallible human being like the rest of us. His whole philosophy requires us to struggle constantly to make the right decisions, and he never said that this was easy. Every step we take along the right or wrong path—the "Way"—is our decision and ours alone:

Confucius said: "It is like building a mound: If I stop before carrying a single basket of earth, it is my stopping. It is like levelling the ground: If I continue even after dumping only one basket, it is my continuation."

Analects, 9:19

Thus the important thing about his encounter with the dictator of Lu was not that he was almost tempted to accept his offer, but that he struggled mightily and in the end made the right choice. Instead of feeling shocked and disappointed that Confucius did not immediately say "Get thee behind me Yang Huo," but actually said "yes" and then changed his mind, we can all imagine ourselves in the same situation and hope we would make the same decision. Difficult though it had indeed been to refuse Yang Huo, Confucius had managed in the end to abide by his own principles:

Confucius said: "When the Way prevails in the world, show yourself. When it does not, then hide. When the Way prevails in your own state, to be poor and obscure is a disgrace. But when the Way does not prevail in your own state, to be rich and honored is a disgrace."

Analects, 8:13

After he had once more turned his back on riches and honors, no more suckling pigs came his way and Yang Huo left him alone to get on with his teaching, causing him no further trouble.

The Ji family, themselves marginalized, were now on much friendlier terms with Confucius and may even have recommended paying him a grain allowance. Zilu, who still worked for them, had made great play of the fact that his Master had refused to work for Yang Huo, and the new Lord Ji made a public demonstration of support by sending his own eldest son, Ji Kangzi, who was then about twenty-five, to study at Confucius' school. One day Ji Kangzi would be Lord Ji himself, but unlike his father and grandfather before him the young man saw his destiny as a leader as a responsibility rather than an opportunity to make his family even wealthier. From this time onwards Kangzi often consulted Confucius about the responsibilities of the powerful, and several of the most often quoted passages in the *Analects* about governing are records of conversations between the Master and this youngest scion of the Ji household. The most famous of these is probably Confucius' celebrated testament of opposition to capital punishment, which he made to Ji Kangzi:

"In doing government, what is the need of killing?"

Analects, 12:19

In the state of Lu from 505–501 BC, the years of Yang Huo's dictatorship, the killing certainly did not stop, and as Mencius put it: "Oppressive deeds waxed rife again." Every day newly severed heads were set up on poles as a feast for the flies and an example to all of what happened to anybody who dared oppose the dictator. Confucius rejoiced that he had not thrown in his lot with his dark twin now that he had showed his real face, but he still hungered for a place in government so that he could try to realize his dream of a "new Zhou," and began to look elsewhere.

Although Yang Huo controlled the capital and the central area of the state of Lu, which included Qufu where Confucius' school was situated, the rest of the state had begun to break up into small feudal areas controlled by different warlords. At the beginning of 501 BC one of these warlords, Gongshan Fujao, seized the fortified city of Bei, which had been a fiefdom of the Ji family, and like Yang Huo invited Confucius to help him create an "ideal state." Once more Confucius was sorely tempted, and once more his self-appointed "conscience"—Zilu—opposed the idea vociferously:

> Gongshan Fujao issued an invitation to Confucius to join his government when he was holding Bei in an attitude of rebellion, and the Master was rather inclined to go.
>
> Zilu was displeased, and said, "Indeed, you cannot go! Why must you think of going to see Kungshan?"
>
> The Master said, "Can it be without some reason that he has invited ME? If any one should employ me, may I not make a new Zhou in the east?"

Analects, 17:5

Head to head: Zilu argues with his master on a question of principle. Detail from Ming Dynasty painting. *Qilu Press*

Zilu just snorted in disbelief. He was going to create a "new Zhou" in some petty little fortified city in the middle of Lu? A city which had been taken by force? Ridiculous!

The first Zhou king took power by force, Confucius argued …

> "The founders of the Zhou Dynasty, King Wen and King Wu, had small beginnings but succeeded in founding a kingdom. Now Bei is, of course, but a small place, but perhaps, even so, much may be possible."

Sima Qian, Records of the Grand Historian

Zilu shouted at him that he was always going on about the two heroes who had starved to death rather than serve the usurper King Wen, so how could he even think about going cap-in-hand to some brigand who had taken over a one-chariot town in the middle of nowhere? What would people think?

After a lot of argument Confucius eventually gave in to Zilu, even though he still yearned to try and bring back the lost golden age of the Zhou—somewhere—some time. Then a few months later he got another invitation, this time from another warlord who had seized yet another small fortified city, Zhongmu.

> Bi Xi invited him to visit him, and the Master was once again inclined to go.
>
> Zilu said, "Master, formerly I have heard you say, 'When a man in his own person is guilty of doing evil, a superior man will not associate with

him.' Bi Xi is in rebellion, holding possession of Zhongmu; if you go to him, what shall be said?"
>
> The Master said, "Yes, I did use these words. But is it not said, that, if a thing be really white, it may be steeped in a dark fluid without being made black?"

Analects, 17:7

In other words he could go and serve this warlord but not be corrupted himself, and then lead the people of the small city into a new golden age by his example.

Zilu merely snorted at this. That was all very well but what would people say? What would they say? If Confucius were to go, nobody would ever take him seriously again—no matter how pure his motives everybody would think he just wanted power like everybody else.

Confucius, sighing, knew in the end that Zilu was right, and refused to go to Zhongmu as he had refused all the other leaders who had taken power by force. Nevertheless he was feeling even more frustrated than ever and seemed to have lost the last opportunity he would ever get to have a real say in governing. Was this to be his fate, he asked his students bitterly?

> Confucius said: "There are some who sprout but do not blossom, some who blossom but do not bear fruit."

Analects, 9:22

As it happened it was very lucky that he had taken Zilu's advice. As the spring of 501 turned into summer and the creamy apricot blossoms on the trees outside the school-house ripened into fruit, this familiar sun-dappled scene was for the first time to become an appropriate metaphor for his life instead of a source of melancholy and regret. The situation in Lu was about to change, and very much in his favor.

The previous year old Duke Meng died, and Nangong Jingshu's elder brother Meng Yi (a former student of Confucius) had succeeded him as head of the family. Although Yang Huo still controlled the army of the Ji family, Meng Yi was far more determined than his father to bring an end to the upstart's dictatorship. He persuaded his counterpart, Ji Huan, to show a bit of spunk for a change and join him in getting rid of Yang Huo once and for all, guaranteeing the support of the Shu family as well. Ji Huan tried to get his soldiers over to his side but only succeeded in getting himself arrested by Yang Huo once again. Meng Yi marched on the capital in a replay of the coup of 517 which had forced Confucius into exile, only this time the feudal families had right on their side as they were fighting to restore the Duke to power, not overthrow him.

In the confusion Ji Huan somehow managed to escape, while his own soldiers, who had been mobilized to defend Yang Huo, saw which way the wind was blowing and changed sides. According to Zhuangzi, Yang Huo managed to escape from Lu dressed as a woman—this is probably apocryphal but is rip-roaring stuff (thanks to Zhuangzi the whole history of Chinese philosophy plays like an action movie). We do know that, wearing women's clothes or not, he ended up in the neighboring state of Qi—that perennial haven for exiles where Confucius spent seven years himself. Meanwhile, back in Lu, Duke Ding was triumphantly restored to authority and paraded the streets in a chariot, flanked by soldiers waving banners emblazoned with green dragons. Bonfires blazed in celebration all night, and the next day the Duke announced he would form a new government.

The three families, rejoicing like everybody else at Yang Huo's ignominious departure, imagined that it would once again be business as usual, the business in question being the milking of the populace for grain tithes while the Duke sat quietly in his palace doing nothing about it. They received a rude shock. Duke Ding, having spent the past four years a virtual prisoner in his own house with plenty of time to think, had decided that from now on he would be nobody's puppet, and it was time for new blood in his government. Although Ji Huan (Lord Ji) was once more invited to be the prime minister, many other posts were filled by men who were not members of the upper nobility, and Duke Ding did this to counterbalance the undue influence of the feudal families, which in his opinion had caused all the problems in the first place. As Confucius had said, "a ruler should be a ruler, and a minister a minister," and the Duke was determined to start acting like a real duke for a change instead of merely stamping decrees with his crimson seal for the benefit of the rich barons. Accordingly, one of the first people whom he invited to join his new administration was Confucius.

Once again a messenger arrived at the door of the school-house, this time with a silk scroll bearing the ducal seal, which offered him the post of governor of the district of Chungdu, the central area of Lu which included the capital. Zilu's immediate reaction was "Is that all?"—believing that his Master deserved the post of prime minister immediately—but Confucius shook his head and told him that being inside the halls of power in any position was far better than peering in through the window from outside as he had done all his life.

Confucius said: "If you don't have an official position, you can't plan the affairs of government."

Analects, 8:14

He patted Zilu on the shoulder and told him to be patient: one day he would lead the government and all his students would be his ministers. They would remember this impossible dream when both were near their deaths. Now, both Master and student made confident fists in the air as they celebrated this triumph, but then they would be weeping. Confucius penned a quick reply of acceptance on a bamboo-slip, handed it to the Duke's messenger, and bowed twice, telling him that he would attend the Duke at his court as soon as he had put his affairs in order.

At long last Confucius had been invited to the banquet. He had waited a long time—he was now in his fifty-first year—but this time the door would not close in his face …

Confucius accepting office as a Minister of State. Tableau in City of Six Arts Qufu. *Photo: Jonathan Price*

At the Summit

Confucius said: "… at fifty I knew the mandate of heaven."

Analects, 2:4

The "mandate of heaven" was the ancient Zhou concept of the right to rule, granted by the gods but nevertheless revocable if the ruler proved unworthy of the responsibility. Confucius' mandate had been granted by the Duke of Lu, and he knew that if he failed to do a good job he would be fired. Once again he was a *manager*, not this time of cattle-breeding but of a whole district which included the capital, Chungdu, and its surrounding area, and once again he seems to have been an immediate success.

Duke Ding appointed Confucius ruler of the middle district (Chung Du). At the end of a year his neighbors on all sides took him as a model. From the management of Chung Du, he was advanced to the post of minister of public works.

Sima Qian, *Records of the Grand Historian*

Since Chungdu was the capital, Confucius was in frequent contact with Duke Ding, who started asking his advice on governmental matters in the same way as Duke Jing of Qi had done more than ten years before:

Duke Ding asked how a ruler should employ his ministers and how a minister should serve his ruler.

Confucius replied, saying: "The prince employs his ministers with propriety; the ministers serve their prince with good faith."

Analects, 3:19

Duke Ding asked if there were a single phrase which could uplift a country.

Confucius replied: "Words in themselves cannot

Confucius in his official robes as Minister of State
Ming Dynasty painting. *Qilu Press*

have such an effect."

The Duke asked further: "Is there a single phrase which could ruin a country?"

Confucius answered, "Again, words in themselves cannot have such an effect. But if you are evil, and no one disagrees with you, perhaps you could destroy the country with a single utterance."

Analects, 13:15

Slogans in other words are never enough, but on the other hand can be extremely dangerous. As always (or at least as most of the time) Confucius was right about this. When the miserable survivors of the Third Reich picked their way across the ashes of Berlin in 1945 they must have heard the empty slogans echoing across the rubble from the ruins of the Olympic stadium: *"Deutschland, Deutschland, uber alles!" "Ein Reich! Ein Volk! Ein Führer!"*

Confucius repeatedly warned of the dangers of absolute power, and characterized a dictator as somebody who says:

"I do not enjoy ruling; I only enjoy people not disagreeing with me."

Analects, 13:15

The true ruler, Confucius told Duke Ding, is always ready to accept criticism:

"When he makes a mistake, he doesn't hesitate to correct it."

Analects, 1:8

The mere fact that Duke Ding was at last listening to him must have encouraged Confucius to feel that eventually he could make a real difference in the state that he considered was "only one step from the Way." His hidden agenda, which he confided only to his students, was to put and end to the quarrelling between

Power dinners: Confucius discussing good government with the Duke of Lu. *Qilu Press*

Right: Confucius in his official robes as Governor of Chungdu. Ming Dynasty Painting. *Qilu Press*

the feudal clans and abolish their private armies, but this would have to wait until exactly the right moment. For now he concentrated on being a good administrator.

"What do you think if all the people in a town like someone?"

"Not too good," said Confucius.

"What if they all hate you?"

"Also not too good. It is better if the good people in a town like you, and the evil ones hate you."

Analects, 13:24

Although very busy now, he still found time to teach some classes, and all the students were very eager to hear his first-hand experience of governing. Many of the remarks he made at this period have now been adopted by the "Confucian management" enthusiasts of our own day, since managing an administrative district is little different from the challenge of managing a modern company.

Confucius said: "Expect much from yourself and little from others and you will avoid incurring resentments."

Analects, 15:15

Above all he stressed the ethical responsibilities of management, and never wavered in his belief that others will always follow a good example:

Confucius said: "If those in authority behave correctly, the people under them will be easy to manage."

Analects, 14:43

The Master said, "If you put the honest in

positions of power and discard the dishonest, you will force the dishonest to become honest."

Analects, 12:22

In his first year as governor, he fired several people whom he considered to be dishonest, incurring a lot of resentment as a result. Although as a teacher he preferred all his students to like him, he already knew from his previous managerial experience that for an administrator, courting universal popularity could be fatal:

Confucius said: "If a person lacks trustworthiness, I don't know what he or she can be good for. When a pin is missing from the yoke-bar of a large wagon, or from the collar-bar of a small wagon, how can it go?"

Analects, 2:22

At the same time as sorting out those in his employ, Confucius also used his own inimitable combination of formal politeness and professional confidence with his superiors, especially the Duke himself, who began to rely on him more and more.

Confucius said: "If you use every single courtesy while serving your ruler, the people will call you a toady."

Analects, 3:18

Sima Qian wrote this glowing report about Confucius'

Confucius supervising the imposition of fair prices for live-stock during his period as Governor of Chungdu district.
Qilu Press

Official 4-horse traveling carriage for high official.
Replica of Qin Dynasty vehicle, Museum of Chariots, Linzi.
(Although this replica is based on archaeological remains from a slightly later period, the official carriages used in Confucius' time would have been very similar to this.
Photo: Jonathan Price

achievements as governor of the capital:

> After Confucius had conducted the governorship for three months, the sellers of lambs and of suckling pigs no longer falsified their prices, lost objects were not picked up on the streets.
> Strangers who came from all sides did not need to turn to the officials when they entered the city, for all were received as if they were returning to their own homes.
>
> Sima Qian, *Records of the Grand Historian*

This is probably a slight exaggeration but he certainly acquitted himself well enough to be promoted to minister of works. Then, in the year 500, only a year after taking his first public office, Confucius was given the

Understanding Confucius' famous metaphor from *Analects* **2:22:** If the pin is missing (shown here inserted through the yoke-bar) the horses will not be connected to the vehicle strongly enough. Thus a tiny fault – for example the acceptance of one single bribe – will prevent an administrator from operating effectively. Replica of Spring and Autumn Period chariot, Museum of Chariots, Linzi.
Photo: Jonathan Price

biggest chance of his career and was appointed by Duke Ding as acting secretary of state for an important diplomatic mission. This was to travel back to the state of Qi and negotiate with Duke Jing, who had taken advantage of all the upheavals in his neighboring state and had quietly annexed two districts belonging to Lu immediately to the south of the Great Wall of Qi. Confucius was chosen rather than anybody else because of his known close relationship with Duke Jing. Duke Ding of Lu wanted to avoid war at any cost, but on the other hand it was totally humiliating to lose territory and do nothing about it. Could Confucius please see what he could do?

Confucius travelled in great state this time, leaving his old ox-wagon at home and making the journey in a carriage pulled by four horses. He wore minister's robes and an official hat trimmed in scarlet and black with a large decorative pin piercing the top—every inch the statesman.

Duke Jing was as always delighted to see him. He had no intention of returning the territories he had seized but with his characteristic bonhomie suggested an informal get-together—just Duke Ding, himself, and possibly Confucius? Not to mention a few girls—wink-wink—he was sure they could work something out? They could have this meeting at his hunting lodge at Jiagu (Chia Ku) just inside the Qi border.

> Duke Jing wished to go thither in a simple chariot, as if to a friendly reunion. Confucius, who was acting secretary of state, said: "When the princes leave the boundaries of their territories, they must take with them their entire official retinue."
>
> Sima Qian, *Records of the Grand Historian*

"You think so?" Duke Jing replied.
"Oh yes," Confucius insisted. It had to be a formal

"**Marshals of the right and left**". Model of Spring and Autumn Period army of Qi state on parade in the City of the Six Arts, Qufu. *Photo: Jonathan Price*

Performance on replicas of the ancient musical bells. Huaxia Ancient Music Ensemble, Henan Museum. *Photo: Jonathan Price*

summit. Duke Ding insisted on that. Of course—no doubt they could resolve the situation—but it had to be done according to protocol.

"All right. All right. Arrange it."

Confucius agreed, and told Duke Jing he would have to appear with his marshals of the "right and left" together with their troops with their dragon flags attached to their helmets. Everything had to be done according to the rules specified in the *Book of Rites*.

"Whatever …" Duke Jing agreed wearily, as always deferring to Confucius' superior knowledge of traditional ritual. Then he brightened, and told Confucius about his latest passion—"barbarian dancers." While visiting the state of Zhao to the west of Qi he had seen a performance by dancers from the steppes far to the west of the ancient Zhou Empire, and they were, he assured Confucius, an absolute knockout. Such passion … such … movement—well, Confucius just had to see them for himself. Duke Jing had brought a whole troupe of them to his court, and treated Confucius to a performance that evening.

The "Duke Jing Dancing Ensemble" was not exactly to Confucius' taste—he preferred the classical music of the ancient Zhou Empire called the *Shao* music—but out of politeness he expressed his enthusiasm. The

An ancient Chinese juggler keeps four swords and four balls in the air at the same time, while a tumbler performs cartwheels on right. Han Dynasty relief. Shandong Museum. *Photo: Jonathan Price*

Ancient Chinese acrobats. Han Dynasty bronze figures. Henan Museum. *Photo: Jonathan Price*

"barbarian" dance routines included belly dancers and tumbling dwarfs and reached a climax in a number called "The Four Cardinal Points" in which the dancers formed human pyramids at the four corners of the stage, then extended their arms and shouted "Hi!" bringing forth tumultuous applause. Very Central Asian—but extremely un-Chinese.

All this was recorded by Sima Qian in the *Records of the Grand Historian*, and also in four other independent historical records. Sima's account of this whole incident is so detailed (the dwarf tumblers and the name of their dance for example) and is so much in character with both Confucius and Duke Jing as we know them from the *Analects* that it seems to be authentic, and must be

based on contemporary records which are now lost. In the account here I realize I can be accused of "novelization" but this is what Sima Qian himself was doing and I am simply fleshing out the details as he himself did—I remain convinced that this is exactly what happened since Sima Qian's account fits the characters so perfectly, even though as always he could not quite get inside Confucius' head.

Confucius returned to Lu and told Duke Ding that the Duke of Qi had agreed to an official summit:

"So I beg you also to take the marshal of the right as well as the marshal of the left." Confucius said. Duke Ding said: "Yes," and commanded his marshals of the right and of the left to accompany him.

Sima Qian, *Records of the Grand Historian*

So the famous Jiagu summit was convened, and the two sides met in neutral territory with all their formal retinues as Confucius had insisted.

A terrace was built, to which a threefold staircase led. Then the princes met together, according to the rites, for a meeting. After the princes had bowed, and each had offered the other precedence, they mounted the steps.

Sima Qian, *Records of the Grand Historian*

After the appropriate ceremonies of welcome which Confucius supervised exactly according to the rules of protocol as laid down in the *Book of Rites*, the two sides sat down for the first conference.

Duke Jing had still had no intention of giving back the land he had seized and argued that because the territories were near to the border of Wu, a state which threatened both Qi and Lu, it was in both their interests to have Qi soldiers stationed there. He offered a

Site of the Jiagu Summit 500 B.C. Duke Jing of Qi had annexed territory to the south of the Great Wall of Qi (ruins seen on left). The peace talks were held on the lowlands seen in the distance in this picture, very close to this section of the wall.

Deadlock at the Jiagu Summit: Duke Jing of Qi on left, Duke Ding of Lu on right. Confucius bottom right presiding over proceedings. Ming Dynasty Painting. *Qilu Press*

Duke Jing of Qi holding court. Ming Dynasty Painting. *Qilu Press*

guarantee of protection to Lu in the event of any invasion by Wu forces in return for Lu formally ceding the seized territories to Qi, which Duke Ding of Lu refused to do. So far the summit had only resulted in "meaningful discussions and a frank exchange of views" (has anything ever changed?)—in other words they had decided absolutely nothing and were in a state of complete deadlock.

The Duke of Lu was very disappointed that Confucius had been unable to make the other Duke give way on anything, but at this point all his acting secretary of state could do was shrug his shoulders and say he had done his best. Then, after the evening's formal banquet, Duke Jing blundered and played into Confucius' hands.

First of all, the Duke proposed a toast: "To peace and friendship!" The words echoed around the hall as everybody drained their drinking cups. So far, so formal, but then Duke Jing announced that since he was hosting the summit, he would like to offer a surprise after-dinner entertainment which he was sure everybody was going to love—his dance ensemble. With a wink at Confucius, who remained impassively formal, Duke Jing summoned his chamberlain to introduce the performance.

> After the ceremony was concluded, in which each drank to the other, an official of Qi advanced.
>
> Sima Qian, *Records of the Grand Historian*.

"Your majestic eminences, my lords, ladies and gentlemen," announced the official, "we now humbly present … direct from the capital of Qi … the music of the four cardinal points!" A cymbal clashed, followed by frenzied drumming, and then, amid wild applause:

> … a crowd of dancers appeared, decked in feathers and tails of fur, spears and lances, swords and shields, and these advanced amid drumbeat and outcry.
>
> Sima Qian, *Records of the Grand Historian*.

Dusky belly-dancers writhed to the sensuous rhythms

in pink pantaloons, tumblers performed back-flips, and acrobats jumped over whirling and flashing swords.

> There appeared jugglers and dwarfs, with their dances.
>
> Sima Qian, *Records of the Grand Historian*.

As the dancers formed a human pyramid for the spectacular climax Duke Jing beamed proudly and the whole hall erupted into tumultuous applause. Confucius had at first been horrified by the performance, which he considered vulgar in the extreme and totally inappropriate to the formality of the occasion, but suddenly he had a flash of inspiration. Remembering how he had once saved the life of the forester in Qi he realized that he might be able to use the same ploy here to break the deadlock at the talks. It might just work … and in Duke Jing he was sure he knew his man. As soon as the guests started to depart he requested a private word with his own Duke. What they said was not recorded but it must have gone something like this:

Confucius: "Pretend to be outraged."

Duke Ding: "Outraged? I thought it was wonderful …"

Confucius: "Trust me on this one. You're outraged—insulted—you've never been more insulted in your life."

Having been assured that if he played the outraged monarch he might get his territories back, Duke Ding agreed to go along with his minister's plan. Confucius next requested a private audience with Duke Jing. The other Duke received him in his private chambers with great bonhomie and offered him a drink. They were after all old friends.

"Master," Duke Jing said magnanimously as he raised his drinking cup, still confident that he himself was still the master of the whole situation. "You are welcome. You see—they loved the dancers. It is the new style, it is the future. The old music is dead. You should come back to Qi my friend. Lu is … finished."

Confucius nodded, sipped his millet wine, and then got down to the business: "We have a problem. The dancers—wonderful—fantastic—I loved the 'barbarian' style, but … the Duke of Lu is very upset. He's even thinking of complaining to the King of Zhou. Two state leaders meeting—the dancing should be traditional. No question—it's in the *Book of Rites*. You've lost face here."

"Lost face?"

"Yes. Big-time I'm afraid…"

"I see. Well—what should I do, apologize?

Key player: Confucius in full regalia as Acting Secretary of State for the state of Lu. Ming Dynasty Painting. *Qilu Press*

Confucius shook his head. "Not enough I'm afraid." "If a person of noble character has committed a fault, he excuses himself by means of something actual; if a person of low character has committed a fault, he excuses himself with words alone. If you have regrets, excuse yourself by means of an actual deed."

Sima Qian, *Records of the Grand Historian*.

Duke Jing: "So—what do you suggest?"

Confucius: "As far as I see it you've got to—well—return the territories."

(Long pause)

Duke Jing: "All right. If you say so ..."

Thereupon the Duke of Qi, in order to make good his fault, returned the territories Yun, Wen Yang, and Kuei Yin, which he had stolen from the state of Lu.

Sima Qian, *Records of the Grand Historian*.

The treaty was signed the next day. After this diplomatic triumph Confucius' stock rose dramatically and Duke Ding informed him that he was to be promoted to minister of justice. Sima Qian adds one more detail which really jars in this otherwise credible narrative. According to the Grand Historian, Confucius asked the two dukes to order the officers of the day to execute all the members of the barbarian dance team, and this was carried out in the most bloodthirsty manner—the dwarfs and jugglers were not simply beheaded but first had all their limbs hacked off:

Agreement is reached: Duke Jing of Qi (left) agrees to give back the annexed territories to Duke Ding of Lu (right). Confucius (foreground) insisting that Duke Jing observes correct protocol and apologizes. Ming Dynasty Painting. *Qilu Press*

Then hands and feet flew about separated.

Sima Qian, *Records of the Grand Historian*

This is so at odds with Confucius' whole creed of humanity and avoidance of punishment that it must have been one of the vivid little details Sima was so fond of inserting into his historical writing. This was the man after all who claimed that Confucius was nine feet tall. Sima Qian himself had of course been castrated by his emperor so he would understandably have had a slightly warped view of human nature. If we discount the severed hands and feet, however, the Jiagu summit must have played out more or less as described.

After returning to Lu Confucius took up his post as justice minister. This job did not really suit him because he always held that it was more important to deal with the root causes of crime rather than concentrate on punishing the criminals in order to deter others. What he really wanted to do was attack the fundamental problems in his society, and he proved so over-eager about this that it ultimately proved to be his downfall. While the leaders of society—the feudal barons—were engaged in very publicly lining their own pockets, was it surprising that the common people became pickpockets? So went Confucius' argument, and even though his idea that criminals can be "shamed" into honesty might be utopian, this second idea is still valid. It is no coincidence that even today those rulers who are the most corrupt are always the most vociferous advocates of law and order, and this is what Confucius was talking about. He was not in fact opposed to punishment as such, only its excessive use as a remedy for society's ills, and accepted that sanctions were still necessary if justly applied:

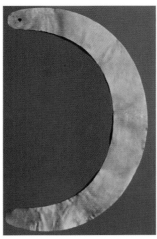
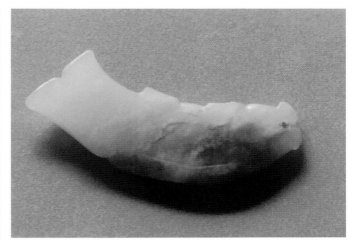

Someone said: "What do you think of the saying: 'Repay harm with virtue'?"

Confucius replied, "Then how will you repay virtue? Repay harm with Justice and repay virtue with virtue."

Analects, 14:34

He had already said that "In doing government, what is the need of killing?" However, Confucius saw that the complete abolition of the death penalty was hardly possible in his own time, and instead looked towards a gradual phasing out of what he saw as the most inhumane of punishments:

Confucius said: "If good men were to govern a country for a hundred years, they could overcome cruelty and do away with capital punishment. How true this saying is!"

Analects, 13:11

Despite his opposition to capital punishment he was obliged to preside over at least one execution during his term as justice minister:

Thereupon he executed, from among the dignitaries of Lu, the trouble-maker, Shao Cheng Mao.

Sima Qian, *Records of the Grand Historian*

Targets for thieves: valuable objects from the Spring and Autumn Period, around the time of Confucius. Left: Fragments of officially stamped gold bars used for trading (Shanghai Museum). Centre: Man's gold ear-ring as worn by the aristocracy (Capital Museum Beijing). Right: Jade dress ornament (Capital Museum Beijing). *Photos: Jonathan Price*

Forced to spend his days hearing endless criminal and civil cases, Confucius was quickly tiring of his job. In his opinion robbery, fraud, disputes over property, and even murder were symptoms of a general malaise in society and it was the root causes of this that he really wanted to address, not the petty details:

Confucius said: "In hearing lawsuits, I am no better than anyone else. What we need is to have no lawsuits."

Analects, 12:13

Ji Kangzi (the son of Lord Ji and one of Confucius' students) eventually became Chancellor of Lu. Alarmed by the growing number of robberies in the state, he

Confucius expounding his theories on government to his students. Tableau in the City of the Six Arts, Qufu. *Photo: Jonathan Price*

The Master said:

"If you put the honest in positions of power and discard the dishonest, you will force the dishonest to become honest."
Analects 12:22

asked the master what could be done to control crime. Confucius' reply was not quite what Ji Kangzi expected:

Confucius said, "If you, sir, were not covetous of your property, nobody would steal from you, even if you were to offer them a reward to do so."

Analects, 12:18

In other words if you place a notice outside your unlocked door saying "Please come inside and help yourself to anything you want, I don't need all these things" nobody would take anything. Although this seems to be one of Confucius' more outlandish remarks, there is still something in it—property theft and even violent crime always increases as a population becomes more materialistic, and this is certainly happening in his own homeland today. Petty thieves from time immemorial have always felt they were being denied their fair share of the goodies, and believe they are performing a social service by redistributing wealth. As an experiment take a high-value banknote in your own currency, go out into the street and try and give it away. Almost certainly, just as Confucius said, nobody will take the money.

Confucius, like many state attorneys, was also aware that he was wasting his time prosecuting the small fry.

A "conventional townsman" and his wife. Confucius hated the hypocritical complacency of the 'respectable citizens' even more than he despised corrupt rulers. They are still alive and well today. Han Dynasty figurines, Capital Museum Beijing. *Photo: Jonathan Price*

Confucius lecturing. Ming Dynasty Painting. *Qilu Press*

The really successful criminals always live in big houses with state-of-the-art security, appear to be model citizens, and usually avoid being caught.

Confucius said: "The 'conventional townsman' is a thief of virtue."

Analects, 17:13

In this, one of his most celebrated remarks, he attacks not only those true criminals who hide behind a cloak of conventionality but all the other respectable citizens who wallow in their own self-righteousness but in fact do nothing to help those outside their gates who are less fortunate. It is these "conventional townsmen" (today they would be members of the Rotary Club) who always support the government of the day and are the loudest supporters of a tough law-and-order policy. Mencius was once asked to explain what Confucius meant when he said that these respectable burghers were "thieves of virtue":

If you would blame them, you find nothing to allege. If you would criticize them, you have nothing to criticize. They agree with the current customs. They consent with an impure age. Their principles have a semblance of right-heartedness and truth. Their conduct has a semblance of disinterestedness and purity. All men are pleased with them, and they think themselves right.

Book of Mencius, Book 7, Part 2, Chapter 37:11

Infuriated by the smugness of the "conventional townsmen," while greed, rapacity, and oppression flourished as never before, Confucius was becoming very impatient. After only a year of hearing cases against pickpockets and thieves, he told his students (he still found time for teaching although lawsuits took up most of his time) that the moment had arrived to act. Everybody kept throwing up their hands, saying that this was an impure age and nothing could be done about the crime wave and the greed and the killing, but Confucius insisted this was not true, something *could* be done. Everybody looked back to the golden age of the Zhou, but were men any different in their essential nature at that time? Of course not, the Master said:

"The common people were the ground upon which the rulers of the Three Dynasties manifested the correct Way."

Analects, 15:25

It was time to raise the flag of humanity, Confucius told his young disciples. The state of Lu was "one step from the Way," they could do it, they could make a difference—they could change things. Zilu led the students in a round of wild applause and cheering. *The Way! The Way! The Way!*

For Confucius, this was the beginning of the end …

Memories of an ancient town: the Drum Tower Qufu (Ming Dynasty) *Qilu Press*

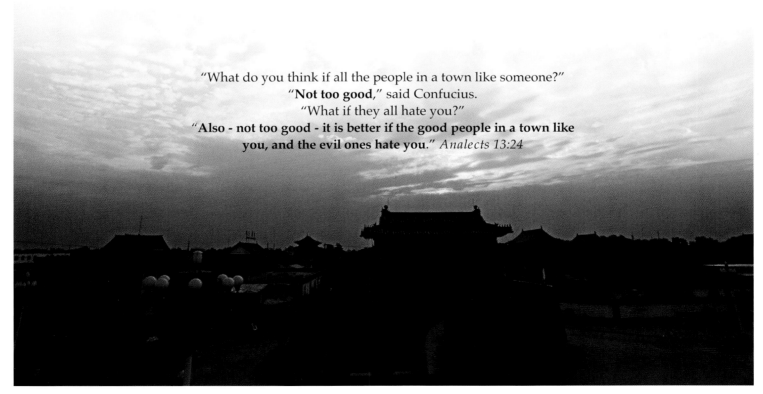

"What do you think if all the people in a town like someone?"
"Not too good," said Confucius.
"What if they all hate you?"
"Also - not too good - it is better if the good people in a town like you, and the evil ones hate you." *Analects 13:24*

Tearing Down the Walls

Unaware that the world was not yet ready for his ideals, Confucius came into the year 498 on an all-time high. With their beloved teacher now a powerful minister, all the students wanted to talk about at the school was the ideal state they all dreamed of bringing into existence.

> Zigong asked about government.
>
> The Master said, "Enough food, enough weapons and the confidence of the people."
>
> Zigong said, "Suppose you had no alternative but to give up one of these three, which one would be let go of first?"
>
> The Master said, "Weapons."
>
> *Analects*, 12:7

It was in fact weapons reduction—specifically the disarmament of the warlords—that Confucius was starting to see as the crucial first step in the establishment of his ideal state, which he could see would never happen while the powerful families expended their energy and resources in fighting amongst themselves all the time.

The young man who had asked this very perceptive question, Zigong (Tzu Kung), was a new member of the class who quickly became one of Confucius' two all-time star students—the other was Yan Hui who was even younger, only about sixteen, when he enrolled the following year. Zigong, who appears in a large number of the *Analects*, was certainly among the liveliest members of the classes, the embodiment of Confucius' ideal student who "continually asks *what is it, what does that mean*?" (*Analects*, 15:15), and indeed many of the Master's most celebrated pronouncements were in response to Zigong's questions including his second reiteration of the "golden rule":

> Zigong asked: "Is there a single concept that we can take as a guide for the actions of our whole life?"
>
> Confucius said, "What about 'reciprocity'? What you don't like done to yourself, don't do to others."
>
> *Analects*, 15:24

Confucius rightly praised Zigong above all others except Yan Hui, his all-time star student who was shortly himself to join the class:

Wall of Qufu

Zigong asked: "What do you say of me?"

Confucius said, "You are a vessel."

"What kind of vessel."

"A gemmed sacrificial vessel."

Analects, 5:4

What Confucius meant was that Zigong as a "vessel"—or "urn"—absorbed his ideas as no other had done up until this point. Although Yan Hui was to surpass him, as even Zigong himself modestly acknowledged, nevertheless Zigong was a gem indeed, and could be said to be Confucius' biggest success-story: he went on to become one of the most successful diplomats of the Warring States Period. His old teacher would have been proud had he lived to see this, especially as his own efforts to disarm the barons, towards which he was now gearing up, ultimately failed.

Zigong's family were struggling merchants, but still they would have been unable to get their son into government work without the new opportunities provided by Confucius' school. Their son's "fees" would have been a little more than a dried sausage, and their contribution would have helped support poorer students like Yan Hui who was Zigong's classmate. Zigong himself also had a great talent for business, and used his instinctive ability to buy low and sell high to help support his Master during the years of hardship which lay ahead. He supported his Master unequivocally, and shared his passionate belief in action rather than words, believing that together they could change society for the better.

In the spring of 498 Confucius still thought he could succeed in bringing about this change. He knew it was not going to be easy to get the powerful families to stop their feuding and unite

Zigong presenting his Master with food. Statue outside Confucius Temple, Nanjing. *Photo: Jonathan Price*

behind the Duke, but he was confident that he was now in a position to persuade them to do this. Not only was he himself a government minister but he had also managed to get more and more of his students established in key state posts as governors of towns and cities, while many others occupied influential positions within the households of the big three families, the Ji, Meng, and Shu clans.

The Master said: "The perfected man, wishing himself to be established, sees that others are established, and, wishing himself to be successful, sees that others are successful."

Analects, 6:30

This is another of the fundamental lessons of his educational philosophy. Great teachers will always glory in their students' success, and this is one of the fundamental differences between Chinese and Western education even today. The Western saying "those who can't—teach," implies that teachers are by definition pathetic failures who teach others to be successful. A Chinese teacher by contrast (and this is because of the ongoing influence of Confucius) is still regarded in Chinese society as the ultimate success story.

Confucius himself, having got his students jobs, now urged them to use their positions to promote his "Way"—the way of humanity and helping the poor and disenfranchised:

Yuan Si being made governor of his town by the Master, he gave him 900 measures of grain, but Si declined them.

The Master said, "Do not decline them. May you not give them away in the neighborhoods, hamlets, towns, and villages?"

Analects, 6:5

Confucius kept tabs on all of them, and it really seemed in this brief summer of 497 that his Way was going to work and that he and his students were

"You are a vessel, a gemmed sacrificial vessel": Confucius likened his brilliant but sometimes brash and over-confident student Zigong to a vessel used for sacrifices like this one. Like Zigong himself, the vessel is somewhat flashy but would certainly have attracted attention! Reconstruction of *'dou'* bowl from Eastern Zhou period. Capital Museum Beijing. *Photo: Jonathan Price*

on the brink of ushering in a new golden age in the state of Lu:

> Ziyou became the governor of Wucheng. The Master said, "Have you got any good men working for you?"
>
> He answered: "I have Dantai Mieming, who never takes short cuts in his work and does not come to my office unless he has real business to discuss."

Analects, 6:14

Almost every city in Lu now had a Confucius graduate in command:

> Hsia, who was serving as governor of Qufu, asked about government.
>
> Confucius said, "Don't be impatient, and don't look for small advantages. If you are impatient, you will not be thorough. If you look for small advantages, you will never accomplish anything great."

Analects, 13:17

Because the biggest obstacle to any sort of social progress was still the endless feuding between the powerful families, Confucius was now determined to attack this problem at its root. Zilu (Yu) and Ranyu (Qiu), who had been among his first batch of students, were now in their late thirties and occupied senior positions in the Ji family—Qiu was now actually head of the Ji military organization. Although Qiu had once been temporarily expelled from Confucius' inner circle he was now on reasonably good terms with his former teacher. Lord Ji

had ordered Qiu to organize an attack on the fortified town of Zhuanyu, which did not in fact come under his feudal suzerainty but was strategically important because is was near to the city of Bei which had been captured from the Ji family by another warlord, and they wanted it back. All this had to stop, Confucius told his former students, the feudal barons could not go around taking territory just because they were able to—might was not right.

> Confucius said, "Qiu, is it not you who are in fault here? Zhuanyu is in the midst of the territory of our state; and its ruler is a minister in direct connection with the Duke: What has your chief to do with attacking it?"
>
> Ranyu said "But at present, Zhuanyu is strong and near to Bei; if our chief does not now take it, it will hereafter be a sorrow to his descendants."

Analects, 16:1

Confucius sighed with exasperation.

> Confucius said. "Now, here are you, Yu and Qiu, assisting your chief to plan these hostile movements within the state!

Analects, 16:1

Now at last Confucius unveiled his grand plan: he

Feudal fortifications: The petty warlords ringed the cities they controlled with high walls guarded day and night by sentries, which enabled them to defy the central authority of the Duke. This magnificent example – built during Confucius' lifetime – still stands near Chanqing in Shandong. *Photo: Jonathan Price*

Inset pictures: **Tearing down the walls**: the crumbling ruins of the Great Wall of Qi are almost all that remains of the massive fortifications built during Confucius' time – which he vehemently condemned as a pointless activity. *Photos: Jonathan Price*

would persuade the Duke to enforce the demolition of the fortifications that all the petty warlords had constructed around the cities they had seized. That meant Lord Ji would get his city of Bei back, but Zilu and Qiu had to make sure Ji Huan did not jeopardize the situation by attacking another city in the meantime. The great families had to be seen to be doing the right thing, and then all the petty warlords would be forced to follow, according to Confucius' principle that if the most powerful set a good example they would force the dishonest to become honest.

Zilu and Qiu were very dubious about their chances of persuading Lord Ji but agreed to try.

Zilu asked how to deal with a leader. Confucius said, "If you have to oppose him, don't do it by deceit."

Analects, 14:23

Leaving his followers to try and persuade their chief to abandon his plans for war and "give peace a chance," Confucius sought an audience with Duke Ding to explain what he had in mind.

In the summer of the thirteenth year of Ding [498 BC], Confucius spoke to Duke Ding: "Among the officials, there must be none who have concealed stores of weapons; among the nobles, there must be none who possess cities with walls more than three thousand feet long."

Sima Qian, *Records of the Grand Historian*

The authority of the state, Confucius argued, must be the Duke and his state government, and not the nobles.

Confucius said: "When the Way prevails in the realm, then social organization, the arts, and military campaigns are all initiated by the Ruler.

Lethal weapon: Razor-sharp blades mounted on long poles (specially designed to inflict the most horrific injuries) were standard issue in the feudal militia which Confucius wanted disbanded. Bronze pike, Warring States Period. Shanghai Museum. *Photo: Jonathan Price*

When the Way declines in the realm, then these things are initiated by the nobles, and when this happens the ruling house will usually lose its power within ten generations."

Analects, 16:2

Confucius was in fact prophetically correct about this—within ten generations all the ruling houses of the Warring States, still racked by feuding, lost their power when the Qin Dynasty was established in 221 BC.

He was not, he explained to the Duke, suggesting total disarmament, but the fact that each feudal family maintained its own army was an incredible waste of resources and a completely unnecessary waste of human lives. Confucius' position was that the state of Lu should be capable of defending itself, but this should be with a professional army. In his opinion it took at least seven years to train a professional soldier:

Confucius said: "Only when qualified men have instructed people for seven years, may they take up arms. To lead untrained people into battle is the same as throwing them away."

Analects, 13:29 / 13:30

Instead each feudal clan conscripted farmers and ordinary people into their armies every time they picked a fight with one of the other warlords, which was more or less every year. This not only had a disastrous economic effect, since the farmers were frequently taken

Confucius supervising the dismantling of the walls around the fortified cities. Ming Dynasty painting. *Qilu Press*

off their fields during the planting and harvest season, but was also literally throwing away lives because most of these farmers were untrained in archery and could not hit a target accurately even from a few paces away. As a result these feudal skirmishes were simply exercises in carnage:

When contentions about territory are the ground on which they fight, they slaughter men till the fields are filled with them. When some struggle for a city is the ground on which they fight, they slaughter men till the city is filled with them.

Book of Mencius, Book 4, Part 1, Chapter 14:2

The Duke was initially very enthusiastic about Confucius' proposals, and appointed him "acting chancellor" in charge of the disarmament program. Zilu, Ranyu, and all his other former students who were working for the three families began lobbying intensely with their own feudal lords for a handing-in of weapons and the dismantling of fortifications around the cities they controlled.

Confucius had his disciple, Ranyu, steward of the Ji family, promote the intention of razing the city walls of the cities of the three clans. Thereupon, the Shu-Sun family first dismantled the walls of Hou.

Sima Qian, *Records of the Grand Historian*

Amazingly, at first the idea seemed to be working. Through his former students and other influential connections Confucius was telling the nobles that by disarmament everybody wins. His best friend Nangong Jingshu argued on his behalf with his elder brother, who was now Lord Meng. Meng Yi also miraculously agreed to get behind the program and conscripted his vassals to start dismantling the walls surrounding the cities he himself controlled. For a few brief months, the state of Lu echoed not with the screams of dying soldiers but the thudding of sledgehammers and the crumbling of masonry as the walls came down amid clouds of dust. Swords, pikes, and even chariots were handed in by the clans to the central armoury of the state. At last, Confucius' ideal state seemed to be coming into being, and everybody awaited the dawn of the new golden age. Then, everything started to go wrong…

The Ji family was about to raze the walls of Bei, but Kung-Shan Pu Niu and Shu-Sun Che put themselves at the head of the citizens of Bei and fell upon the Duke of Lu and the three barons. These latter retreated into the fortress of the Ji family.

Sima Qian, *Records of the Grand Historian*

礼隋三都
孔子言於定公曰
臣無藏甲大夫無
百雉之城今三家
過制請損之公曰
然於是隳三都為

Resistance to Confucius' disarmament initiative: fighting around a fortified city as Confucius (seen on left) and the Duke of Lu (right) attempt to dismantle the fortifications of a feudal city. *Qilu Press*

Aided by a renegade member of the Shu clan, the warlord Kung Shan Piu Niu successfully drove away the Ji demolition squad, together with the inspection team comprised of the Duke of Lu, Lord Meng and Lord Shu, and Confucius himself, who had all come to watch the walls come down. Furious, Duke Ding ordered an all-out attack on the rebel city:

> The citizens of Bei were conquered, and the state troops pursued them and annihilated them near Ku Mieh. The two insurgents fled to Qi, and the walls of Pi were razed.
>
> Sima Qian, *Records of the Grand Historian*

Bodies and dismembered limbs now littered the open spaces in front of the city and were already being eaten by dogs, while smoke poured from many houses behind the rubble of the dismantled walls. Confucius could see that his peace initiative was crumbling and had simply resulted in the very thing it was intended to prevent—unnecessary bloodshed. The plan still could have worked if all three of the feudal families had continued to cooperate, but the fragile accord broke to pieces when the Meng clan suddenly refused to demolish the fortifications around their main city in the extreme north of the state, near the border of the state of Qi.

When they were about to raze the walls of Cheng,

Kung-Lien Chu-fu said to the Meng family: "If the walls of Cheng are razed, the people of Qi will surely soon arrive at the North Gate. And Cheng is the fortress of the Meng family. Without Cheng, there will be no Meng family. I will not let the walls be razed."

> Sima Qian, *Records of the Grand Historian*

Lord Meng agreed with the governor of his city, despite being himself a former student of Confucius, and the war standards of Meng were raised on the battlements. By the end the year 498, the state of Lu was embroiled in all-out civil war, with the Duke and the Ji family laying siege unsuccessfully to the Meng stronghold.

> In the twelfth month, the duke beleaguered the city of Cheng, but could not take it.
>
> Sima Qian, *Records of the Grand Historian*

That winter many of the petty warlords took advantage of the chaotic situation and rebuilt the walls around their own small cities. From behind the snow-covered Great Wall of Qi Duke Jing also wondered whether this might not be a good time to launch an invasion, and mobilized troops all along the wall, waiting for spring and the campaign season. The disarmament initiative had ended in a fiasco.

Confucius was naturally blamed for the whole mess and now became the most unpopular person in the whole state. The three families decided that his motives had never been altruistic and he had all along been trying to strip them of their power in preparation for taking power himself as Yang Huo had done eight years before. Others even suggested that Confucius had been in the pay of his friend Duke Jing of Qi for years, and the demolition of the city walls had been part of a long-term plan which was to culminate in an invasion from the north, with Confucius scheduled to become the "governor" of Lu which by then would have been swallowed up by its larger neighbor.

Yan Hui – Confucius' all-time star student. Statue in Confucius Temple, Nanjing.
Photo: Jonathan Price

For the first time Confucius' life was in real danger. He still retained the nominal support of Duke Ding, but the Duke, although not firing him from any of his official positions as yet, no longer sought his advice about anything and once again Lord Ji became the number two man in the state. Confucius spent most of his time with his students, but even in the school house the atmosphere had changed. The door, once open to all, now had to be guarded in the daytime and locked securely at night, and some of the students even got into street brawls defending the honor of their master.

Even Zilu, who had advocated the disarmament plan to his employer, Lord Ji, was being accused of being part of Confucius' cunning plot to destabilize the state and take power himself. One of the students offered to break a few heads on Zilu's behalf, but his teacher called for calm:

> Gongbo Liao had said bad things about Zilu to Lord Ji. Jingbo told Confucius about it, saying: "Lord Ji is certainly being deceived by Gongbo Liao. But I have enough power to drag his carcass out into the middle of the marketplace."
>
> Confucius said, "It is up to fate as to when the Way is going to function, and when it isn't. What can Gongbo Liao do about fate?"
>
> *Analects*, 14:36

My students, Confucius begged, let us all be wise about this and not let our tempers get the better of us. If the world is not yet ready for the Way then so be it—one day it will be ready.

> Confucius said, "Those who do not let slander get under their skin and who are not wounded by unfair accusations can be called 'enlightened.'

> Indeed, such people may be called 'far-seeing.'"
>
> *Analects*, 12:6

Many of the students ignored their Master's advice and went around getting into arguments with anybody would listen:

> Zigong, having heard that Wushu of the Shu clan had disparaged Confucius, said: "It is ridiculous talking this way. Confucius cannot be slandered. The virtue of other men is like a small hill, which can be climbed over. Confucius is like the sun and the moon. There is no way they can be climbed over. Even if you want to cut yourself off from the sun and moon, how can you hurt them?"
>
> *Analects*, 19:24

A boy of only sixteen who had recently joined Confucius' classes was alone among the students in sharing the Master's calm forbearance, and simply got on with his studies as if nothing had happened, always with a smile on his face. He was the poorest of them all, and Confucius had accepted the barest minimum contribution from his father, who himself had been one of his original students more than twenty years before. The boy's name was Yan Hui—possibly a relation of Confucius through his mother's family—and it was this young man whom Confucius was later to call the true son of his heart, and the only student who truly understood what he was trying to say.

Although the exact chronology of Confucius' life and that of his students is notoriously uncertain, the majority of records say that Yan Hui died age 30 in the year 483 and joined Confucius' classes at the age of sixteen: he would therefore have become one of the students early in the year 497, just after the disarmament fiasco. Certainly at this moment Yan Hui seemed to know instinctively that there was no point in ranting like the others about the injustices of the world, and it did not matter that nobody else understood them. The time for action had passed but there would be another opportunity; for the moment they would be wise to keep a low profile:

> Confucius said to Yan Hui: "When called to office, that is the time to act. When not called, retire and wait—only you and I can do this."
>
> *Analects*, 7:11

Yan Hui. Ming Dynasty painting. *Qilu Press*

Even as a teenager Yan Hui showed a precocious aptitude for scholarship, like Confucius himself at the same age, and was tireless in his studies. Confucius realized immediately that he had at last found a student truly after his own heart. In this quiet young man he saw a potential successor who would lead society into a new golden age, even if he himself never had another opportunity to do so. Had this happened perhaps the subsequent history of Confucianism would have been totally different, since most of his ideas were distorted beyond recognition by his successors. Tragically Yan Hui was to die four years before his Master, but neither of them could have foreseen this.

As a very young man Yan Hui worshipped his teacher, almost excessively so as Confucius often complained that he never disagreed with him about anything:

> **Confucius said: "I can talk with Hui for a whole day without him differing with me in any way— as if he is stupid. But if I observe him after class it is quite clear that he is applying my teaching in the most creative way. He is not stupid at all."**
>
> *Analects*, 2:9

This was simply a case of a great teacher meeting an ideal student, and Yan Hui paid this tribute to his Master:

> **Yan Hui sighed in admiration saying: "My master is impeccable in his skillful guidance. He has broadened me with literature, disciplined me with good behavior. I want to give up, but I can't. I**

> **think I have exhausted my ability, yet it seems as if there is something rising up in front of me, so I want to follow it …"**
>
> *Analects*, 9:11

Yan Hui followed Confucius until his death.

Devoting much more time to his students now, Confucius was still officially minister of justice but found that there were no more cases for him to try—clearly he had been sidelined. More ominously, many people wanted to get rid of him once and for all before he caused any more trouble. Confucius escaped assassination, but only just, and a short time after the disarmament debacle, in the summer of the year 497, he fled from his home state and did not return for thirteen years. Exactly why he was forced to do this is still shrouded in mystery.

Sima Qian's "official" version of his departure—that Confucius left on moral grounds—utterly beggars belief, but for what it is worth here is the tale of "Confucius and the Dancing Girls of Qi" as set down in the *Records of the Grand Historian*.

According to Sima, Duke Jing of Qi wanted to destabilize the Lu government preparatory to an invasion, and hit upon the idea of sending a bevy of nubile dancing girls to tempt the Duke of Lu and his court. While the Duke and his ministers were wallowing in an orgy of sensuality with the girls, he would strike swiftly from the north and the state of Lu would be history:

> Thereupon the people of Qi chose eighty of their most beautiful maidens, dressed them in magnificent garments, and had them practice the dances to the music of Kang; besides this, they chose thirty sets of four magnificent horses, and sent them as a gift to the Duke of Lu.
>
> Sima Qian, *Records of the Grand Historian*

The sexy sirens and the prancing steeds (in Sima's account) suddenly appeared outside the city walls of the capital of Lu. Sima Qian does not explain how they managed to cross the border, and makes a factual gaffe, saying that they were cavorting outside the south gate, whereas if they were coming from Qi they would have appeared from the north:

> The female dancers and the splendid steeds were exhibited in front of the South High Gate of the capital of Lu. Lord Huan of Ji went there two or three times incognito to see them … then the Duke went to behold them, and remained the whole day. He neglected the government.
>
> In the end, Lord Huan of Ji actually accepted

the dancing girls who had been sent as a present, and for three days all the business of government ceased. Thereupon, Confucius departed.

Sima Qian, *Records of the Grand Historian*

What can one say? Horses outside the walls, the leaders of the city falling for the ruse, haven't I read this somewhere before? The story is so eerily reminiscent of the tale of the wooden horse of Troy that one wonders whether this folk tale of Ancient Greece had somehow made its way to China and was then incorporated into the legend of Confucius. This is not entirely impossible: the Trojan War occurred 800 years before Confucius while Homer's account predates him by 400 years, and certainly this was enough time for such a story to filter slowly eastwards from campfire to campfire across the steppes of Asia.

The eighty nubile dancing girls are certainly a spicy addition, but familiar as it sounds, the story has no real motivation nor even a proper ending. "Confucius departed" is a real anti-climax, when one is expecting at least a surprise attack from Qi while the rulers of Lu were busy in their three-day orgy or (even better) the "maidens" revealing themselves as men in disguise and taking the city *à la* the Trojan Horse.

A far more likely scenario is that Duke Ding had finally come under too much pressure from the nobles and had decided that Confucius had to go. Like King Henry II of England many years later when he wanted to be rid of his former Chancellor, Thomas à Becket, Duke Ding may also have turned to his courtiers and said "Who will rid me of this meddlesome scholar?"

So I would suggest that we forget the dancing girls. What probably happened is that somebody—perhaps his friend Nangong Jingshu who was the number two in the Meng clan but still Confucius' loyal ally—turned up at the schoolhouse one day and said: "They're going to kill you—you have to get out—now …"

Echoes of Troy: The 'gift horses' and the voluptuous girl musicians – supposedly presented to the State of Lu by Duke Jing of Qi. Ming Dynasty Painting. *Qilu Press*

Adventures in Exile

According to Mencius Confucius went into exile on Midsummer Day 496. This detail is repeated in Sima Qian's *Records of the Grand Historian* and seems to be authentic. If we leave aside the dancing girls and assume that Confucius had been warned that he was in danger, it is possible that he still could not believe this, even though his students begged him to flee.

Ignoring his followers, Confucius dressed himself in his ceremonial robes of office and prepared to attend the midsummer festival, which was held in the main square of the capital. Bulls were sacrificed and the square echoed to the sound of drumming. After the meat had been cooked, portions of the cooked flesh were distributed to the high officers. This was for them to offer to the gods on their own altars at home—roast beef was for some reason considered inedible by humans in ancient China.

Confucius, however, received nothing and thus was pointedly ignored and publicly shamed—as far as the Duke was concerned he no longer existed. Confucius warily darted his eyes around the crowded square—the Duke was not there, neither was his prime minister Lord Ji: they should have been but they were not. It was all too convenient, and if something happened they could deny all knowledge of it, the assassin could be arrested and immediately beheaded, the great Master could be publicly mourned and nobody would be any the wiser …

"Master!" Zilu repeated. "We must go …"

Realizing at last that his students were right and he really was in danger, Confucius allowed himself to hustled away by Zilu and Zigong, who had already

Confucius and his followers leaving Chungdu, the capital of Lu, as they begin their long exile. Ming Dynasty painting. *Qilu Press*

Pottery model of an ox-drawn traveling wagon from the Han Dynasty. The vehicle is identical to the 'exile-wagon' of Confucius, as depicted in countless paintings. Capital Museum, Beijing. *Photo: Jonathan Price*

made ready their Master's old travelling wagon. According to Mencius he left in such a hurry he was still wearing his minister's robes:

After the summer solstice sacrifice, when a part of the flesh presented in sacrifice was not sent to him, he went away even without taking off his cap of ceremony.

Book of Mencius, Book 6, Part 2, Chapter 6:6

Once again Confucius' old ox-wagon trundled northward along the road out of Lu, carrying him into exile, but this time several of his students accompanied him. These included the ever-faithful Zilu, who took it upon himself to organize everything, Zigong the merchant's son who remained the fiercest champion of his master, and the still very young Yan Hui. In all the descriptions of Confucius' long exile, not only in the *Records of the Grand Historian* but also in the "anti-biography" by the Daoist writer Zhuangzi and in many of the *Analects*, these three appear to have been with him the whole time. Zilu must have quit his job with the Ji family in order to accompany his master, Yan Hui, who never owned more than the ragged clothes on his back, had nothing to lose anyway, while Zigong used his considerable skills as a merchant to buy and sell things as they travelled in order to keep them alive.

Zigong said: "We have a beautiful gem here.

Should we hide it away, or look for a good price and sell it?" Confucius said, "Sell it! Sell it! But I would wait till I got a good price."

Analects, 9:13

Together they endured many hardships and lived through many adventures. Young Yan Hui remained cheerful even when they went hungry or faced extreme danger, and inspired the others with his fortitude:

Confucius said: "Hui was indeed a worthy! Hui never changed from his happy disposition. Hui was a worthy indeed!"

Analects, 6:11

Zilu was not so cheerful and often moaned about the privations they had to endure, but none the less he stuck it out for thirteen years—if not without complaining then at least without complaining too much:

The next day, Confucius and his disciples continued their travels. By the time they got to Chen, they had run out of provisions, and Zilu was obviously angry about it.

He said, "Must the Superior Man suffer such dire straits?"

Confucius said, "The Superior Person remains stable when in dire straits. The inferior person falls apart."

Analects, 15:2

On the way to the border they had to skirt the foothills of Mount Tai, which were thickly forested, and here they encountered a woman who was laying flowers on a grave at the foot of the mountain. She was an exile from another state, and told Confucius and his followers that her father-in-law, her husband, and now her son, had all been eaten by a tiger. Zilu asked her in amazement why she did not get away from this dangerous place and return home? The woman replied that the ruler of her home state was a cruel despot who fleeced his subjects with heavy taxes and executed people on the merest whim. She would rather take her chances with the tiger.

"You see!" Confucius exclaimed. "This is truly a wise woman. An oppressive government is more to be feared than the fiercest tiger!"

> Incident from life of Confucius related in Han Dynasty biographies

The danger from wild animals was something which Confucius and his little band of wandering scholars would now have to face on a daily basis as they journeyed in search of a ruler who would give them asylum. However, even though tigers (and a particularly aggressive species of rhinoceros) were quite common in this part of China at that time, most people would pass their whole lives without ever seeing one in the wild and, as Confucius had pointed out, humans were a far greater threat. Just after leaving the poor woman whose family had been eaten by the tiger, Confucius is supposed to have encountered the ferocious bandit warlord Tao Ki in the same area, as Zhuangzi relates with his usual flair for vivid detail and realistic dialogue:

> With Yan Hui as his charioteer, and Zigong seated on the right, he saw Tao Ki, whom he found with his followers halted on the south of Mount Tai, mincing men's livers which he gave them to eat.
>
> Tao Ki flew into a great rage; his eyes became like blazing stars, and his hair rose up and touched his cap. "Is not this fellow," said he, "Kong Qiu, that artful hypocrite of Lu?"
>
> *Zhuangzi*, Book 29, Part 3:7

Having become particularly unpopular with the warlords after the disarmament debacle, Confucius decided that an exaggerated show of respect was called for if they were all to escape with their lives:

> Confucius alighted from his carriage, and said, "I, Kong Qiu of Lu, have heard of the general's lofty

Tigers of Lu: A Chinese Tiger cub and his watchful parent in their original natural habitat – the mountains on the northern border of ancient Lu – now home to Jinan Wild Animal World. *Photo: Jonathan Price*

Realm of tigers: These forests on the foothills of Mount Tai were in Confucius' day the habitat of ferocious man-eating tigers. It was here that he and his followers encountered the woman whose whole family had been eaten by the beasts. *Photo: Jonathan Price*

Confucius in his traveling wagon, accompanied by his loyal followers. Ming Dynasty painting. *Qilu Press*

righteousness," bowing twice respectfully to the man as he said so.

"You wag your lips and make your tongue a drum-stick, leading astray the princes throughout the kingdom, take yourself off at once! If you do not do so, I will take your liver, and add it to the provision for to-day's food."

Zhuangzi, Book 29, Part 3:7

Zigong pulled his Master away and helped him back onto the wagon while Yan Hui whipped the oxen frantically and the travelling scholars made a hasty escape to avoid ending up in the warlord's cooking pot.

When they reached the Great Wall of Qi they found that Confucius was no longer welcome in that state, and were refused entry. Duke Jing, Confucius' old friend and former student had heard all about his failed disarmament plan in Lu and wanted no more to do with him—he was sure that the next thing his old tutor would suggest would be the dismantling of his own Great Wall, the result of 200 years' labor and still only half finished. No thank you, Master.

The Duke Jing of Qi said, "I am old; I cannot use his doctrines any more."

Analects, 18:3

Zilu suggested they try the state of Wei just to the west. Many other *shi* travelled from state to state seeking employment, and Zilu was sure that Confucius stood a good chance of a job with Duke Ling of Wei. Not only this, he had family connections there himself: his brother-in-law was a minor government official in Wei so at least they would have somewhere to stay. So they headed for the Yellow River, crossing by ferry, and told the border guards they were "visiting relatives."

Thereupon, Confucius betook himself to the state of Wei, and dwelt in the house of the brother of the wife of his disciple, Zilu, whose name was Yan Chou Zou.

Sima Qian, *Records of the Grand Historian*

Bandit country: the ferocious warlord Tao Ki, famed for his unbridled savagery (and possible cannibalism) made his camp in these wooded foothills on the slopes of Mount Tai – now part of the Taishan National Park. *Photo: Jonathan Price*

Refused entry: When Confucius and his followers reached the Great Wall of Qi – shown here in a very well-preserved section near Chanqing, Shandong, they were turned away from the gate. *Photo: Jonathan Price*

Confucius managed to get an interview with the Duke of Wei through Zilu's brother-in-law—in China connections then as now were always paramount.

> When he was in Wei, he lived with Yan Chou Zou. The wives of the officer Zou and Zilu were sisters, and Zou told Zilu, "If Confucius will lodge with me, he may attain to the dignity of a high noble of Wei." Zilu informed Confucius of this, and he said, "That is as ordered by Heaven."
>
> *Book of Mencius*, Book 5, Part 1, Chapter 8

When he finally got an audience, however, Duke Ling told Confucius he was really looking for a military expert, and was very disappointed when the Master told him he knew no more about commanding an army than the next man. The Duke had expected Confucius as an acknowledged "sage" to include the "art of war" in his repertoire; the most successful freelance "wandering scholars" of this period were in fact specialists in military strategy. The tenor of the times had changed. The era of the "Warring States" was dawning and Confucius was more than ever out of kilter with his own age: peace had gone out of fashion. Duke Ling thought for a moment, but finally agreed to employ him. Confucius was after all quite famous now, and it would be one in the eye for the other dukes if he added the sage to his court.

> Duke Ling of Wei questioned Confucius as to what salary he had received in Lu? Confucius replied: "I received 60,000 bushels of grain." Thereupon, in Wei, likewise, he was given 60,000 bushels of grain.
>
> Sima Qian, *Records of the Grand Historian*

The students celebrated—they had somewhere to live, Confucius had a generous (if not to say huge) salary which would support all of them, and it looked as if the Duke of Wei was prepared to be sympathetic to their Master's ideals. Confucius was not optimistic about this, however, and he eventually came to regard Duke Ling as an evil ruler. He was reputed to have taken power by murdering his brother, although nothing had ever been proven. With a mansion full of concubines, he preferred the pleasures of his bed to the responsibilities of ruling, and left the government of his state in the hands of three corrupt and self-serving henchmen:

> **Confucius was speaking about the evils of Duke Ling of Wei.**
>
> **Ji Kangzi said, "If he is such a person, how can he stay in power?"**
>
> **Confucius said, "Zhongshu Yu takes care of his guests; Zhu Tuo handles the temples and Wangsun Jia is his military commander. With ministers like these, how could he fall from power?"**
>
> *Analects*, 14:19

Although he was occasionally called for meaningful talks, as in the case of the other leaders Confucius had advised, the evil Duke Ling did not actually put any of this advice into effect. Instead Confucius concentrated on supervising court ceremonies, which was what he was being paid for, and of course his teaching. It was during this period that Yan Hui emerged as the star student, which Confucius' older followers did not resent as the young man was so modest and unassuming and in fact they were all full of praise for him:

> **Confucius, speaking to Zigong said, "Who is superior, you or Hui?"**
>
> **Zigong answered, saying: "How could I compare myself to Hui? He hears one point and understands the whole thing. I hear one point and**

understand another."

Confucius said, "You are not equal to him; you
are right, you are not equal to him."

Analects, 5:9

**Confucius said: "I teach him and he never slacks
off. Aah, Hui!"**

Analects, 9:20

Hui also seemed to "get" Confucius' main idea in a
way that none of the others ever quite mastered: that
there is only one basic principle—humanity—which is
needed in all our dealings with others.

**Confucius said: "Hui could keep his mind on
humaneness for three months without lapse.
Others are lucky if they can do it for one day out
of a month."**

Analects, 6:7

**Yan Hui asked about the meaning of humaneness.
The Master said, "To overcome selfishness
completely and keep to correct behavior is
humaneness. If for a full day you can overcome
selfishness and keep to correct behavior, everyone
in the world will return to humaneness."**

**Yan Hui asked: "May I ask in further detail how
this is to be brought about?"**

**Confucius said, "Do not watch what is
improper; do not listen to what is improper; do not
speak improperly and do not act improperly."**

**Yan Hui said, "Although I am a dull fellow, I
will try to live by these words."**

Analects, 12:1

Ladies' man: Duke Ling of Wei taking a drive with his
concubine-du-jour. Ming Dynasty painting. *Qilu Press.*

Many have found this passage from the *Analects*
difficult to understand, as Confucius seems to appear
hopelessly naïve if he really believed that if one person
achieves "humaneness" then the whole world will
magically follow. However, on many occasions he
stressed that perfection is impossible and all we can do
is strive for it, so all he meant was that the more we strive
for humanity the more the world around us will change,
something which is in fact self-evidently true although
few people act on this principle—Yan Hui was one of
those who tried to live his life in this truly Confucian
way. Confucius himself was unstinting in his praise for
his young disciple, who gave so much inspiration to the
others by being an embodiment in his own person of his
Master's principles:

**Confucius said: "… Yan Hui … did not transfer
his anger to the wrong person, and he did not
repeat his mistakes. Unfortunately he died
young."**

Analects, 6:3

**The Master, speaking of Hui, said: "How rare is
his type! I have seen him striving, and have never
seen him rest."**

Analects, 9:21

Other students lacked Hui's instinctive understanding
of "humanity," and had to have everything explained to
them, even though Confucius always told them that if

you have to talk about it, you are not doing it:

Sima Niu asked about the meaning of humaneness.

Confucius said, "The humane person is hesitant to speak."

Niu replied, "Are you saying that humaneness is mere hesitancy in speaking?"

Confucius said, "Actualizing it is so difficult, how can you not be hesitant to speak about it? The Superior Person desires to be hesitant in speech, but sharp in action."

Analects, 12:3 / *Analects*, 4:24

"Don't talk about it. Just do it." He said this again and again and often chided those students who talked about how humane they were instead of proving it by their actions:

Zigong said: "What I don't want done to me, I don't want to do to others."

Confucius said, "Si [Zigong], you have not yet got to this level."

Analects, 5:12

Instead, Confucius always pointed to the example of Hui who never boasted but was simply quietly and unassumingly good.

Yan Hui said, "I would like not to be proud of my good points and not to show off my good works."

Analects, 5:26

Zigong by contrast was always boasting about his good works and was such a powerhouse of energy that as well as trying to act on his Master's principles in his own life he also took it upon himself to correct other

Duke Ling of Wei enjoying the fruits of office. Tableau in the City of Six Arts, Qufu. *Photo: Jonathan Price*

people's behavior:

Zigong was always criticizing other people. Confucius said, "Are you perfect yourself? I myself have no time to do this."

Analects, 14:29

Zigong devoted the rest of his energy to making money and, unlike Yan Hui, who did not mind being

Confucius and his loyal followers on their travels: Zilu (left), Confucius, Zigong (centre) and Yan Hui (right). Ming Dynasty painting. *Qilu Press*

Master and disciples. Zigong (left), Confucius (centre) and Yan Hui (right). Tableau in the City of Six Arts, Qufu. *Photo: Jonathan Price*

poor, Zigong started doing deals as soon as the wandering scholars arrived in any new state, and was always buying and selling something.

> Confucius said: "Hui is completely full, yet always possession-less. Si is not wealthy by fate, so he has to contrive in order to enrich himself, and is usually very successful at it."
>
> *Analects*, 11:19

Unfortunately it was only a few months after their arrival in Wei that the usual pattern repeated itself: other courtiers and scholars started to resent Confucius' growing influence with the Duke, not to mention his high salary, and tongues began to wag:

After some time, a certain man traduced

Confucius to Duke Ling of Wei. Thereupon, Duke Ling commanded Kung-Sun Yu-chia to accompany Confucius wherever he went. Confucius feared that he had fallen into disfavor, so he left Wei after having been there ten months.

Sima Qian, *Records of the Grand Historian*

It is hard to understand why Confucius hastily quit a job worth 60,000 bushels of grain per annum unless he seriously believed that once again his life was being threatened, and this was probably what had happened. They had all heard that Confucius had been declared an outlaw in Lu which meant that anybody could kill him without fear of reprisal, and there was probably a bounty on his head all over the Warring States. As long as he remained in favor in any one state its ruler would protect him, but the fact that Duke Ling had started to have Confucius followed by a minder looked too ominous to be ignored. Injustice lived, and the only practical course was to keep on the move, so the travelling scholar-wagon trundled once more out of the city's gates, accompanied by the three faithful students who took turns to ride on the cart. Confucius himself remained philosophical, Zilu grumbled a lot as usual, while Zigong—the group's self-appointed business manager— swiftly calculated what they had left to sell. Yan Hui shared his Master's indifference to privations:

> Confucius said: "I can live with coarse rice to eat, water for drink and my arm as a pillow and still be happy. Wealth and honors that one possesses in the midst of injustice are like floating clouds."
>
> *Analects*, 7:16

Travelling again: Confucius and his followers at the Yellow River ferry. Ming Dynasty painting. *Qilu Press*

Dire peril: Confucius and his followers captured by the ferocious inhabitants of the Kuang district. Ming Dynasty painting. *Qilu Press*

They decided to journey to the very small state of Chen, and on the way had to pass through a district called Kuang. This area, although nominally part of the state of Wei, was in fact, like many other places at the time, under the control of a local warlord. As the cart jolted along the muddy road they were passed several times by roughly dressed men who looked suspiciously like bandits, and during one of these encounters Yan Hui became separated from the main party. Confucius was very worried but the others told him they should push on to the safety of the nearest town—Yan Hui could look after himself and would catch up with them.

The Master tried to encourage his faithful followers:

Confucius said: "The Superior Man… risks his life in the face of danger, and in times of hardship keeps to his promise."

Analects, 14:12

Several more times armed men in approached the scholar-wagon, looking keenly at Confucius and muttering amongst themselves. Confucius nodded and smiled serenely at them. It was always his theory that since he and his students meant no harm to anybody no harm would come to them, especially as they were carrying nothing worth taking.

There was fear for the Master's life when he was in the district of Kuang.

He said, "I carry the ancient culture within me. If Heaven does not want to destroy this culture, what can the men of Kuang do to me?"

Analects, 9:5

When they had almost reached the main town of Kuang a detachment of soldiers surrounded Confucius' wagon and ordered him to climb down. "You are under arrest!" the leading officer shouted.

"On what charge?" Zilu protested.

"Banditry, murder, and sedition!"

"Murder?" Zilu started shouting at the soldiers. Did they not know? They had just arrested the famous scholar and advisor of princes, Kong Fu Zi, and they were his disciples. What were they talking about? Their

WANTED for banditry and sedition: Yang Huo of Lu. The men of Kuang arrested Confucius in the mistaken belief he was Yang Huo – the two men were supposed to closely resemble each other. Detail from Ming Dynasty painting. *Qilu Press*

Confucius despairingly banging the musical stone in the State of Wei.
Ming Dynasty painting. *Qilu Press*

Master had never harmed a fly! The soldier told him to be quiet, adding that they knew very well their so-called "Master" was none other than the infamous Yang Huo, who was wanted for murder in five states!

> The citizens of Kuang thought it was Yang Huo of Lu. Now Yan Huo had cruelly dealt with the citizens of Kuang. Therefore the citizens of Kuang detained Confucius. Confucius resembled Yang Huo in form; therefore they took him prisoner.
>
> Sima Qian, *Records of the Grand Historian*

Confucius was bundled off to the town lockup, and the Kuang authorities remained convinced that he was Yang Huo—his double and former dictator of Lu. Huo it will be remembered had fled to the state of Qi dressed as a woman when he was finally ousted from power. He had eventually been thrown out of the state of Qi as well and now led the life of a free-booting warlord with a small gang of followers, moving from state to state pillaging and stealing and hacking off the heads of anybody who resisted. A witness who had seen Yang Huo raiding a farm was produced, and swore blind that Confucius was the same man.

> The people of Kuang kept Confucius in ever stricter confinement. His disciples were terrified. But Confucius said: "What can the people of Kuang do to me?"

Sima Qian, *Records of the Grand Historian*
He told Zigong to hire a chariot and ride back to Wei, in order to bring some officials who would identify him. Zigong pawned a jewel in exchange for horses, and rode off. The next day Yan Hui finally turned up.

> Confucius said, "I was afraid they had killed you."
>
> Hui said, "While you are alive, how can I dare to die?"
>
> *Analects*, 11:23

Zigong eventually returned with a business acquaintance from Wei, Kung-Liang Ju, who came accompanied by his own detachment of very professional-looking mercenary soldiers. Kung was able to identify Confucius and demanded his immediate release. The mix-up was finally sorted out and they all returned to the Wei capital, Di Qiu, lodging in a different house since Confucius had lost his official job after leaving and they did not want to embarrass Zigong's brother-in-law. This time they took rooms in the house of a man described by Mencius as an "ulcer doctor." Mencius, who unlike his idol seems to have been something of a snob, in fact denies the story that Confucius "lodged with unsavoury characters" in Wei as a "malicious rumor":

> Wan Chang asked Mencius, saying, "Some say that Confucius, when he was in Wei, lived with an ulcer-doctor, was it so?"
>
> Mencius replied, "No; it was not so. Those are the inventions of men fond of strange things."
>
> *Mencius*, Book 5, Part 1, Chapter 8

At this time doctors were considered to be members of the lower class, and it was therefore inconceivable to

Confucius' neighbour complains to Zigong about his Master's annoying performance on the musical stone. Detail from Ming Dynasty painting. *Qilu Press*

Performance on replicas of the ancient musical stones at Henan Museum. *Photo: Jonathan Price.*

Mencius that his revered Master would have mixed with such unworthy people. Confucius himself was unaffected by such niceties as after all most of his students, including Zilu and Yan Hui, came from the so-called lower orders. Rooms in the doctor's house would have been all Confucius could have afforded at this time.

Continuing his teaching as the only means of support (aided by Zigong's wheeling and dealing) Confucius grew a little mournful, as no more official job offers seemed to be coming his way. One day he was playing a musical stone outside his lodging house, an instrument meant to accompany a flute or zither, but Confucius was simply banging the stone monotonously like a funeral dirge, and succeeded in annoying his neighbor (this story is related both in the *Analects* (14:39) and the *Records of the Grand Historian*).

"Your heart must be full of sadness" said the neighbor, who was wearing a straw hat and carrying two baskets of grain to his house on a yoke across his back. Confucius did not reply and continued his mournful banging. Dong! Dong! Dong!

"What obstinacy!" the man exploded. "Bong—bong—bong—have you only got one idea in your head? If

nobody is noticing you then give up your wish for public employment! Do you not know the proverb? If you can't swim find an easier place to cross the river where you may go across by simply holding up your robe!"

"He's right," Confucius said, and cheered himself up.

It was during this short stay in Wei, after his escape from captivity in Kuang, that Confucius paid his notorious visit to Duke Ling's concubine Nanzi, which incurred so much displeasure from Zilu. Nanzi had a lot of influence and Confucius may have been hoping that she could somehow engineer another job for him, and an incident which occurred shortly after this indicates that in fact, despite Zilu's horror, nothing untoward occurred.

Duke Ling was showing no inclination to give Confucius his job back, but nevertheless he received him socially and one day invited the Sage for a drive in the countryside. Confucius was sure that he would be sitting next to the Duke in his carriage, and this would publicly mark his return to favor. Instead, to his extreme annoyance, Confucius was seated in a carriage following the Duke, while Duke Ling himself occupied the leading carriage with his concubine-de-jour, indulging himself in an orgy of playful kissing while his erstwhile ritual advisor had nothing to do but look at the scenery. This provoked one of Confucius' more bitter remarks when he returned to his students:

Confucius said: "I have never met a ruler who loves virtue as much as he loves beauty."

Analects, 9:18

It seems that he was rather prickly about his position and reacted badly to any sort of slight—this may have been one of the reasons why he made himself so consistently unpopular in all the states. Very soon after this demeaning carriage drive he and his students once again quitted the state of Wei:

Since he found this humiliating, he left Wei.

Sima Qian, *Records of the Grand Historian*

Neither Confucius nor his followers had any sort of job; they had not succeeded in attracting any students in Wei; the ulcer-doctor was threatening to increase the rent—this time none of them really had anything much to lose. Yan Hui flicked his whip across the ox's back and they moved off, heading for the ferry across the Yellow River which would take them into the territory of Song.

A fresh start in another state, that is what they needed,

they all decided, and for the few days it took them to reach the river everybody remained cheerful—even Zilu—and they sang a repertoire of traditional songs as the old wagon jolted down the rutted road. Surely, in the state of Song, their fortunes would at last begin to change for the better?

They were wrong. They got much worse.

Sex versus philosophy – no contest: Confucius humiliatingly forced to ride behind the Duke of Wei as the potentate entertains his latest concubine. Ming Dynasty painting. *Qilu Press*

The Years of Wandering

After crossing the river by the ferry, they moved south into the state of Song, the original homeland of Confucius' father. Once clear of the river plain and onto the higher ground in the district of Shang they halted to eat. Before the meal Confucius celebrated the rites under a tree with his students, offering a sacrifice to the gods in thanks for their safe arrival. Suddenly they were surrounded by helmeted soldiers of the Song government armed with bows, swords, and pikes. Their commander, Marshal Huan Tui, ordered Confucius to stop his ceremony. Confucius refused, so the Marshal ordered his men to cut down the tree over their heads. Then the soldiers surrounded Confucius and his followers, bows at the ready, waiting for the order to fire. Confucius, still defiant, proceeded to give a lesson based on the *Book of Songs*.

Marshal Huan sent one of his chariots back to the

Confucius and his followers at the Yellow River. Ming Dynasty painting. *Qilu Press*

Song capital, Shang Qiu, to report that he had captured the notorious outlaw "Kong Qiu", and asked his messenger to bring back an authorization for Confucius' execution bearing the seal of the Duke of Song. Luckily for Confucius as it turned out, the Marshal was reluctant to kill him without official authority.

The standoff continued for several days, and neither Confucius nor the students were able to get any food. Fortunately Zigong had slipped away unnoticed in the confusion when the tree came down, and had taken the ferry back over the Yellow River to Wei. Here he once again persuaded his friend Kung-Liang Ju to muster his small detachment of troops for another rescue

Public enemy number one: soldiers of the State of Song pull down a tree over Confucius' head as he attempts to perform a thanksgiving ritual. Ming Dynasty painting. *Qilu Press*

Humiliated by the military: the Song soldiers manage to get the tree down. Ming Dynasty painting. *Qilu Press*

attempt. By the time they arrived, Confucius and the students were almost too weak from starvation to stand up, but the Song soldiers backed off.

> Kung-Liang Ju joined Confucius with five of his own chariots. He was of ripe age, competent, and full of courageous strength. He said: "When I formerly joined the Master, we met with difficulties in Kuang. Today we again meet with difficulties here. That is fate. I will fight and die rather than again see the Master caught in difficulties."
>
> Sima Qian, *Records of the Grand Historian*

Kung-Liang escorted Confucius and the disciples back to Wei with his own troops as a bodyguard.

It seems that this latest attempt on Confucius' life originated in his home state of Lu, where in the same year (494 BC) Duke Ding had died, to be replaced by Duke Ai, known in the *Spring and Autumn Annals* as "Duke Ai the Lamentable." The new duke was under pressure from the feudal families who still wanted Confucius eliminated—they were afraid that with the change of ruler he might take the opportunity to come back home and start mouthing off about disarmament again. Duke Ai knuckled under. With the collaboration of the rulers of the other states he had Confucius declared a wanted man and an outlaw all over the

former Zhou Empire (like his double Yang Huo) in the hope that somebody somewhere would do the honors and get rid of him. This time at least, the assassination attempt had failed.

After recuperating for a short time at a lodging house in Wei, Confucius went to the small state of Chen, where he kept a low profile for a while, but it was becoming increasingly dangerous for him to stay in any one place for very long. For the next few years he travelled from one state to the next, doing a bit of teaching here, a bit of advising there, until either a local war or a direct threat to his own safety forced him to move on again.

> Confucius said, "I was twice driven from Lu; the tree was felled over me in Song; I was obliged to leave Wei; I was reduced to extreme distress in Shang and Kuang; my intimate associates are removed from me more and more; my followers and friends are more and more dispersed—why have all these things befallen me?"
>
> *Book of Zhuangzi*

Although he often wondered why he was treated as pariah by everybody except his loyal followers, Confucius usually managed to keep a cheerful face on things despite the hardships. Although he often had to endure hunger, imprisonment, ridicule, and attack, the period he spent wandering the countryside with his beloved student family was in a paradoxical way one of the happiest times of his life.

> When Confucius was reduced to extreme distress between Khan and Tsai, for seven days he had no cooked meat to eat, but only some soup of coarse vegetables without any rice in it. His countenance wore the appearance of great exhaustion, and yet he kept playing on his zither and singing. Yan Hui was selecting the vegetables, while Zilu and Zigong were talking together.
>
> Zilu said to Hui, "The Master is reduced to extreme distress—anyone who kills him will be held guiltless; there is no prohibition against making him a prisoner! And yet he keeps playing and singing, thrumming his lute without ceasing? How can he bear it to this extent?"
>
> Confucius heard this and asked him: "Where is the proof of my being in extreme distress? I hold to the principles of benevolence and righteousness, and with them meet the evils of a disordered age. I do not lose my virtue."
>
> He then took back his zither so that it emitted a twanging sound, and began to play and sing. At the same time Zilu hurriedly seized a shield, and

Marshal Huan Tui of Song orders Confucius and his followers to stop their ritual under the tree. Tableau in the City of the Six Arts, Qufu. *Photo: Jonathan Price*

began to dance, while Zigong said, "I did not know before the height of heaven, nor the depth of the earth!"

Zhuangzi, Book 28, Part 3:6

They have passed into legend—Master Confucius, fighter Zilu, business-wise Zigong, and gentle Yan Hui—the wandering scholars of ancient China who danced and sang under the trees and travelled their world in search of somebody to understand them, but this is one legend which is true. This folk memory has become embedded in the Chinese consciousness to such an extent that it can never be destroyed. Despite repeated attempts to eradicate this memory (notably during the Cultural Revolution of the 1960s) they have lived on for ever because they actually did it, endured unbelievable privations because they believed in humanity, and still they could dance and sing—and this is not a fairy tale but genuine history.

The years passed, and the time they spent in any one state grew shorter and shorter, usually because they became caught up in one of the endless skirmishes between the petty states or the warlords, the very thing that Confucius was always saying should stop although nobody ever listened. These years really marked the beginning of the Warring States Period, as there were several quite large skirmishes between many of the states

while he was wandering about with his students, and it was at exactly this time that Sun Tzu (Sun Zi) wrote his classic treatise on strategy *The Art of War*. Sun like Confucius was a "scholar for hire" who travelled from one state to another giving advice to rulers, but he managed to make a much better living at it, which is not surprising as war is a much more marketable commodity than peace. While Confucius preached disarmament and

Confucius arrested by the soldiers of Song. Tableau in the City of the Six Arts, Qufu. *Photo: Jonathan Price*

honest government, Sun advised on the best way to win battles—if necessary by dishonesty, deception, and disinformation. *The Art of War* is still quoted by military strategists, and Sun's long section on the use of spies could be used as the official CIA handbook—in fact it probably is. There is no evidence that the two ever met, even though they were operating in the same areas at exactly the same time, and in any case Confucius the scholar of peace would have had nothing to say to Sun the scholar of war, and he often got very annoyed when rulers asked him about military matters.

Every time they returned to the state of Wei for example, which they did quite often, Duke Ling would question Confucius closely about the military strength and fortifications of the other states he had visited in case he needed to attack them, but never about whether such an attack was right or wrong.

> When Duke Ling of Wei heard that Confucius was coming, he went outside the city as far as the open common to meet him. Duke Ling asked him: "Can Pu be attacked? Pu is the place where Wei must offer resistance to the states of Qin and Chu. If now we attack it from Wei, is not that, after all, not feasible?"
>
> Sima Qian, *Records of the Grand Historian*

Confucius sighed when he heard this. No longer just a travelling scholar, he was now expected to be a travelling spy as well.

> "Concerning the arrangement of sacrificial vessels, I am informed. Concerning the arrangement of

Zigong to the rescue: aided by the mercenaries of Kung-Liang Ju, Confucius' loyal disciple gets his Master and his starving followers released from the Song militia. Ming Dynasty painting. *Qilu Press*

armies, I have as yet learned nothing."

> On the following day, Duke Ling had another conversation with Confucius. Then Duke Ling saw a wild goose. He looked up at it, and seemed to be paying no attention to Confucius. Thereupon, Confucius prepared to travel again to Chen.
>
> Sima Qian, *Records of the Grand Historian*

Sun Zi - author of 'The Art of War'. *Qilu Press*

Confucius defiantly playing the zither as he and his followers face starvation. Ming Dynasty painting. *Qilu Press*

It was all very disillusioning. Clearly no more walls would be coming down in his lifetime and nobody wanted to listen to him—apparently even a wild goose was more interesting than his ideas.

Before they left Wei once again, Yan Hui asked the Music Master Kin, who had always been friendly to Confucius, why it was that nobody seemed to want to pay any attention to his master any longer?

The Music Master replied, "Alas! It is all over with your Master!"

"How so?" asked Yan Hui.

The other said: "To seek to practise the old ways of the Zhou nowadays is like pushing along a boat on the dry land. He has not learned that in handing down the ways of one time he is sure to be reduced to extremity in endeavoring to adapt them to the conditions of another. Alas! It is indeed all over with your Master!"

Zhuangzi, Book 14, Part 2:6

Confucius in other words was an old-fashioned has-been, out of touch with the modern world—a charge which is still made against him nowadays. Yan Hui did not believe this. How could believing in humanity and fairness and refraining from unnecessary warfare be "old-fashioned"? Confucius' principles, in Hui's mind, were universal truths which could never become irrelevant with changing times.

All of them in fact except the tireless and idealistic Hui were becoming weary and disillusioned. Even Confucius was given to sighing and shaking his head and saying that he was the right man in the wrong place at the wrong time:

I have sought to find a ruler who would employ me for a long time, and that I have not found one, shows the character of the time.

Zhuangzi, Book 17, Part 2:10

Zilu's theory was that they had not succeeded in becoming good enough people themselves, and this was why nobody took any notice of them. He suggested they retire from the world for a period of intense self-improvement. Confucius pooh-poohed this idea, telling him that even if they achieved utter perfection it still would not necessarily mean they would be heeded—history was full of examples of men of extreme virtue who starved to death.

Zigong, a pragmatist and realist—qualities which gave him the edge in his business dealings—begged Confucius to lower his sights and tailor his teaching more to the market. Practical management advice which led to a good job and a high salary was what people wanted these days. All right, throw in a few general moral platitudes as a bonus but for heaven's sake lay off the disarmament angle—it just gets everybody's backs up and is never going to happen anyway.

Duke Ling of Wei consulting Confucius. Ming Dynasty painting. *Qilu Press*

Duke Ling of Wei more interested in some passing wild geese than Confucius' opinions. Ming Dynasty painting. *Qilu Press*

Zigong said: "The Master's teaching is so overpowering that no one on earth can bear it. You must, I think, bring it a little lower."

Confucius said: "Su, a good farmer can sow the seed, but he cannot guarantee the harvest. A good workman can be clever, but he cannot always meet people's taste. The Sage may cultivate his doctrines, may arrange them and simplify them, but he cannot bring it to pass that they be accepted. If you strive only to have them accepted, then, Su, you do not have long-term vision."

Sima Qian, *Records of the Grand Historian*

It was the youngest of them all who brought them back on track, inspiring even his weary Master:

"What does it matter if we are not understood?" Hui said. "If we do not cultivate our doctrines, then that is our error. But if we painstakingly cultivate our doctrines, and these doctrines are not accepted, that is the fault of the rulers of the land. In the very fact that he is not understood, the Sage is recognized."

Confucius rejoiced and smiled. He said: "Son of the house of Yan, if you had great riches, I should wish to be your overseer."

Sima Qian, *Records of the Grand Historian*

Zhuangzi included many descriptions in his pseudo-biography of Confucius of both Master and disciples abandoning their principles in the face of all their privations, but this is merely anti-Confucian propaganda. According to Zhuangzi, Confucius abandoned his followers for many years and lived as a hermit in the forest, while Yan Hui rejected his Master's beliefs and became a Daoist:

Yan Hui said, "I am making progress, I have ceased to think of benevolence and righteousness … I have lost all thought of ceremonies and music … I am become one with the Great Spirit."

Confucius exclaimed: "You have, indeed, become superior to me! I must ask leave to follow in your steps."

Zhuangzi, Book 6, Chapter 6:14

This is pure fiction—in fact none of them ever showed any sign of being sympathetic to the Daoist ideal of withdrawal from the world—they wandered around the countryside not because they wanted to but because they were forced to.

Zilu's celebrated encounter with two farmers who were sympathetic to the Daoists shows Confucius' unwavering contempt for those who chose to live as hermits, and there is no reason to think he ever changed his mind about this:

Changju and Jieni were working together in the fields when Confucius was passing by. He sent Zilu to ask them where he could ford the river. Changju said, "Who is that holding the carriage?"

Tzu Lu said, "It is Confucius."

Zilu meets some Daoist supporters near a ford as Confucius waits in his carriage. Ming Dynasty painting. *Qilu Press*

Chang said, "The Confucius of Lu?"

"Yes."

"Well, if that's the case, then he knows the ford."

Analects, 18:6

What the man meant was that if Confucius were a sage as his supporters claimed, he would by definition know *everything*—so why ask? If he really did not know then he was not a sage and was therefore a fraud. The man muttered some more derisive remarks along these lines and continued hoeing his vegetables. Zilu sighed and turned to the other man.

"Who are you?" Jieni said.

"I am Zilu."

"The follower of this Confucius of Lu?"

"Right."

Jieni said, "Disorder, disorder throughout the realm! And who can change it? Rather than following a *shi* who flees from evil men, you should follow one who flees from the world altogether!" With that, he went back to his hoeing and wouldn't stop.

Analects, 18:6

This is of course a clear reference to the Daoists who advocated "escaping from the world," and is the only time that the rival philosophy is mentioned anywhere in the *Analects*. Significantly, Confucius' negative reaction

to the man's suggestion that Zilu abandon his master and follow a Daoist hermit instead is omitted from Zhuangzi's pro-Daoist account and only appears in the *Analects*:

Zilu went back and reported this to Confucius. Confucius sighing, said, "I can't form associations with the birds and beasts. So if I don't associate with people, then who will I associate with? If the Way prevailed in the realm, I would not try to change anything."

Analects, 18:6

Although he agreed with the man that there was "disorder everywhere," he still believed that it was the duty of right-thinking people to try and change the situation. Indeed, although "shunned by everybody" he had no desire to "escape from the world" altogether and often bewailed bitterly the fact that this very situation had been forced upon them. Confucius, despite everything that Zhuangzi wrote about him, was never a Daoist:

Confucius said: "In the *Book of Songs* it is written: 'We are neither rhinoceroses nor tigers that we could stay in this wilderness.' How is it that this befalls us?"

Sima Qian, *Records of the Grand Historian*

Apart from his suggestion that the disciples should go and live in the woods, the farmer's idea that if Kong Qiu were a sage he would know everything there is to know about absolutely everything—including the whereabouts of the nearest ford—was another thing that infuriated Confucius. He was often asked to pontificate about almost any subject under the sun and if he had failed to come up with an instant pronouncement would no longer have been taken seriously as a philosopher, so pervasive was the belief in the omniscience of sages.

The most unusual request Confucius dealt with during his time as a wandering freelance scholar-sage was when he was consulted about an unusually large bone, which had been found in one of the states to the far south of the old Zhou Empire in what is now Zhejiang Province. This indicates that his fame had really spread far and wide even though he was ignored and persecuted for most of the time, because the Duke of Wu sent a messenger on a long journey which must have taken many weeks in order to find the renowned Master and get his opinion about the bone.

The state of Wu fought the state of Yue and destroyed the mountain Kuai Chi [upon which, in the year 494 BC, the capital of Yue was situated]. There they found a bone of such a size that it filled

Shantungaur giganteus, a giant dinosaur which roamed the area near Confucius' home 70 million years ago during the Cretaceous Period.
Shandong Museum. *Photos: Jonathan Price*

an entire wagon. The state of Wu sent a messenger to Confucius to ask why the bone was so large.

Sima Qian, *Records of the Grand Historian*

This story was previously thought to be one of Sima Qian's more fanciful inventions but in fact we now know that it may well be scientifically accurate—clearly the huge bone was part of the vertebrae or thighbone of a dinosaur, as these fossils are always discovered by "destroying a mountain" as he recorded. In fact in exactly the same area in the year 2000 the complete skeleton of an entirely new species of dinosaur was unearthed by workers excavating a hillside for a new freeway near the town of Lishui in Zhejiang, very near the site of the discovery of Confucius' bone, and this was christened *Zhejiangosaurus Lishuiensis*.

China has become known as the "nation of dinosaurs" because so many have been discovered there—specimens of more than 120 of the 900 known species of dinosaur have been found within its borders, and more new species are unearthed every year. This is because during the Jurassic and Cretaceous periods, when the giant reptiles ruled the earth, the whole of what is now China was continuously a land mass, unlike other parts of the world which were alternately sea or land. Finding dinosaur bones has been a common occurrence throughout recorded Chinese history, although it was not until relatively recently that anybody knew what these giant skeletons actually were—for thousands of years they were known as "dragon bones." One of the most sensational

discoveries in recent years was in 2007, when the skeleton of a gigantic bird-like reptile was found in the Gobi Desert. Named *Gigantoraptor Erlianensis*, this terrifying prehistoric eagle would have weighed 3,100 pounds, and stood up to 16.5 feet high.

Powdered dinosaur bones in fact feature in many traditional Chinese medicine recipes ("add a sprinkling of powdered dragon bone") and it was not until 2006 that the sale of dinosaur powder was made illegal in Henan Province, site of the ancient state of Zhou which Confucius visited with his friend Nangong Jingshu. Indeed it was in Henan that the heaviest dinosaur ever discovered in Asia was unearthed, with part of its vertebrae measuring in at 4 feet 3? inches, and certainly as Sima Qian records a "wagon" would be needed to carry a single bone of this colossal creature.

Confucius may be forgiven for being slightly stumped over this find and if time-travel is ever developed somebody should take him to the Henan Dinosaur Museum (which is very close to the place where he is supposed to have met Lao Tze) in order to bring him up to speed on the latest discoveries. As it was he suggested that the bone was from a member of a race of gods who used to inhabit the area, since even the tallest man could not possibly have a thighbone as large as the one they had discovered.

The messenger asked: "What are the limits of stature to a man's body?"

Confucius answered: "The Chiao Yao are three feet high; that is the extreme of smallness. The tallest men are at most ten times as tall as this."

Thereupon, the messenger of Wu said: "Magnificent! He is a philosopher."

Sima Qian, *Records of the Grand Historian*

Remembering that Sima Qian is the man who said Confucius was nine feet tall, it is very unlikely that the Master would have said that the tallest men were 30 feet high—he never went in for this sort of thing. So Confucius' opinion that the bone was of a "race of gods" is the best that anybody in 496 BC could have come up with and he was enough of a rationalist to avoid identifying it as a dragon bone, something which is still believed in remote Chinese villages to this day where the trade in powdered dinosaur bones continues—illegally.

It is a pity that he did not venture to suggest that the bone was from a race of animals which no longer existed or he might have had a species named after him called *Stegosaurus Confuciencis*, but all in all he did his best in the circumstances and deserved whatever fee Zigong no doubt insisted the Messenger from Wu had to pay—in gold. Yan Hui (and his Master) considered that wisdom has no price and should be dispensed freely, but Zigong always insisted that consultancy costs money and the fee he was demanding was a bargain considering the wealth of information his Master had dispensed. The representative of Wu shelled out, Confucius feigned embarrassment, and the wandering scholars had made enough to live on for six months from five minutes of consultancy. Zigong was not his Master's self-appointed business manager for nothing.

Six years after Confucius went into exile, in the year 491, there was news from home. Ji Huan (Lord Ji) had died and been succeeded by Ji Kangzi, who had attended Confucius' classes and was a supporter of his ideas. Ji Kangzi was appointed the prime minister of Lu, like his father before him, and for a brief time it seemed that Confucius would be allowed to return home. Ji Kangzi tried to make this happen but the political situation was delicate and the Ji family did not have the supreme influence that they had once enjoyed. Ji Kangzi's feudal vassals told him that if Confucius returned they would turn against him. Zigong travelled to Lu and conferred with Confucius' former student, Ranyu (Qiu), who was now the commander of the Ji army, and was about to be appointed as the assistant chancellor to Ji Kangzi in the state government.

Zigong knew that Confucius was thinking of returning home. He met Ran Qiu, and warned him, as follows: "When you enter upon your official duties, see to it that Confucius is summoned."

Sima Qian, *Records of the Grand Historian*

Qiu ran true to form: he was a "company man" through and through. Once expelled by Confucius for milking taxes for the Ji family, he now told Zigong that there was no deal. Zigong returned to Confucius, who was once again residing in Wei, and told him the bad news.

On this day, Confucius said: "I want to go home, I want to go home!"

Sima Qian, *Records of the Grand Historian*

It was a sad moment—Confucius was not to be allowed to return home for another seven long years. Instead of yearning for home, the faithful disciples began to look around for a state that might accept their Master permanently, after which they would persuade him to settle down and try not to upset people too much. By the year 489 BC it looked as if they might have found somewhere in the state of Chu, a powerful state to the south of Lu, which covered the present-day provinces of Anhui and Hubei including the fertile basin of the Yangtze River, and was the largest of the Warring States.

The ruler of Chu, Duke Zhao, had offered Confucius a large fiefdom of 700 square miles in exchange for his acting as a government advisor. This time things looked very hopeful. As the scholar-wagon trundled into the state, Duke Zhao sent an armed escort to accompany them to the capital.

Unfortunately, as they approached the capital they were met on the road by a lunatic named Jie Yu whose ravings struck uncomfortably close to home. Jie Yu, known as "the madman of Chu" (this incident is recorded in three independent historical sources including the *Analects* so can be presumed to be authentic) screamed at Confucius that he was finished and nobody would ever listen to him again:

Jie Yu, the madman of Chu, passed by Confucius, singing:
Phoenix! Phoenix!
How your powers are fading!
The future will never come; the past is not to be sought again!
Give up! Give up!
You are in peril! You are in peril!
The cinnamon tree can be eaten, and therefore it is cut down!

Above: Emissaries of the State of Chu invite Confucius to come and be the advisor to their Duke. Ming Dynasty painting. *Qilu Press*

Left: Jieyu – the 'madman of Chu' – raving that Confucius is 'finished'. Ming Dynasty painting. *Qilu Press*

The grease which lights the fire fries itself!
Those who involve themselves in government now
Will be in danger!
    Confucius jumped down, wanting to talk to
him, but he ran away, so Confucius couldn't talk
to him.

Analects, 18:5 / *Zhuangzi*, Book 6, Part 1, Section 4:9

This prophetic warning proved to be correct. Even before his arrival, the courtiers surrounding Duke Zhou of Chu persuaded their ruler that Confucius' hidden agenda was to restore the authority of the King of Zhou, and he would thus thwart the ambitions of Chu to become the dominant state. Interestingly, part of the courtiers'

Confucius forced to leave the State of Chu. Ming Dynasty painting. *Qilu Press*

argument was that Confucius and his team were *too* talented. Prudent rulers surround themselves with mediocrities and the scholar-wagon now approaching was carrying an undeniable A-team, the members of which, the Duke's courtiers argued, would be unlikely simply to follow orders, as they themselves did.

Then Minister Tze Hsi of Chu said: "Is there among your ambassadors, O Duke, any man who is the equal of Zigong?"

The Duke answered: "No"

"Is there among Your Majesty's generals any who is the equal of Zilu?"

The Duke answered: "No."

"Confucius makes glorious the work of the Kings of Zhou. If Your Majesty should appoint him, how then would it be possible for the state of Chu to extend itself, proud and prosperous, from generation to generation, over thousands of square miles?"

Sima Qian, *Records of the Grand Historian*

Thinking about it, the Duke of Chu decided that he did after all prefer advisors who prostrated themselves, performed the kow-tow, and did exactly what they were told. Later on, when Confucius was long dead, the Chinese emperors were able to have his ideas rewritten in such a way that it appeared that doing what your ruler told you without question was a Confucian virtue. While he was inconveniently still alive such revisionism was not possible, so Duke Zhao thanked his prostrated courtiers for their timely advice and revoked his offer of land. When Confucius and his followers finally arrived, they found that there were no estates awaiting them as

promised and no job for the Master either. Furious, Zilu turned the ox-cart around and they set off back the way they had come.

Thereupon, Confucius left Chu and returned to Wei. In this year [489 BC] Confucius was sixty-three years old. It was the sixth year of Duke Ai of Lu.

Sima Qian, *Records of the Grand Historian*

Despite his failure to influence the rulers of his time, Confucius' ideas nevertheless were gaining increasing ground among ordinary people, and this presaged the future in a way that the Master himself could not have foreseen. It was to be in the hearts and minds of ordinary people and not their leaders that his ideals lived on for thousands of years, and as a result the attempts by various governments to expunge Confucius from all memory have always failed. An example of this is the incident recorded in the *Analects* when a humble border guard asked to have a talk with Confucius when the scholar-wagon passed through his gate on the way back to Wei after the wasted trip to Chu.

The border guard at Yi requested an audience with the Master, saying: "Whenever a Superior Man comes here, I never miss the opportunity to see him." The disciples sent him in. When he came out, he said, "Friends, don't have any doubts about your master failing. The world has certainly lacked the Way for a long time now, but Heaven will use your master to awaken everyone."

Analects, 3:24

When they got back to Wei it looked for a short time as if the encouraging words of the border guard were indeed prophetic. Old Duke Ling, the womanizing despot, had died, and had been succeeded by another member of the same family, Duke Che, who was hesitant and inexperienced and now formally requested Confucius to help him form a government. Zilu especially was wildly excited about this prospect, imagining that this would at last be an opportunity for them all to become government ministers, if not in their own state at least in somebody else's. He particularly fancied the post of defense minister for himself, as he had never completely abandoned his dream of military glory—always in defense of the right of course—something Confucius had always chided him about.

Zilu said: "The ruler of Wei is anticipating your assistance in the administration of his state. What will be your top priority?"

Confucius said, "There must be a correction of terminology."

Analects, 13:3

Zilu stared at his Master with his mouth open. Confucius told Zilu, "Come on—don't be slow—you know what I mean." and then proceeded to explain. Now in his early sixties, but still at the height of his powers intellectually and with a lifetime of experience behind him, Confucius proceeded to deliver to Zilu the most influential statement about government that he ever made:

"If the naming of things is not corrected, then what is said cannot be followed. If what is said cannot be followed, then work cannot be accomplished… therefore, the Superior Administrator needs to have his terminology appropriate to what is being described, so that what he talks about may be carried out appropriately. The speech of the Superior Administrator cannot be indefinite."

Analects, 13:3

Countless books have been written about this single saying from the *Analects*, not only in the centuries following Confucius' death but right up into our own day—it was this passage that Peter Drucker cited as the most important for managing a modern company. What Confucius meant was that everything about government or management should be precisely defined and not "indefinite." Goals should be specified in the clearest possible language and everybody's role in achieving these goals should be equally clearly laid out.

Obvious? Of course—yet this idea became one of the most misunderstood of all the statements Confucius ever made, and became the basis of an abstruse theory called "The Rectification of Names" (*Zhenming*) which was used to enforce the authoritarian rule of the dynasties supposedly in the name of Confucius. Quite clearly, however, he was talking about changing and improving a system, not enforcing an existing one as was later claimed—nowadays we call this "management restructuring."

We do not know if the new Duke of Wei ever applied any of Confucius' suggestions, probably not as he had serious problems with his own feudal barons who were secretly planning to take power in a coup. The following year, however, 488 BC, Confucius and his team were able to use their talents in another area they had already dabbled in—preventing an armed conflict—and this time they were successful.

A serious diplomatic crisis had erupted between the states of Lu and Wu, and for a time it looked as if there was going to be an all-out war. As is common with border incidents then or since, this one was sparked by a trivial dispute. The large and powerful state of Wu (which included the sites of the modern cities of Shanghai and Hangzhou) had extended its territory all the way up the eastern coast as far as the Great Wall of Qi, and had a very short frontier with Lu. In order to gain a foothold in Lu, the rulers of Wu demanded access to a sacred site—a burial place which they claimed belonged to one of their heroes. Lu refused. When Confucius heard about this he sent Zigong back home to Lu with an undertaking from the new Duke of Wei that the state of Wei stood behind Lu. According to Sima Qian the message Zigong carried was as follows: "Confucius says: 'The governments of Lu and of Wei are brothers.'"

In the following year [488 BC], Wu held a conference with Lu in Tseng. Wu demanded the tomb. Chancellor Pi of Wu demanded it of Baron Kang of Ji, the Chancellor of Lu. Baron Kang had Zigong accompany him, and thus the matter could be avoided.

Sima Qian, *Records of the Grand Historian*

This was Zigong's first major recorded success as a diplomat—turning his considerable skill at deal-making in business to good use in the political field—and war was averted. Although barely mentioned in most biographies, this incident was in fact the only time Confucius succeeded in realizing his ideals in his own lifetime so it is in fact highly significant. Zigong was an ideal pupil because he translated his Master's ideals into concrete action, and after Confucius' death he repeated

Emissaries from Chancellor Ji Kangzi inviting Confucius to return home to Lu. Ming Dynasty Painting. *Qilu Press*

this success by averting another unnecessary war through diplomacy.

Lu's chancellor—Ji Kangzi, the new Lord Ji—was extremely grateful and tried to get Confucius rehabilitated, something he had been attempting to do for several years as he remained his fervent admirer. The feudal barons still objected, however, and Confucius had to spend another three years in exile. Although all the barons in Lu were glad a major war had been prevented (they might well have lost in an all-out conflict with the much larger state of Wu) they still did not want Confucius back again and telling them to stop fighting amongst themselves. Little wars were good for business.

One of the feudal barons—Lord Shu, the leader of the number three family in Lu—even went as far as saying that Zigong was far superior to his Master, especially after his recent diplomatic triumph. Zigong got very angry and retorted that he was simply putting his Master's words into action, and by comparison he himself was nothing!

Zigong commented: "If I am a castle then my wall is only shoulder high, and you may look over it easily. My Master's wall is several tens of feet high and if you can't find the door and enter by it, you will not see the beauty of the ancestral temple inside. Those who find the door are few indeed!"

Analects, 19:23

Confucius' school was still running in his absence, and several of his former students including Hsia (who now styled himself "Master Hsia") had been standing in as teachers. Zigong reported back to Confucius, however, that the tradition of serious scholarship combined with moral education had slipped, and the current students were rowdy and undisciplined.

Confucius said, "I must return! I must return! My young disciples are wild and unbridled."

Analects, 5:22

Finally, in the year 485 or 484 (the exact date is uncertain), Ji Kangzi managed to persuade the vacillating Duke Ai of Lu to lift the *in absentia* death sentence on Confucius and allow him to return home. Duke Ai was still very nervous of the other feudal barons who were making threatening noises about this proposed rehabilitation. Eventually he told his chancellor that Confucius could return but only on condition he never involved himself in politics again. Ji Kangzi bowed, and immediately sent emissaries to the state of Wei to tell Confucius the good news.

Baron Kang of Ji sent the honorable Hua, the honorable Pin, and the honorable Lin to receive him with gifts of silk. Then Confucius returned to Lu.

Sima Qian, *Records of the Grand Historian*

Confucius is supposed to have wept when he was told the news, and composed an ode called the *Qiu Ling*, which he accompanied on his zither as the scholar-wagon headed at last for the border of Lu. He was now sixty-seven years old, and had another six years to live.

The Phoenix and the Turtle

Confucius returned to live in his old school-house (there is no mention in any of the records of any reunion with his actual family). Although he was not allowed to participate in government officially, Ji Kangzi certainly asked Confucius for advice informally on many occasions, and many of these conversations found their way into the *Analects*.

> **Ji Kangzi asked Confucius about government. Confucius replied saying: "To 'govern' means to 'rectify.' If you were to lead the people with correctness, who would not be rectified?"**
>
> *Analects*, 12:17

It was also to Ji Kangzi that Confucius made his celebrated statement of opposition to capital punishment:

> **Ji Kangzi asked Confucius about government saying: "Suppose I were to kill the unjust, in order to advance the just. Would that be all right?"**
>
> **Confucius replied: "In doing government, what is the need of killing? If you desire good, the people will be good. The nature of the Superior Person is like the wind, the nature of inferior people is like the grass. When the wind blows over the grass, it always bends."**
>
> *Analects*, 12:19

This advice has never been heeded in most of the Asian countries which have claimed at one time or another to have based their governmental system on Confucian ideas, all but one of which still retain the death penalty. In fact from this passage alone is it is easy to see how easily his ideas can be distorted. If you take only the last two sentences, omitting the first two, Confucius appears to be enthusiastically endorsing authoritarian rule, whereas in the complete passage he is clearly talking about government by good example rather than by excessive punishment, one of his favorite themes.

Even Duke Ai "the Lamentable" occasionally asked for advice from the venerable sage, although he remained careful not to give Confucius any real power.

Phoenix relief, Shandong Museum. *Photo: Jonathan Price*

Turtle supporting stele, Qufu. *Qilu Press*

The Duke Ai asked: "How can I make the people follow me?" Confucius replied: "Advance the upright and set aside the crooked, and the people will follow you. Advance the crooked and set aside the upright, and the people will not follow you."

Analects, 2:19

The Duke did give Confucius the harmless task of sorting out the official music which was supposed to be played on ceremonial occasions. This was both a labor of love and a welcome supplement to his income.

Confucius said: "Only after I returned to Lu from Wei did the music get straightened out, with the Royal Songs and the Praises being played at the proper place and time."

Analects, 9:15

Confucius, when talking with the Grand Music Master of Lu, said, "In my understanding of music, the piece should be begun in unison. As it proceeds, all should be in harmony but with individually distinct and flowing parts."

Analects, 3:23

In his darker moments Confucius sometimes felt that his life had not been as successful as he had hoped.

Confucius said: "Aah! No one understands me!"

Zigong said, "What do you mean, 'No one understands you'?"

Confucius said, "I have no resentment against Heaven, no quarrel with men. I study from the bottom and penetrate to the top. Yet who understands me? Only Heaven does!"

Analects, 14:35

His life had turned full circle. Long ago he had spent the three years after his mother's death cut off from the world, his only companions his beloved books. Now once again he watched the leaves turn outside his doorway as he leafed through bamboo manuscripts and worked on the final volumes of the records of Lu—the *Spring and Autumn Annals*—while the great world passed him by. Nevertheless, as he spent the autumn of his days surrounded by his beloved students, arranging music, and writing, Confucius was happy and contented enough; he was after all doing what he loved doing most:

Confucius said: "…at seventy I could follow my heart's desire without compromising my principles."

Analects, 2:4

When not teaching, he naturally reminisced a good deal, and most of the material which ended up in the *Analects* would have been based on what he told his students during these twilight years, together with first-

The young Zengzi (Zeng Shen) with his master Confucius. Ming Dynasty painting. *Qilu Press*

hand contributions from the now gray-haired Zilu who had been with his Master ever since he gave his first public class forty years earlier. The others hardly noticed the new student who was assiduously taking notes in one corner as the Master recalled his long and eventful life. The young man was barely twenty and had only recently joined Confucius' classes. Intimidated by the brilliance of the others, he was too shy to say very much but made up for it by scribbling all the time—his name was Zeng Shen.

Zeng, known to posterity as Zengzi (Master Zeng), was by his own admission not the brightest of students, yet he went on to become the most prolific author of Confucian texts after his teacher's death, and among the

Bestseller: Zengzi (shown here in a statuette in the Shanghai Jiading Confucius Temple) is the author of more manuscripts than any other of Confucius' disciples in the recently discovered bamboo manuscripts. *Photos: Jonathan Price/ Shanghai Museum*

bamboo-slip manuscripts discovered in the Guodian tomb more are attributed to his name than to any other of the disciples. Being so young (even Zigong was old enough to be his father) Zengzi became fast friends with Yan Hui who was also still only in his twenties, and tried to model himself on his slightly older fellow student, whom he much admired:

> **Zengzi said: "Having ability, yet learning from the clumsy. Having much knowledge, but learning from the unlearned; possessing, yet seeming to lack, being full yet seeming empty, able to accept harm without retaliation: in the past I had a friend [Yan Hui] who could do this."**
>
> *Analects*, 8:5

Later Zengzi set down what both his Master and his friend Yan Hui had taught him in what was to become perhaps the most often quoted guide to behaving in the Confucian Way:

> **Zengzi said: "Each day I examine myself in three ways: in doing things for others, have I been disloyal? In my interactions with friends, have I been untrustworthy? Have I not practised what I have preached?"**
>
> *Analects*, 1:4

Unlike Zigong and Zilu, who were both brashly self-confident, Zengzi seems to have been like Hui rather endearingly modest. He is recorded in the *Xiao Jing* (*Book of Filiality*), a work supposedly written by Zengzi himself, as having apologized to Confucius one day in class after failing to answer a question with the words: "I, Zeng, am very-dull-witted." In the same work Confucius is said to have exclaimed, when Zengzi actually answered a question: "Zeng is not so smart, how can he know this?"

He can hardly have been as dull-witted as he claimed since he later became the first person who is known to have suggested that the world is round, about a hundred years before Eratosthenes made the same claim in Greece. His idea about this is quoted in the *Dadai Liji*—an edited version of the *Book of Rites* which is supposed to have been originally compiled by Confucius and annotated by Zengzi. Perhaps Zengzi, like Einstein, was simply not very good at school.

However badly he may have performed in class, Zengzi is almost certainly responsible for the bulk of the *Analects* as we have them, and without him Confucius might have been forgotten. Perhaps he was no Plato, but Zengzi is certainly the Boswell to Confucius' Johnson, and he had a particular knack of being able to convey his Master's ideas in a very clear and simple way:

Zengzi said, "Our master's Way is to be sincere and fair, and that's it."

Analects, 4:15

Zengzi not only became his Master's principal biographer but succeeded Confucius as head of the school after his death. His teaching style was quite different to Confucius', which we know because the bamboo-slip manuscripts bearing Zengzi's name have two distinct styles. When he is quoting Confucius (using the familiar "Confucius said" tag) none of the sayings is more than a few lines long—in the style of the *Analects*— so clearly the Master did actually speak like this, firing off remarks on one subject or another, changing the subject frequently, and expecting input from his audience. By contrast those passages which follow "Zengzi said" are very long and occupy many slips of bamboo so would have covered several "pages" in the original books. Clearly therefore Zengzi gave lectures more in the style of a modern professor rather than teaching in Confucius' own unique and more intimate style which lives on through the *Analects*.

Zengzi did in fact become the tutor to Confucius' grandson Zisi, but not until after the master's death—the little boy would only have been three or four years old at the time his grandfather returned to Lu. That he had a grandson at all would have come as a surprise to Confucius when he got back home; it seems that the rift within his family had never healed and Confucius' son Bo Yu, who was now in his forties, had no wish to pay his father more than the barest courtesy and kept his family apart from the old man. Zisi, who himself wrote many books, never included any sort of personal reminiscence of Confucius in any of his writings, and so may only have met his grandfather once or twice—at least while his father was alive. This was of course a great pity as grandchildren are one of the joys of autumn.

Zengzi (Zeng Shen) as a child in a poor village. Like many of Confucius' most famous students, he was given his great chance in life by the Master's 'education-for-all' system. Illustration from the classic Confucian work '24 Examples of Filial Piety', in which the young Zeng is held up as a shining example of a devoted son. His father brought him to Confucius when he was still in his teens. *Painting by Bo Jingzhen.*

Little grandson Zisi with Confucius – the theme of countless paintings down the ages. *Painting by Bo Jingzhen.*

As it was, Confucius' life had played out differently to other people's, and as always the family which surrounded him in his old age was composed of his favorite students, especially the loyal three who had accompanied him on his travels. Zilu, only about eight years younger than himself, had always been like his energetic and somewhat naïve younger brother, who even now was going round telling anybody who would listen that in his opinion Confucius should be made chancellor of Lu. Zigong, just into his forties, had become the success story of the Confucius family, the favorite nephew who had not only made a fortune in business but had become renowned as a diplomat all over the Warring States. Still fiercely loyal, he refused all offers of official appointment unless his Master was also appointed above him. Meanwhile Yan Hui continued unassumingly studying and helping the other students, and now that Confucius' failed relationship with Bo Yu showed no signs of mending, Confucius came to regard Hui more and more as his real beloved son. Hui, like the others, could have had his pick of the plum government jobs on offer after they all returned, but like Zigong he always refused.

Confucius said to Yan Hui, "Come here, Hui. Your family is poor, and your position is low; why should you not take office?"

Hui replied, "I have no wish to be in office. Outside the suburban district I possess fields to the extent of fifty acres, which are sufficient to supply me with my needs; and inside it I have ten acres, which are sufficient to supply me with silk and flax. I find my pleasure in playing on my lute, and your doctrines, Master, which I study, are sufficient for my enjoyment; I do not wish to take office."

Confucius changed countenance, and said, "I have long been preaching this; that he who cultivates the path of inward development is not ashamed though he may have no official position—but today I see it realized in Hui: this is what I have gained."

Zhuangzi, Book 28, Part 3:6

At this time most people did not reach the age of seventy and Confucius was considered very energetic for his age—having spent most of his life surrounded by much younger people had probably kept him young. Like all older people in their declining years, however, Confucius began to see old friends fall away around him, and this filled him with foreboding that his own days were numbered:

Boniu was sick and Confucius came to see him. He held his hand through the window and said, "He is dying! How awful it is that this kind of man should be sick like this!"

Analects, 6:10

He began to have strange dreams, and lamented the fact that he no longer dreamed he was living in the golden age of the Zhou, as he had often done in the past:

Confucius said: "I am really going down the drain. I have not dreamed of the Duke of Zhou for a long time now."

Analects, 7:5

For the first time in his life he became interested in the *Book of Divination* (*Yi Jing* or *I Ching*), sometimes known as the *Book of Changes*, which contains a system of foretelling the future through the use of divining sticks. He had always been skeptical of this sort of thing, but now read the book from cover to cover so many times that Sima Qian records that he "wore out the leather bindings" and the bamboo slips fell to the floor in a heap. He is supposed to have said that:

"I wish I could add fifty years to my life, so I could properly study the *Book of Changes*."

Analects, 7:17

In his heart he knew that he could not have much more than fifty months left to him, but perhaps his sudden interest in the future was because he wondered if and how his teachings would survive in the coming ages, or whether his life (as looked very likely at that moment) had been completely in vain.

It is unlikely that the *Book of Changes* would have been

"Humble Alley" Qufu – traditionally supposed to be the site of Yan Hui's home. *Photo: Qilu Press*

Confucius in old age – worryingly prone to strange dreams and visions. Ming Dynasty painting. *Qilu Press*

forty-six. In death Bo Yu was spared his usual nickname of the "little fish"; he was buried as Kong Li and was given a proper funeral appropriate to the son of a man who had once served as the minister of justice. The funeral procession included various government officers riding in carriages, followed by Confucius himself in another wagon. At the head of the cortege, however, Bo Yu was carried to his grave in a simple wooden coffin, without the ornate and beautifully decorated outer shell, which would have been provided when showing great honor to the deceased. Confucius was criticized for this in the same way that he was criticized earlier for giving his mother the kind of extravagant funeral which was considered appropriate for the father of a family.

He gives a rather lame excuse in the *Analects*, saying that he had not had time to have an outer shell made, and it was not proper for him to be seen rushing through the streets to get one at the last minute on the actual day of the funeral:

> **The Master said, "Kong Li, when he died, had a coffin but no outer shell. I could not walk on foot to get a shell for him, because, having followed in the rear of the great officers, it was not proper that I should walk on foot."**

Analects, 11:8

Whatever his excuse, he was demonstrating extremely publicly that Kong Li was his son only in name, for whom he would perform the ritual demanded by society, but nothing further. By this time he saw Zilu, Zigong, and Yan Hui, his companions in exile, as his real family, and the death of Bo Yu did not prostrate him as might have been the case if there had been any sort of closeness between father and son. He is not recorded as

able to reveal his future, even if he had studied it for fifty years. And even if the divining sticks had predicted the exact progression of events, Confucius back then would have assumed they were in error…

"In 250 years time all books about you will be burned. In 1,000 years time you will be worshipped as a god. In 1,500 years time you will be declared Emperor of all China. In 2,447 years time (which will then be known as 1967 AD) your statue in Qufu will be torn down and smashed by a screaming mob of students yelling 'Confucius is dead!' In 2,487 years time (then known as 2007 AD) the best-selling book in China will be about the relevance of the *Analects of Confucius* to the modern world. "Confucius' is the name by the way by which people outside China will know you—and yes, you will become famous all over the world which is much bigger than you thought it was …"

Did he have any sense of this? One hopes so, yet it is hardly likely, and Confucius' last years were unutterably sad. He expected to fade away slowly, leaving behind grieving disciples who would carry on his work, but instead everybody began dying before him.

The first to go was his son Bo Yu, who died four years before his father in 483, at the relatively young age of

Confucius studying the *Yi Jing* – the 'Book of Changes' – in his final years. *Qilu Press*

The burial mound and monument of Kong Li (Boyu) Confucius' son, beside his father's grave to the north of Qufu.
Photo: Jonathan Price

having displayed any signs of grief, and although he would have worn mourning robes he continued with his teaching and his work on the state archives.

Despite the loss of his son and the fact that he had no family around him, he was still looking forward to a peaceful and even happy old age surrounded by his books and his beloved students. The gods had other ideas in mind for him (he later made a famous outburst against heaven for causing all his misery) and there now began the most terrible period of Confucius' long life.

He had intended to pass on his school to Yan Hui, his beloved "son," whom he was sure would be his worthy successor. None of the other students seemed to resent this and all acknowledged Hui's brilliance. Having grown up in extreme poverty, Hui was a living symbol of Confucius' new world of equal opportunity, and his Master expected him to carry the torch for the succeeding generations. Still not quite thirty, Hui was around the age that Confucius himself had been when he started teaching. Unlike the others he had never wanted to take public office, was admired by all the students, and was also a very accomplished musician—several pieces written for the *guqin*, which was Confucius' own instrument, are traditionally attributed to Yan Hui. Who knew what he might achieve in the future?

Then, one day at the beginning of winter of the year 483, only a few months after Bo Yu's funeral, Yan Hui did not come to the school house—it was the first time that he had ever been known to miss any of Confucius' lessons. When he did not appear the following day or the next, his teacher sent one of the students to Yan Hui's house, which was on the outskirts of the city of Qufu, to enquire after him. When the student returned, it was with bad news: Yan Hui had succumbed to a fever and was very sick—the doctor did not expect him to recover. Confucius immediately set out in his old travelling wagon, but by the time he arrived at Yan Hui's humble house it was already too late—the young man had died in the early hours. When he heard the news Confucius screamed out loud:

"Heaven is killing me! Heaven is killing me!"

Analects, 11:9

Yan Hui had lived with his brother and his wife and family. His father, who had been among the first students of Confucius, had died some years previously. Their house was dilapidated and some of the walls of the outhouses were falling down. A few chickens pecked about in the yard and a goat grazed unconcernedly on a tether of rope while from inside the house echoed the sound of wailing and weeping. Yan Hui's brother came out, and begged Confucius to help them—they could not

Lavish funeral offerings: Examples of objects left in tombs from Confucius' time. Above: bronze funeral offerings from Spring and Autumn period, Shandong Museum. Below: *Ding* tripod (Early Warring States period), Shanghai Museum; *Photos: Jonathan Price*

The tomb of Yan Hui on the outskirts of Qufu. *Photo: Qilu Press*

even afford to give the younger son of their family a proper funeral.

When Yan Hui died, Yan Lu begged the carriage of the Master to sell and get an outer shell for his son's coffin.

Analects, 11:8

"Sell my travelling carriage?" Confucius hardly heard him. "Of course—but it is not necessary …" He put his hand on the brother's shoulder, and told him not to worry. The school would arrange the funeral, they would cover all the expenses. Confucius was not in fact sure whether their finances would enable them to do this, but he was sure that his business manager Zigong would be able to think of something.

When he got back to the school house Confucius told his followers the terrible news, and asked Zigong if he could drum up enough money for a proper funeral? No

problem, Zigong assured him. He would sell a few things—Yan Hui would have a funeral befitting a noble, because that what he was. Not by birth but by spirit. Confucius held up his hand for silence. "No. I want to bury him as my own son. Do it." The students murmured in protest. They could not do that. The Master was not his father; he had a family of his own, they would be bitterly offended. *"He was my son! Arrange it!"*

Confucius had buried his mother as his father, showed no sign of grief at the death of Kong Li only three months previously, and now he wanted to bury Yan Hui as his son. This flew against the conventional ordering of society to such an extent that for the first time his students rebelled. They knew the Master often had unconventional ideas, but this time he seemed to be going too far:

The temple of Yan Hui in Qufu. *Photo: Qilu Press*

When Yan Hui died, the Master wept uncontrollably. The disciples said, "Master, you are going overboard with this!"

Confucius said, "Going overboard?! If I can't cry now, when should I cry?"

Analects, 11:10

Zigong quickly came up with the money for the funeral and before Confucius could intervene, Yan Hui was given a sumptuous funeral as the son of his parents, with a pompous ceremony and burial gifts to place in the tomb as lavish as if he were the son of a lord. Yan Hui's family were naturally extremely happy, in fact everybody was happy except Confucius himself, who for the first and only time in his life railed in fury against his own students.

When Yan Hui died, the disciples wanted to give him a lavish funeral. The Master told them not to, but they did it anyway. Confucius said, "Hui treated me like a father. Now I have not been able to treat him as a son, and it is the fault of you students."

Analects, 11:11

He was against giving Hui a lavish funeral because the young man had lived poor and died poor in terms of material things, and had been proud of this. Zigong had auctioned off a few pieces of furniture and called in some debts (in the event they had not needed to sell the travelling-wagon) just so that some vulgar baubles could be placed in the tomb and Hui's family would not lose face. Mass-produced cast-bronze models of horses and chariots, crudely-painted tripod urns and cast-iron statuettes were popular burial gifts at this time, and funerals were an opportunity for a family ostentatiously to display their status—or lack of it. Zigong had even managed to afford an elaborately decorated outer shell for Yan Hui's coffin, as his brother had wanted.

Confucius felt that the students had capitulated to the material values of the time by sending off Hui in this way, something which the young man, who in life had despised displays of wealth, would never have wanted. He had intended putting only a copy of the *Book of Songs* into the tomb, and in his funeral oration he had wanted to tell the mourners that they were saying farewell to a prince among men, who had owned nothing but yet had possessed everything, who had always been poor yet was richer in spirit than all the kings of the world. Farewell to the prince of scholars, the best of men, the beloved younger brother of all the students—my son …

Instead Yan Hui departed on his journey to the afterlife accompanied by a cacophony of out-of-tune drums and pipes played by some hired musicians, with a collection of cheap trinkets balanced on top of the coffin in case he should lose face in the next world. Confucius did not speak to any of his followers for several days. Eventually Zigong came to apologize. "I don't want all that when my time comes," he told Zigong firmly.

"I would prefer dying in the streets [to a pompous funeral]!"

Analects, 9:12

The ailing Confucius refuses to accept medicine from Chancellor Ji Kangzi, fearing that it may be poisoned. Ming Dynasty Painting. *Qilu Press*

Zigong promised. When the time came—and he was sure it was a good few years off yet—they would bury the Master as their father. It would be simple and dignified. No vulgar music or cheap trinkets. He would not repeat his mistake, and he was very sorry. The Master accepted his apology.

Confucius was often ill that winter, and when the blossom appeared on the apricot trees outside the school house in the spring of the year 482 he showed no sign of regaining any of his old zest for life. The death of Yan

Hui seems to have felled him completely, and he no longer even wanted to talk very much. The gods had succeeded in doing what men had always failed to do—shut him up.

> **Confucius said: "I wish I could avoid talking."**
>
> **Zigong said, "Master, if you did not speak, what would we disciples have to pass on?"**
>
> *Analects*, 17:19

He occasionally had distinguished visitors—some of the *Analects* which record him speaking to Duke Ai and the prime minister Ji Kangzi clearly post-date the death of Hui. Although this indicates that he was highly respected in his old age, nevertheless he was never given any sort of honorary appointment, neither was his school officially acknowledged in any way. In the eyes of those in power he had conveniently become a harmless old man. All he seemed to want to talk about was the tragic passing of his best student:

> **Ji Kangzi asked which of the disciples loved to learn.**
>
> **Confucius replied: "Yan Hui did. Unfortunately he died young, and there has never been anyone like him."**
>
> *Analects*, 11:7
>
> **The Duke Ai asked which disciple loved to study. Confucius answered: "There was Yan Hui. I have not yet met anyone who loves to study the way he did."**
>
> *Analects*, 6:3

Confucius once again devotes his time to editing the great classics. Ming Dynasty painting. *Qilu Press*

Although he tried to keep on with his teaching and his work on the records of Lu, Confucius was still bowed down with grief over the loss of Hui and the following autumn he fell ill again, this time more seriously. Ji Kangzi came to his house with a gift of medicine. Confucius refused the gift, fearing it was poisoned. It was a sad moment, for Ji Kangzi sincerely admired him.

Ji Kang having sent him a present of physic, he bowed and received it, saying, "I do not know it. I dare not taste it."

Analects, 10:16

Zilu came too, very worried about his Master, and for a little while his students feared he might die.

The Master was very sick, and Zilu said that he would pray for him.

Confucius said, "Is there such a thing?"

Analects, 7:35

This curious little riposte seems to indicate that even at the end of his life Confucius was not a religious man in the sense that many of his contemporaries were, and still did not believe that Heaven heard prayers or answered them. If this was to be his time, then so be it; no amount of prayers to the Almighty were going to give him an extension. He closed his eyes and seemed to be fading. Weeping, Zilu told his old teacher that for all of them he was the true leader of the country, he was still the acting chancellor of Lu, he had never been formally

Zilu, killed in a coup in the State of Wei, 480BC. Confucius Temple, Nanjing.
Photo: Jonathan Price

dismissed and they were not just his students, they were his ministers!

The Master was extremely ill, and Zilu wanted the disciples to become Confucius' "ministers."

Analects, 9:12

Confucius opened his eyes and smiled sadly.

Confucius, during a remission in his illness, said, "Ah, Yu has been deceitful for a long time. Though I don't have ministers, you would make it appear that I have them? Who would I be fooling? Heaven? I would much rather die in the hands of my students than in the hands of ministers."

Analects, 9:12

This passage is always cited as the strongest evidence we have that Confucius was totally estranged from his own family, and had been for many years. Most people would express the wish to die quietly at home with their family, yet there is no mention of his wife (if she was still alive) or of his son's family who bore his name and had given him a grandson. It was always the students.

As it turned out this was not to be his time after all, and all the disciples were very happy when their Master seemed to make a partial recovery, and even regained some of his old energy. This was because something happened which took his mind off his incessant brooding over the tragic loss of Yan Hui, and gave him a reason to get out of his bed in the morning: for the last time he became involved in politics.

Eight years earlier his old friend and student, Duke Jing of Qi (the aficionado of barbarian dancing) had died, and had been buried together with 600 of his horses and chariots underneath what is now the expressway between Beijing and the seaside resort of Qingdao, site of the sailing events for the 2008 Olympic Games. Duke Jing had been succeeded by his cousin Jian, but as always across the Warring States, the death of a ruler signalled a fierce struggle for power among the feudal barons. Qi was no exception and in the year 481, two years before Confucius' death, Duke Jian was assassinated and a warlord, Chen Heng, took power.

Confucius, who always insisted that the states should be nominally under the old Zhou Empire and usurpers be prevented from taking power, felt unable to remain silent despite the ban on his acting politically and requested an audience with Duke Ai in order to press for

Monument and burial mound of Zilu – Confucius oldest and most loyal disciple.
Photo: Qilu Press

Little Zisi visiting his elderly grandfather Confucius. Detail from Ming Dynasty painting. *Qilu Press*

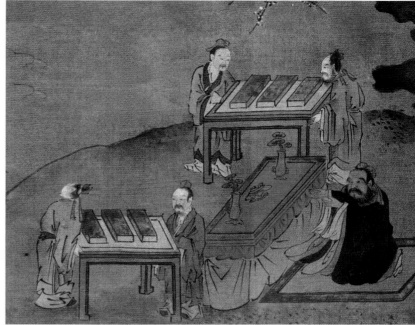

Confucius has strange visions just before his death. Ming Dynasty painting. *Qilu Press*

intervention by the other states.

> **Chen Heng murdered the Duke Jian of Qi.**
> **Confucius bathed, went to court and informed the Duke Ai, saying: "Chen Heng has slain his ruler. I beg that you will undertake to punish him."**
> **The Duke said, "Inform the chiefs of the three families of it."**
> **He went to the chiefs, and informed them, but they would not act.**
> **Confucius retired.**
>
> *Analects*, 14:21

Still in fear of his life, Confucius had known that as always nobody would take any notice of him. Might was right, that was the way of the world, but Confucius had felt obliged to stand out against it one last time. Tired and disillusioned, he went back to work on the dusty state records; clearly it was now only as a humble archivist that he was allowed to play any sort of role in government.

According to Sima Qian in the *Records of the Grand Historian*, he completed his work on the state records of Lu (the *Spring and Autumn Annals*) in the autumn of that year, 481 BC, bringing them right up to date until the current year which was the fourteenth of Duke Ai. Despite the weariness and sadness of his last years, Confucius seems to have retained something of his old sense of humor. After completing the *Annals* he told his students with an arch smile that the previous annalist had used the word "king" to describe the rulers of Lu, all the way from "King Yin" in 722 BC until the present

"King Ai," and had also referred to the feudal lords as "princes." Confucius had taken the liberty of replacing all entries referring to the "kings" of Lu with the word "duke," and had demoted the warlords from "princes" to "barons."

His student Hsia, who was now a scholar and author in his own right, had checked the whole of Confucius' manuscript, and told the others he was in full agreement with these changes. "Hear, hear!" the rest of the students echoed. Not only this, the Master told them, his predecessor had described their current ineffective ruler—who that year had weakly capitulated to the nobles when Confucius had urged intervention after the assassination in Qi—as "Great King Ai the Unique One." "Outrageous!" Zigong snorted.

> Zigong said: "If a territorial prince calls himself by the designation of the Great King, he is in love with his own greatness! The 'Unique One'—that is not the correct name. This Duke will surely not die a peaceful death in his land of Lu!"
>
> Sima Qian, *Records of the Grand Historian*

Have no fear, Confucius told him with another arch smile. In the copy of the *Spring and Autumn Annals* which would be deposited in the archive and handed down to posterity, he had also taken the liberty of replacing "Great King Ai the Unique One" with the words: "Duke Ai the Lamentable." The students burst into hearty applause. Sometimes the pen is mightier than the sword, and it is indeed coupled with the appellation "lamentable" that Duke Ai's name has been passed

Eternal rebirth: Wood carving of Phoenix on the Altar of Confucius' wife, Qufu. *Photo: Jonathan Price*

down through the ages. If Confucius did prepare these records, he had truly taken his revenge.

With the Master apparently almost back to his usual self, Zilu now announced that he had received an urgent request for help from the Duke of Wei, who was having the usual trouble with his own feudal warlords. So far Duke Che of Wei had been luckier than the unfortunate Duke of Qi and had already survived one assassination attempt, but he needed supporters whom he could trust. Would the Master and his loyal team please consider returning to Wei as a matter of the utmost urgency? The Master shook his head. He was tired now.

Confucius said: "It's all over! I have not yet met anybody who can see his own faults and correct them within himself."

Analects, 5:27

Zilu turned to Zigong, who shook his head too. Zigong had made a solemn promise to his Master to supervise the arrangements for his funeral. Although they all hoped he had several more years left to him, Confucius would celebrate his seventieth birthday very shortly, and "three-score years and ten" was indeed a venerable age at a time when most people died much earlier.

Symbol of longevity: the legendary turtle Bixi carrying a heavy stone inscription on his back for all eternity. The Qingshou Stele, Qufu. *Qilu Press*

Zilu, however, decided to go. A few days later he said his farewells. Confucius took his hand and wished him luck. He had wanted his oldest and most faithful student to stay till the end which, he knew in his heart of hearts, would not be far off. He said nothing, however, for Zilu had always dreamed of making some sort of heroic stand in defense of liberty, and having already passed the age of sixty he would never get another chance like this. By the time he returned, hero or not, Confucius was not sure that he himself would still be there to greet him.

Zilu embraced Zigong, then all the other leading disciples he had known for so long, and finally his master; and he was gone. None of them would ever see him again.

The gods had still not yet finished with Confucius. In the summer of the following year (480 BC) heaven delivered him another near-fatal blow—he heard the news that Zilu had been killed in Wei. Confucius' impetuous and enthusiastic former student had spent the winter trying to help the Duke of Wei organize things in his state, but the next year the warlords had finally judged that the moment was right and staged their long-awaited coup. Zilu had died on the ramparts defending the capital. Finally at the age of sixty-four Yu had become the hero he had always dreamed of being—but ultimately for nothing because the Duke too was killed and the coup was successful.

Confucius could not believe it. His own time had come—why were the gods letting him live on like this while they callously snatched away all his most faithful followers?

Poor Zilu—they had known each other for more than forty years. Long ago Confucius had predicted this, and had said: "Yu will not die a natural death." He should have prevented him from going to Wei, he could see that now. His most enthusiastic student had always been the same—rushing into things without thinking. Zilu, who as a young man had often left his lute outside Confucius' door so that he would trip over it; Zilu who had accompanied him during all the long years of exile, who had criticized him, shouted at him sometimes, who had often been infuriating but had always been so loyal and so full of life. Zilu, like Hui, was gone.

Confucius tried to continue teaching, but his heart was not in it any more. During the last autumn of his life Confucius is supposed to have been cared for by his son's surviving family, and little Zisi his grandson cut firewood to keep his old grandfather warm through the coming winter.

Before spring came the following year, and while it was still bitterly cold, Confucius became seriously ill, and his followers began to fear that this really was the end. Zigong was away on business, so Confucius sent a messenger to ask him to come. He wanted to say goodbye—Zigong was now the only surviving member of the group of wandering scholars who had accompanied him during his exile; Zigong was the only family he had left.

The other students gathered at his bedside, hoping to hear some final words of wisdom.

Zengzi said, "When a bird is about to die, its song is melancholy. When a man is about to die, his words are excellent."

Analects, 8:4

The Master did manage a few last words of exhortation, which Zengzi dutifully wrote down and included in the *Analects*:

Confucius said: "Be of unwavering good faith and love learning. Be steadfast unto death in pursuit of the good Way."

Analects, 8:13

More often than not, however, they were disappointed, and during his last days the Master either slept or said strange things in a semi-delirious state:

Confucius said: "The Phoenix has not come, a chart [i.e. the shell of a giant turtle] has not come out of the Yellow River. Alas, I am finished."

Analects, 9:8

The phoenix was the legendary bird common in many cultures which is reborn in fire, while the turtle Bixi in Chinese mythology carried the world on his back. The markings on the shell of a turtle resemble a "map of the world," and Confucius's hearers would have understood what he was babbling about. To dream of these mythical creatures was an auspicious sign, but Confucius now dreamed only of coffins lying on the steps of temples and knew that his time had come.

At last Zigong returned from his business trip and hurried to his Master's house.

Confucius was ill. Zigong asked permission to visit him. Then Confucius walked back and forth in the courtyard, supporting himself on his staff, and said: "Si, why are you so late?" Then Confucius sighed and sang:
"The Sacred Mountain Tai is crumbling
The Roof beam is rotting
The Sage is withering."

Sima Qian, *Records of the Grand Historian*

Both men wept. Then Confucius stopped singing, and turned to Zigong, shaking his head. "No one understood how to follow me…"

"I will follow you Master. All of us, we understand, we will follow you…"

"Do you know," Confucius said slowly, "the people of Zhou used to place the coffin on the west steps, but the people of Yin placed it between the two pillars, on the front porch. Last night I dreamed I was lying between two pillars." He placed an arm on Zigong's shoulder and even managed a ghost of his old smile. "Does that mean that after all I am a man of Yin?"

"Master, you are neither a man of Zhou nor a man of Yin nor of any other place. You are a man for all time and all places."

Seven days later, Confucius died. Confucius had attained an age of seventy-three years, when he died, in the fourth month of the sixteenth year of Duke Ai of Lu [479 BC].

Sima Qian, *Records of the Grand Historian*

Confucius' final farewell to his devoted disciple Zigong. Ming Dynasty painting. *Qilu Press*

~The Phoenix Rises~

Confucius was buried by his students near the River Si, a little way north from the site of his school. As he had promised, Zigong took charge of the funeral and it was simple and dignified, with all the students taking part following the prescribed ritual for the death of the father of a family.

There was no official funeral or parade of the coffin through the streets of the capital, as would have been expected for a former minister. Officially, there was absolute silence, and there is also no record that any members of Confucius' family attended the funeral. Although the Kong family, his descendants through his son Bo Yu, jumped onto the bandwagon with a vengeance much later when Confucius began to be revered, at the time of his death they appear to have shared the official line that the so-called sage was simply an obscure teacher who had been an embarrassment to all right-thinking people.

In an attempt to shame the establishment into making some sort of official tribute, Zigong constructed a hut for himself beside Confucius' grave, and declared that he would stay there until the government erected a suitable monument. All the students visited the grave every day, pledging to continue to do this for the full three-year mourning period.

After a year had passed and the government had still done nothing to recognize Confucius' passing, Zigong decided that the time for quiet and dignified mourning was over, and something more spectacular was called for. Accordingly, on the first anniversary of Confucius' death, he organized a huge memorial banquet at the burial site, which included funeral games and an archery contest, as if Confucius had been a deceased head of state. Zigong paid for all this himself; he had been very successful in business in recent years and now used his considerable fortune to mount a massive public relations campaign on behalf of his dead Master.

Zigong was an astute businessman and knew that free food always guarantees the success of a PR bash; according to Sima Qian the funeral banquet attracted hundreds of people. Several more huts and booths were

Confucius' grave: the burial mound and memorial stele in the 'Confucius forest', to the north of Qufu.
Photo: Qilu Press

The students in mourning for their Master: Zigong seen on left inside the hut he built beside the grave. Ming Dynasty painting. *Qilu Press*

Funeral rites: Confucius' surviving students gather around the burial mound to honour their Master. Zigong inside his hut on left. Ming Dynasty painting. *Qilu Press*

erected beside Zigong's temporary dwelling to accommodate all the guests, forming a little village which later became known as the "hamlet of Confucius." All the students participated in the archery contest, drinking a ceremonial cup before their turn came and offering the lees as a sacrifice to their Master. The event was such a sensation that many people began openly murmuring that it was disgraceful that neither the Duke nor any of his ministers had attended, and finally Duke Ai was forced to make some sort of statement.

Better late than never, the Duke finally capitulated and had a modest memorial to Confucius erected near the site of his school, making a pompous and boring speech at the opening ceremony, which he delivered in the form of an ode accompanied by music:

"Merciful Heaven, have you no compassion?
The elderly sage who alone can advise me is gone!
Who can protect me now?
I, the Great and Unique One am truly alone!
Full of mourning am I in my pain! O woe!
Now I no longer have any one who can serve for me as a model."

Quoted by Sima Qian, *Records of the Grand Historian*

Zigong turned to the other students and muttered "This man is full of shit ..." (Sima Qian records him as saying rather more decorously: "He is besotted."). After never taking the slightest heed of Confucius while he was alive

he was now claiming the old man was his "model." At least the Master now had a monument, which was a step in the right direction. Duke Ai's memorial eventually became the focus for the huge Confucius Temple complex which still stands today, although the original

The 'Confucius forest', now a huge grave-site containing the tombs of the Kong family down the centuries. The original trees are said to have been planted by his students using seedlings brought from their home villages. *Photo: Qilu Press*

"The Zigong tree" near the site of his hut, immediately in front of Confucius' tomb in Qufu. This is supposed to be the actual tree planted 2500 years ago by Zigong in honour of his Master. *Photo: Jonathan Price*

government and official positions. Zigong alone remained living in his hut beside Confucius' grave for another three years. After remaining in mourning for a total of six years, and organizing annual memorial events at the graveside which became ever more popular, Zigong was satisfied that the memory of his former Master was being held in suitable reverence, and resumed his own life. The tradition of offering yearly sacrifices to the memory of Confucius, which was astutely started by Zigong, continued for thousands of years and the ceremonies are still held in Qufu to this day. The site of Zigong's hut beside the grave may still be seen, together with the gnarled remains of an ancient tree said to have been planted by Zigong himself.

After his success as a diplomat a few years earlier while the Master was still alive, Zigong became highly respected in this field, and a few years later managed to avert an all-out war between the states of Qi, Lu, and Wei. His Master's anthem (echoed by John Lennon thousands of years later) had always been "Give peace a chance," and in a tireless round of shuttle-diplomacy Zigong travelled from one capital to the next and finally negotiated a compromise. Once again, war was averted and hundreds of thousands of innocent lives were saved; there were very few triumphs of Confucius' ideals in his own time and most of them were down to the efforts of his former student Zigong. Unlike the others he wrote no books containing the Master's sayings and ideas; instead he tried to put those ideas into action. Confucius' cocky and talkative student, who became his business manager, public relations consultant, and finally a peacemaker, simply refused to let the memory of his Master die, and if Confucius proved to be a phoenix who truly rose again burning even brighter, it was Zigong who lit the flame.

The other "disciples" were already busy writing down their reminiscences of the Master, and there shortly appeared bamboo-slip volumes entitled *The Book of Zengzi* and *The Book of Zhonggong*, containing many of the sayings of Confucius that would later be incorporated into the *Analects*.

About ten years after Confucius' death his grandson Zisi became a pupil of Zengzi, almost certainly against the wishes of his relatives who had continued to ignore the "sage" side of the family. Zisi later took over the school which became known as "The School of Zisi," and himself wrote a large number of books, which attempted to impose some sort of system on his grandfather's often random and haphazard ideas. Zisi's work helped immeasurably in popularizing Confucius'

building disappeared long ago. The students are also supposed to have planted trees around Confucius' grave, with seedlings taken from their respective homes, and these formed the beginning of what is now the "Confucius Forest," a beautifully preserved woodland area which still surrounds the site of his burial mound, and where all his descendants are also buried.

After the three-year mourning period was up, all the students except Zigong resumed their lives. Zengzi re-opened the school, Hsia and Zhonggong busied themselves with scholarship and gave lessons of their own, while other former students returned to

Resting in peace: grave mounds in the 'Confucius forest' where his immediate descendants lie buried near their illustrious forbear. *Photo: Jonathan Price*

ideas—bamboo-slip copies of his books have been found in many tombs from the period and he was referred to many times by other Confucian writers who had obviously read everything he wrote. However, the distortion of Confucius' ideas which ended up as orthodox Confucianism many centuries later could be said to have been initiated, although unwittingly, by his grandson.

This is mainly because Confucius' ideas do not lend themselves readily to being incorporated into a coherent system, and when one attempts to do this then one or other of his concepts will be emphasized over the others and inevitably a distorted view of his general philosophy will emerge that owes more to the interpreter's ideas than Confucius himself. For example Confucius almost never explicitly stated what was right and what was wrong—he expects us to know that. Once you start making lists of rights and wrongs you simply get bogged down in detail and lose the thread:

> Confucius said: "My Way is penetrated by a single thread."
>
> Zengzi said, "Yes."
>
> When the Master left, some disciples asked what he meant. Zengzi said, "Our master's Way is to be sincere and fair, and that's it."
>
> *Analects*, 4:15

Nothing could be simpler, as Zengzi, Zisi's tutor had said. Even simpler is the so-called "golden rule":

> "What you don't want done to yourself, don't do to others."
>
> *Analects*, 12:2

Even a five-year-old child is capable of understanding this; there is no need for volumes of interpretation or a PhD in philosophy to grasp the idea. Zengzi himself wrote a work called *Da Xue* (*The Great Learning*) which is often credited to Confucius, although it is highly unlikely that he left any written works about his ideas. *The Great Learning* summarizes Confucius' idea that the goal of human existence is world peace, and that this cannot be achieved by the intercession of gods but by our own behavior, starting with kindness to our family and extending all the way up to the duty of rulers to govern humanely. This "book" must be the shortest ever written, occupying little more than one page of a modern printed volume or a few bamboo strips in ancient times,

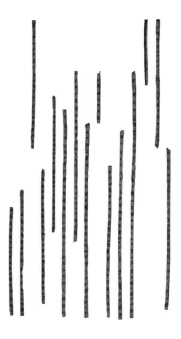

Writing down the legacy: This 4th Century B.C. bamboo-slip manuscript now in the Shanghai Museum collection is a transcription of reminiscences by various disciples entitled 'Students' questions to Confucius'. These works later became the basis for the 'Analects' which appeared several hundred years later. *Photo courtesy Shanghai Museum*

The tomb of Zigong. *Photo: Qilu Press*

Zisi, Confucius' grandson and leading champion in the next generation. Statue in Confucius Temple, Nanjing. *Photo: Jonathan Price*

Zengzi, the youngest of Confucius' major disciples, wrote many "Confucian" texts after his Master's death. *Photo: Jonathan Price*

Unfortunately human beings always seem to crave explicit rules, and most people appear to have an innate aversion to taking responsibility for their own actions, which is what Confucius said we all have to do, all the time. As a result a huge industry arose over the centuries which ground up Confucius' 492 known sayings and kept spewing them out as sets of rules, and his grandson Zisi really started all this.

Zisi's first "system" was what he called the "Five Principles of Confucius" ("*Wu Xing*") and listed them as:

1. Humanity (*Ren*)
2. Appropriate behavior (*Yi*)
3. Observance of ritual (*Li*)
4. Wisdom and knowledge (*Zhi*)
5. Sagacity in Decisions (*Sheng*)

This is all very fine as far as it goes, but begs the question—why write a book about it? Zengzi wrote one page called *The Great Learning* and in his own words "that's it." Starting with Zisi, and for thousands of years since, people have been writing very long books purporting to "explain" Confucius' philosophy, and yet they are all so many wasted words—millions and millions of them—since Confucius' ideas simply do not need to be explained, the difficulty is not in understanding them but acting upon them.

Zisi is also credited with inventing the idea known as the "Doctrine of the Mean," or system of the "middle way" which is now attributed to Confucius as one of his main ideas although he said almost nothing about this in the *Analects*. The couple of times he does mention the idea are in fact pieces of advice about management:

> **Zigong asked who was the most worthy between Shi and Shang (Hsia).**
>
> **The Master said, "Shi goes too far, Shang does not go far enough."**
>
> **"Then is Shi superior?"**
>
> **The Master said, "Going too far is the same as not going far enough."**
>
> *Analects*, 11:16

> **Confucius said: "Since I can't get men who act according to the middle way, I must find the unrestrained and the cautious. The unrestrained go after things regardless, the cautious restrain themselves from doing certain things."**
>
> *Analects*, 13:21

Once again, this advice is fine, especially when making up a team to tackle a specific task—but why write a whole book about it? This is a question which has never deterred a determined scholar, however, and the Confucius industry was well under way only a few

yet it encapsulates the main idea of Confucius' whole philosophy. Zengzi, unlike those who followed him, understood that his Master's teachings did not need volumes of exposition but were breathtakingly simple to understand.

Zengzi was right, Confucianism is not a moral or philosophical system, it is a simple Way—and everything he said can be seen as a guide to following that Way. Confucius was convinced that the more people tried to follow this Way, the better the world would become, but he was always at great pains to emphasize that there were no "rules," only general principles (like the "golden rule") which we apply to each situation. This is what he meant when he said:

> **"The human being manifests the Way. The Way doesn't manifest the human being."**
>
> *Analects*, 15:28

The tomb of Confucius' grandson and ardent supporter Zisi (Kong Ji), who lies just beside his grandfather in the Qufu burial forest of the Kong family. *Photo: Jonathan Price*

years after his death. On the evidence of the bamboo-slip manuscripts so far discovered, former students Zengzi, Zhonggong, and Zixia led the field, followed by other lesser "disciples" like Zigao and Ziyou and of course grandson Zisi, brushing furiously onto their strips of bamboo with such enthusiasm that in only a few years millions of characters on the subject of Confucius had been produced, only a small proportion of which represented the biographical material and transcriptions of dialogues which make up the *Analects*.

Zigong, who distanced himself from all this scholarly activity, would have said quite simply, why write a book about it—just do it. Indeed he was the only one of the surviving disciples who actually succeeded in changing anything. Had Zhonggong or Zixia ever asked him, "How many words have you written today?" Zigong could have simply replied, "How many lives have you saved? I just stopped a war." Which of them would Confucius have approved of the most? The scholar-disciples, though admirable for having preserved their Master's words, seem to have forgotten his celebrated remark:

> **"A man… may discourse profoundly but is he really a Superior Man?"**
>
> *Analects*, 11:21

Zigong did find time to pen the occasional work and a manuscript attributed to him dealing with the political history of the state of Wei is now among the Shanghai Museum's bamboo-slip collections. Alone among the disciples the indefatigable Zigong was a doer as well as a writer; all the others were merely writers and although the pen is said to be mightier than the sword, their scrawling had very little effect on the world around them. One hundred and fifty years later, despite the avalanche of bamboo manuscripts, which were piling up in tombs all over the place full of profound pseudo-Confucian theories like the "Doctrine of the Mean," the world had not changed one iota and Mencius, who attempted to emulate his idol Confucius in the late

Millions of words: This bamboo-slip manuscript entitled 'On Character' is one of the hundreds of works produced shortly after Confucius' death which amplified and interpreted his ideas and became the basis for the 'Doctrine of Confucianism'. Now in the Shanghai Museum Bamboo-Slip collection. *Photo courtesy Shanghai Museum*

Mencius (372-289 B.C.) one of the major Chinese philosophers, who championed and reinterpreted Confucius' teachings a century after he died. Statue in Confucius Temple,
Nanjing. *Photo: Jonathan Price*

fourth century BC in exactly the same area, bewailed the
fact that everything the Master had said was wrong with
society—the killing, feuding, and extortion—had
actually got worse in the intervening years.

To give him his due, Mencius, who was born in a very
small state adjoining Lu, did make some attempt to have
the ideas of his idol Confucius put into concrete action,
but he appears to have been as unsuccessful as his
Master. He did enjoy a few months like Confucius as an
advisor in the state of Qi, but resigned in protest and
spent the rest of his life railing against the rulers of his
time. His major work, the *Book of Mencius*, is basically a
complement to the ideas of the man he called the "Great
Master," which amplifies and explains Confucius'
thoughts and also includes some biographical snippets
that do not appear in any other sources, many of which
have already been quoted. Mencius is supposed to have
been a student in the "School of Zisi"—not of Zisi
himself, who would have died many years before he was
born, but one of his successors.

Mencius was an important thinker in his own right,
and was the first known person in China to speak out on
environmental issues, a topic Confucius never discussed.
Mencius protested against the over-logging of forests,
but naturally nobody listened, and today there are no
almost no trees left in the area where he lived:

> Mencius said, "The greenery on Niu Mountain
> was once beautiful, but since it was near a large
> city, it was attacked by loggers … if people saw
> this barrenness, they might have imagined that
> there had never been any greenery. How could the

mountain be naturally like this?"

Book of Mencius, 6A:8

Like his illustrious predecessor Mencius was
thousands of years ahead of his time in many respects.
He set out to be mainly a publicist for Confucius' ideas
rather than an interpreter, claiming to be only a
"transmitter" of his ideals to posterity, much as
Confucius himself had said he was doing for the wisdom
of the ancient Zhou, and Mencius was very influential
in spreading Confucius' ideas. The disciples and Zisi had
concentrated on specific topics, and the first collection
of all Confucius' known sayings did not appear for
another 200 years, so Mencius' book was in fact the first
comprehensive attempt to summarize the whole body
of his thought. However, in attempting to present his
idol in the best possible light, Mencius started the
tradition of portraying Confucius as a saint or sage who
could do no wrong:

> "Since the beginning of human existence, there
> has never been anyone like Confucius."

Book of Mencius, Part 1, Chapter 2:23

At one point in the book he claims that Confucius could
have been made the sovereign of the whole Zhou
Empire, but declined on the grounds he was not
descended from the line of kings.

> "It was on this account that Confucius did not
> obtain the throne."

Book of Mencius, Book 5, Part 1, Chapter 7:3

This is obviously ridiculous—we know that Confucius
was never in line for any kind of throne and in fact was
hounded from state to state in fear of his life, but
Mencius' idolatry eventually led to Confucius' literal
canonization and then deification, which changed him
from an exceptional human being trying to do his best
into a deity dispensing commandments (usually written
by other people) from on high. This was ultimately very
unfortunate because when Confucius was finally
dethroned from his position as a god in the early
twentieth century all the other useful advice he had for
us as a mere man was thrown out as well, although he
does seem to be making one of his many comebacks as
the new century gets under way.

More seriously, Mencius was something of a snob and
a male chauvinist, and he transmitted these attitudes to
posterity along with Confucius' true ideas about
everything else. It will be remembered that Mencius
claimed that Confucius could not possibly have lived
with a "doctor" (a member of the lower classes) and it
was Mencius not Confucius who said that wives should
obey their husbands, an idea which from his time

onward slipped into the received precepts of Confucianism. Historically, however, the most disastrous effect Mencius had on the development of Confucius' ideas was his behavioral theory.

Mencius was more of an analytical thinker than his Master and could see the possible flaw in Confucius' thinking which has already been mentioned in connection with his ideas about the family—if parents are to be unquestionably obeyed then all parents must by nature have their children's welfare at heart. Confucius never said this but appears to have assumed this was the case. By the same token, if criminals and others can be shamed out of wrongdoing by examples of goodness around them as Confucius claimed, human beings must not only be able to recognize innate goodness but be innately good. Again, Confucius did not specifically state this but going by a couple of things he said he seems to have believed that as infants we are all basically the same and acquire bad habits from our surroundings as we grow up:

Confucius said: "People are straightforward at birth. Once they lose this, they rely on luck to avoid trouble."

Analects, 6:19

Confucius said: "People are similar by nature, but through habituation become quite different from each other."

Analects, 17:2

Thus at any time in our lives we should be able to recognize we are doing wrong and return to the "straightforward" innocence of childhood, and this was the basis for his theory of self-correction through shame:

"If you govern people legalistically and control them by punishment, they will avoid crime, but have no personal sense of shame. If you govern them by means of virtue they will gain their own sense of shame, and thus correct themselves."

Analects, 2:3

Many people on hearing this would agree that this might well apply to most individuals, but what about people who have no sense of shame?

Apparently nobody ever pointed this out to Confucius, but they certainly did to Mencius, and in his book he records how he defended the old Master's idea to some skeptics:

"Everyone has the sense of shame and disgust at their own evil! Everyone has the sense of right and wrong! They are our original endowments—you have really not thought it through, have you?"

Book of Mencius, Book 2, Part 1, Chapter 6

Although nowadays we do not believe this to be true, and call individuals who do not have this sense of shame psychopaths (some of whom end up ruling whole countries), Mencius lived in a more innocent age and felt obliged to declare that the innate goodness of all human beings had to be adopted as a matter of faith by all Confucians.

Mencius said: "When I say human beings are inherently good, I am talking about their most fundamental emotional qualities. If someone does evil, it is not the fault of their natural inheritance."

Book of Mencius, Book 2 Part 1 Chapter 6:6

To prove that innate goodness is an irrefutable fact Mencius used his famous example of a baby who has fallen down a well. Which of us, even the most hardened, would not rush to help after hearing the piteous cries from the bottom of the well, he argues? We would do this neither for hope of reward nor because we fear censure if we do nothing, but simply because we are *good*.

This is one of the oldest questions in the world and people are still arguing hotly about it, but it is unfortunate that Mencius started to turn Confucianism into a doctrine at such an early stage since intellectuals at this time were keener on arguing about doctrinal questions than actually doing anything to help anybody. Confucius' main philosophy was primarily a recipe for action; instead his ideas became mired in pointless debates about nature versus nurture.

As he said himself, the *junzi*—the "Superior Person"—does not get involved in doctrinal controversies or have preformed ideas about anything:

Confucius said: "The Superior Person is not prejudiced for or against anything. The Superior Person does what is Right."

Analects, 4:10

While his supporters argued about the existence or otherwise of innate goodness, another idea was waiting in the wings—the rule of law. Confucius had said that governing people legalistically did not attack the root causes of crime, which may well be true to a large extent, but his opponents maintained that the only thing hardened criminals understood was a damn good thrashing or the threat of beheading. This idea (still very familiar today) was known at the time as Legalism, which did eventually triumph under the rule of the first Emperor, Shi Huangdi, but only for a very short period.

The third century BC in China was a period of often savage debate on these issues. The Legalists argued that only strict laws could control the innate savagery of mankind; the Confucians screamed that if rulers set a good example their citizens would necessarily follow since all humans were basically good; the Daoists held that there was no such thing as good and evil anyway and we should simply drop out and tune in to the cosmos; another school called Mohism opposed music, dancing, and all forms of licentious behavior claiming they were the root of all evil (like the Puritans in England and America 2,000 years later) and sought the answer to the questions of existence in scientific enquiry and logic.

In fact Confucianism was not named as such in China at this time but was known as "Ruism." The origin of this word is obscure and has never been satisfactorily explained, but basically the Ruists claimed to propound Confucius' ideas. It is perhaps significant that they did not use Confucius' name and very quickly Confucianism—or Ruism—had very little to do with the Master's original ideas; it was Ruism rather than true Confucianism that came to dominate China over the next 2,000 years.

What is remarkable is that the intellectual arguments in China at this time, petty though they might have been, pre-dated the equivalent debates in Europe by almost two millennia. While Confucius and Mencius with their concept of innate goodness are aligned with the ideas Rousseau propounded in the 1770s, Daoism came into its own in the 1970s and became extremely popular with the hippie generation. Even more amazingly the Mohists (followers of an obscure sage called Mo Zi about whom nothing is known) were violently opposed to the Confucians because their leader had never asked any scientific questions, but apparently came up with the First Law of Motion 2,000 years before Newton:

"The cessation of motion is due to the opposing force. If there is no opposing force, the motion will never stop. This is as true as that an ox is not a horse."

Mo Jing (*Book of Mo*), fourth century BC

If they had only all settled their differences and stopped squabbling, a truly monumental philosophy might have emerged, but as it was all they did was argue—not only with the opposing schools but with each other. Within each school, whether they were Ruists, Daoists, Mohists, or Legalists, the fanatics attacked erring followers of their own creed with even more savagery than they attacked their opponents. A prime example of this was Xun Kuang (310?–238 BC), known through his (voluminous) writings as Xunzi (Master Xun), a Confucian of the next generation to Mencius who felt obliged to attack his predecessors and

The 'Terracotta Warriors'. Some members of the 8000-strong 'model army' of the Emperor Shi Huangdi, buried with him in his mausoleum in ancient Chang'an (Xian), capital of the Qin Dynasty. *Qilu Press*

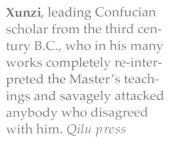

Xunzi, leading Confucian scholar from the third century B.C., who in his many works completely re-interpreted the Master's teachings and savagely attacked anybody who disagreed with him. *Qilu press*

Ying Zheng (259-210 B.C.) who styled himself Shi Huangdi, first emperor of the united China which replaced the old Zhou Dynasty with its collection of autonomous states. *Qilu Press*

Those who today are called "scholars" are base and reckless, given to villainy and anarchy, to self-indulgence and excesses of passion, and to sheer greed … their manner is insolent and rude … such are the base Ru [Confucians] of the school of Zixia [Hsia—a disciple of Confucius].

Xunzi: *Against Twelve Philosophers*

After demolishing all rivals Xunzi then got down to his own take on Confucius, which was that Mencius was "false" because human beings were inherently greedy, selfish, and evil, and therefore Confucianism is a struggle to overcome our inner demons rather than a quest to liberate the inner sage. Whereas Confucius and Mencius had anticipated Rousseau in their belief in innate goodness, Xunzi was the Thomas Hobbes of the third century BC (mankind is "nasty and brutish") and he directed Confucianism away from its idealistic basis towards the idea that, whereas the ruling class should devote themselves to perfecting themselves as "gentlemen," as far as the lower orders are concerned flogging and hanging is the only way to go if all else fails. Although Xunzi no doubt meant well and the "base Confucians" of his time were no doubt as villainous and self-indulgent as he claimed, clearly Confucius' ideals were being totally distorted only 200 years after he died, and this process was to continue for another 2,000 years.

Xunzi was appointed a professor in Linzi, the capital of the state of Qi, where Confucius himself had spent many years. It will be remembered that the ruling dynasty in Qi took power by assassinating the current ruler while Confucius was still alive—their successors

contemporaries viciously before propounding his own theories. In his work entitled *Against Twelve Philosophers* the savagery of his vitriol almost beggars belief, but it is directed not at rival schools, as might be expected, but at several of Confucius' disciples and followers including Mencius and almost all the fellow-Confucian scholars of his own time:

> The scholars of today claim their doctrines represent the genuine words of the gentleman of former times [Confucius]. Zisi provided the tune for them, and Mencius harmonized it. The stupid, indecisive, deluded Ru [Confucians] of today enthusiastically welcome these notions unaware that they are false.

The whirlwind from the west: the invincible Qin cavalry. Pottery figures from Qin Dynasty, Museum of Chariots, Linzi. *Photo: Jonathan Price*

The technological breakthrough that changed the world: iron stirrups plated with gold from the Qin Dynasty. Capital Museum Beijing. *Photo: Jonathan Price*

found it good PR to sponsor a university called the Jixia Academy at which Xunzi was the leading light. Xunzi wrote a huge work about Confucius called the *Book of Xunzi* which was ten times longer than the *Analects*. Included in this work was a long treatise called the *Zhenming—Rectification of Names*—based on the single saying of Confucius in which he had said that "terminology" was crucial to the administration of a state. What he had meant was that a ruler should be specific about the goals he wanted to achieve. Xunzi re-interpreted this to mean that everybody should know their place and do exactly what they are told in order to achieve the ruler's wishes. This was exactly what the authoritarian rulers of the time wanted to hear. He also expounded on the "Doctrine of the Mean," which was an idea of Confucius' grandson Zisi rather than Confucius anyway, and this eventually emerged as the "Doctrine of Mediocrity"—promote the middling, ignore the brilliant, and the ruler rules forever.

The stage was set for the adoption of the re-written Confucianism, which seemed the ideal philosophy to support dictatorship, and even though this was not what Xunzi really meant, the rulers of the state of Qi loved it. During Xunzi's lifetime the Great Wall of Qi was finally completed after 450 years of construction, and Qi was now poised to take over the defunct rule of the Zhou and become the supreme ruler of all China. This was never to happen. Quite suddenly a colossal army appeared apparently out of nowhere, sweeping all before it like a whirlwind, and in only a few years the Warring States were no more.

This army had come from the last place anybody expected, the obscure state of Qin (pronounced: "Chin") which was on the extreme west of the original territory once occupied by the old Zhou Empire. Considered of little account by the other states, whose rulers considered the Qin people to be little better than the barbarians who were their neighbors, the large state to the west nevertheless had one huge advantage over the others: access to the latest military technology. At this time all the significant developments in warfare were coming from Central Asia, immediately to the west of Qin, and it therefore adopted the new technologies far earlier than the other states, which continued waging war according to the old methods—charges by massed chariots and longbow exchanges from infantry.

The new technology was formidable. The invention of stirrups had led to the first use of mounted cavalry riders, who were now able to fire accurately from the saddle while riding at high speed thanks to another

Burner of books: the Emperor Shi Huangdi. He attempted to destroy Confucianism, but ultimately failed.

invention they had adopted from the tribes to the west—the crossbow. The highly-trained Qin cavalry were more or less invincible against the old-fashioned armies of the other states. The mighty Qin army, under the command of the young ruler Ying Zheng, who was still only in his thirties, swept through one state after another conquering every army that was set against them.

Ying Zheng's technique was simple and utterly ruthless. Chariots were not used for fighting but as highly mobile command posts. Given the signal by means of bells from the command chariots, the Qin cavalry would thunder into the massed ranks of infantry opposing them, using crossbows which were able to fire three steel bolts at one time like modern machine guns, and were capable of instantly decapitating somebody if fired accurately. The initial carnage was horrific enough but before the other side knew what was happening, the Qin infantry, responding to another bell, would charge in and finish off the dazed survivors of the cavalry charge. Ying Zheng's motto was take no prisoners, and after one battle 10,000 enemy survivors who had surrendered were butchered.

By the age of forty Ying Zheng had conquered the whole area of the former Zhou Empire and even extended it. The Zhou Dynasty, pathetic survivor of Confucius' lost golden age was no more. Ying Zheng renamed himself Qin Shi Huangdi—the "first emperor of the Qin." We know so much about his battle techniques because he had spectacular life-size models of his whole army—8,000 of them—wearing real armour and bearing real weapons, buried with him when he died.

Discovered accidentally by workmen in the 1970s, the "Terracotta Army" of Shi Huang has become known as the eighth wonder of the world and a must-see on the itinerary of all visitors to China—the name "China" simply means "Qin"—since the whole country had now become part of that formerly obscure state.

A cross between Alexander the Great and Adolf Hitler, Shi Huang set about the complete subjugation of his new empire with great gusto. Although Alexander (who reached India almost exactly a hundred years before Shi Huang conquered all China) also never lost a battle, he saw it as his mission to install Hellenistic civilization in all the territories he conquered. Shi Huang by contrast shared the views of Hermann Göring, who once reportedly said, "When I hear the word 'culture' I reach for my gun." Almost immediately after declaring himself emperor, Shi Huang ordered that every book in China be burned, and the smoke from bonfires of bamboo-slip manuscripts clouded the skies for months. It did not matter whether the bamboo slips contained the works of Confucians, Daoists, Mohists, classical literature, or more modern poetry—reading was now prohibited.

The 'Wall of Lu' inside the Confucius Temple complex, Qufu. Precious Confucian manuscripts were bricked up inside this wall during the Emperor Shi Huangdi's orgy of book-burning, and were thus preserved for posterity. *Photo: Qilu Press*

The Confucian scholars of the time, still arguing over whether goodness was innate and other esoteric questions, were taken completely by surprise. Shi Huang ordered mass executions of all scholars, and thousands of Confucians were buried alive all over the former states which were now provinces of the Qin Empire. The only philosophical school which survived the purges was Legalism. The Emperor announced that his empire would be governed strictly by law, and it was now against the law to possess any sort of book or whisper the slightest words of dissent against his regime. His "Empire of Heaven," he announced confidently, would "last for 10,000 years" (in the event it lasted fifteen years, only three years longer than Hitler's "Thousand Year Reich").

The people cowered in terror. At one point Shi Huang had one and a half million forced laborers working on his two most grandiose projects—the first Great Wall of China and his own mausoleum in the new capital Chang'an (near modern Xian). Nobody talked about books or music or had anything remotely resembling an intellectual discussion for fear of being reported to the Emperor's spies. Confucius was dead and forgotten and Confucianism was finished forever.

Not quite.

Tyrants who ban and burn books have never throughout history succeeded in eradicating the ideas the books stand for, and yet these megalomaniacs have continued to try right up into our own time. When will they ever learn? Apparently never. Typewriters were banned in Iraq, Afghanistan, and Romania in relatively recent history, and books were burned in the streets of Nazi Germany, yet neither Saddam, the Taliban, Ceausescu, nor Hitler was able to erase people's thoughts. Confucius was declared dead for a second time as copies of the *Analects* once more blazed in bonfires in the 1960s. Where are they now, the book-burners and the destroyers of words?

Confucius had said it all well over 2,000 years earlier:

Confucius said: "You might force people to act according to a certain principle, but you won't be able to force them to understand it."

Analects, 8:9

"You can snatch away the general of a large army, but you cannot snatch away the will of even the lowliest of men."

Analects, 9:26

During the Qin Dynasty, far from being dead and buried, Confucianism and the whole ancient cultural tradition simply went underground. Although countless manuscripts were lost—the *Book of Music* for example probably did not survive the book-burnings of Shi Huang—thousands of other volumes were buried in caves and tombs or bricked up into people's walls to await the ending of the madness. In Qufu a very ancient wall, called the Wall of Lu may still be seen and inside this wall many precious Confucian manuscripts were hidden during the terrible years of Shi Huang's purges, not to be rediscovered until several centuries later when they became the basis for the "official" versions of the classic Confucian texts.

It was quite ordinary people who did this, not officials or even scholars (most of whom were killed). Shunned by the governments of his day, the wandering scholar of Lu had nevertheless found a place in the hearts of ordinary Chinese people which has continued throughout history right up to the present time. Despite the efforts of successive governments to erase him from their hearts and minds, and no matter how powerful these governments have seemed at the time, the Chinese people have stubbornly refused to let Confucius die.

From the flames of the burning books, the phoenix has always risen.

Master of Two Millennia

The Emperor Shi Huang died in 210 BC, and was interred in his gigantic mausoleum attended by the Terracotta Warriors, his tomb itself encased in mercury. He is rumored to have died of mercury poisoning after drinking quicksilver pills in a futile attempt to achieve immortality.

The whole population of the new Chinese Empire breathed a collective sigh of relief. The Emperor's son proved so weak and ineffective that the law-and-order machine which had been so terrifyingly efficient under his father's rule began to collapse. People began to break out their book collections and organize concerts and poetry readings. Within another four years the 10,000-year empire was finished, to be replaced by the Han Dynasty, which was much more successful and lasted for the next 400 years.

The new rulers inherited many benefits from the monumental but blood-soaked efforts of their Qin predecessor: a unified empire of China with a centralized government, a common system of weights and measures, a single currency, a standardized official language, and the first part of the Great Wall; they eased up, however, on Shi Huang's fanatical imposition of the rule of law. Confucius' more relaxed ideas about governing were much more palatable to both the new emperors and the huge population they now had to govern, and eventually the Han Emperor Wu (141–87 BC) made Confucianism the official state ideology.

At last the dream of Confucius seemed to have been realized: a united empire covering all the ancient Zhou

The approach to Confucius' tomb, Qufu. *Qilu press*

domains, rulers and ruled working together to create a prosperous and harmonious state in which the arts and culture would flourish and trade prosper in a way not known since the passing of the golden age centuries before.

To a certain extent this did happen. Although the official philosophy was a very watered-down version of Confucianism which could best be described as "Confucius without teeth," the adoption of at least some of his ideas did have many beneficial and very lasting effects. Even though Confucius' reverence for traditional ritual resulted in Confucian China becoming a kind of living museum, it is on the other hand quite remarkable that the civilization based on his ideas lasted almost unchanged for two millennia. Language, customs, even the mode of dress hardly changed from the first century BC until the nineteenth century AD, and in no other part of the world did this happen. Had the same situation prevailed in the west, Greater Europe would still be a united country with the same borders as in the days of the Roman Empire, everybody would still speak Latin, and no European power would have colonized any other part of the world.

Whether this was entirely a good thing is open to debate, but China certainly avoided the violent wars and religious conflicts that engulfed Europe in bloodshed for so many centuries. Even though the imperial dynasties can be accused of having been oppressive to their own people, and over the last two millennia there have been a number of bloody civil wars within China's borders, nevertheless on the international level right up until our own era successive Chinese governments have been avowedly (and officially) pacifist, something which has been unique in human history and is certainly a legacy of Confucius.

When Marco Polo arrived in China in the thirteenth century, he was amazed that such a stable and prosperous society could exist anywhere in the world. Trade was conducted using an elaborate system of canals, there was universal prosperity, and people of widely differing religious beliefs and ethnic origin walked the streets of the Chinese cities he visited. In Europe at this time so-called religious heretics were being massacred or burned and the constant warfare— the Hundred Years War between England and France was still going on—echoing the situation in China during the Warring States Period 1,500 years earlier. Confucianism, for all the criticism it eventually attracted, cannot have been all bad.

One of the main reasons for the social and political

In for the long haul: Beside ancient Chinese tombs, the mythical turtle Bixi is often shown supporting giant steles on which are carved quotations from the *Analects*. Like the stones, Confucius' ideas have endured for thousands of years. Tombs of the Kong family from the Han Dynasty and later, Qufu. *Qilu Press*

stability was that Confucianism as it was practised incorporated the old Zhou idea of the mandate of heaven, which allowed for rulers or even whole dynasties to be replaced if they failed to govern in an acceptable way. Although Confucius himself had been characteristically vague about the actual process of overthrowing a ruler, Mencius had stated categorically that if a ruler became oppressive then he was no longer qualified to hold the title "king" or "emperor" and had become by definition an "ordinary person"; overthrowing such a person did not therefore constitute a usurpation of power but was more in the way of a public service.

This allowed for many changes of rulers and ruling houses to take place over the long history of Imperial China without the changes at the top having any significant effect on society as a whole. The Confucian

system operated by means of a strict hierarchy, but allowed for any individual, even the emperor himself, to be "renamed" and replaced if he did not perform his role according to expectations or had become corrupt.

Even when China was invaded and taken over by foreign rulers, which happened on two occasions, first in the thirteenth century when the whole country was conquered by the Mongols led by Genghis Khan and his successor Kublai, and then again in the seventeenth century when the Manchu rulers from Manchuria took over and founded the Qing Dynasty, this still did not have any major effect on the ordering of society as a whole. The Chinese system seemed to work so well that the invaders simply left it intact, the only difference being that they themselves were now in charge, so that their seizure of power was not so much an invasion but a Confucian leadership change. Indeed the new emperors from both Mongolia and Manchuria were so dazzled by the whole Chinese way of doing things that they very quickly became Confucian gentlemen themselves.

Genghis Khan's successor, Kublai Khan, moved his capital to Khanbalik (now Beijing) but instead of imposing the rough and military Mongol ways on the Chinese he immediately employed a Confucian scholar as his advisor who was supposed to teach him the

Officially Confucian: The Han Emperor Wu (reigned 141-86 B.C.) and his court. *Qilu Press*

Chinese way of doing things. Instead of displaying severed Chinese heads on poles all around the capital, which was what everybody had expected of a Mongol ruler (Genghis had been notorious for doing this sort of thing) Kublai's first act was to declare through his Confucian interpreter that he was the first emperor of the new "Yuan" Dynasty.

In fact when Marco Polo arrived in what he called Cathay, the ruler was not Chinese at all but was still the Great Khan Kublai, who ruled from 1260–94. The advanced civilization and harmonious social order of Cathay, descriptions of which Marco's biographer excitedly communicated back to European readers, were, however, uniquely Chinese. They were the result, for better or worse, of more than a thousand years of "Confucian" rule.

Although Kublai Khan never bothered to learn Chinese, successive Mongol emperors became so Confucianized that they adopted Chinese names and regularly visited Qufu to offer sacrifices to the memory of the great Chinese sage. The Mongol Emperor Wu Zong, who ruled briefly from 1307–11 and whose Mongol name was Khaishan, was such a devotee of

Unchanged for centuries: This modern re-enactment in Qufu of sacrifices by the Emperor to Confucius is based on a ceremony from the Qing Dynasty (19ᵗʰ century) – but the Qing ritual was itself closely modelled on the original observances first started in the Han Dynasty 2000 years earlier.
Qilu Press

Confucius that he took his sister to visit the Confucius Temple in Qufu. She was in fact the first woman ever to set foot inside the temple, which had been the exclusive preserve of men for over a thousand years.

Wu Zong's predecessor Genghis, whose very name has become a byword for uncivilized barbarity, would have been turning in his grave had he known that in only a few generations his successors were to become so softened by the ongoing influence of some namby-pamby Chinese philosopher that they would begin to feel that world domination was not the behavior of a gentleman.

In the event, while the Mongol emperors and their courtiers themselves became Confucianized, the only lasting effect the Mongols had on Chinese society was in the field of cookery. The Mongol soldiers used to use their helmets to boil up meat and vegetables with a few tasty spices after a hard day of riding or massacring their opponents, and this method of cooking is now so popular that "hot pot" restaurants can be found in every Chinese town or city. The traditional shape of the dish

used for cooking, which is done at each table by the customers themselves, is exactly the same as Genghis Khan's helmet.

It was at the same time that Mongolian hot-pot became popular in China that Chinese noodles travelled west to Italy, possibly even in Marco Polo's backpack. Ancient Chinese noodles, which were very similar to spaghetti, were a staple dish enjoyed by the wandering scholars on their travels—it will be remembered that Yan Hui and Zilu used to prepare the vegetables.

The Mongol Emperors also retained the Imperial Examinations System, which was another direct legacy of Confucius and lasted for an astonishingly long period of time from its introduction around 150 BC during the Han Dynasty until being finally abolished in 1905—the idea of written exams, which now exist in almost all countries, derives from the ancient Chinese model. Until British merchants visited China in the early nineteenth century nobody in the West had ever thought of holding written examinations for candidates who wished to work in the civil service or attend university. Seeing this system as theoretically a much fairer way of selection

Marco Polo (1254-1324). He spent over 17 years in China, from 1274-1292

'In Xanadu did Kublai Khan a stately pleasure dome decree…'
Kublai Khan, first Emperor of the Yuan (Mongol) Dynasty established the Chinese capital on the site of modern Beijing. The 'pleasure dome' at his summer residence, Xanadu, was described by Marco Polo and later immortalized in the poem by Coleridge. *Qilu Press*

than simply accepting the sons of wealthy families, the British East India Company was the first Western institution to copy China and introduce competitive written exams in 1806, the British Civil Service followed in 1853, and written examinations were finally started for the American civil administration in 1883.

The hope of the family: A young man says farewell to his mother before leaving to sit the Imperial Examinations during the Qing Dynasty. Success would guarantee a job in the civil service and a huge increase in status for the whole family. Tableau in Shanghai Jiading Museum. *Photo: Jonathan Price*

Written exams had in fact existed in China for 2,000 years before this. Quite soon after Confucianism was declared the official state philosophy in the Han Dynasty, the Confucian scholars who were now becoming increasingly powerful in the running of the state began to urge their rulers to embrace Confucius' educational philosophy as well as his social and political ideas. By this time the *Analects* had appeared and Sima Qian had written his life of Confucius in the *Records of the Grand Historian*, so both the sayings of the Master and the events of his life were widely known.

The Master had said: "In education there should be no discrimination" (*Analects*, 15:38), and as everybody knew Confucius had accepted students from all walks of life, many of whom had gone on to work in government and administrative positions. The scholars argued that the same principle should now be applied to the whole Chinese civil service, which should accept people on merit, regardless of their birth or financial position.

The idea was admirable in principle but the problem was how to select the candidates? Confucius had literally accepted anybody, but he had only been running a tiny academy in a tiny little state—if the civil service was opened to all in what was now a huge country, hundreds of thousands of people would apply for what could only be a few thousand available jobs.

Confucius said: "Among people, who should I criticize and who should I praise? If I praise someone it is because I have had some way of testing him."

Analects, 15:25

Confucius did not reveal exactly how he tested students, so his later followers during the Han Dynasty, who could think of no fairer or better way of doing it, introduced the system of written examinations to test candidates for the coveted civil service positions and for admission to the newly founded Imperial University in the capital, Chang'an. The system was gradually made more sophisticated and organized under the succeeding dynasties until it reached its final form under the Song emperors (960–1279 AD) with a gruelling competitive exam in three parts. Candidates were required to have an extensive knowledge of classical literature and in particular the "Four Confucian Books," which were *The Great Knowledge* (*Daxue*), *The Doctrine of the Mean* (*Zhongyong*), the *Book of Mencius*, and of course the *Analects*. They were also expected to be able to write in the prescribed classical style themselves.

The system certainly succeeded at least in theory in supplying the Chinese emperors with the brightest and the best of each generation, regardless of their backgrounds. In practice of course only those from relatively wealthy families could afford to spend several years studying for the notoriously difficult exams, but nevertheless the continuous intake of fresh talent to help administer the huge empire was one of the reasons Imperial China lasted for such a long time. The alternative—a ruling elite which recruits its members from a limited number of wealthy families—has been the downfall of many empires. Such a ruling class quickly becomes effete if only from the biological effect of in-breeding—the number of mad monarchs among the European royal families is a case in point—but the Chinese system managed to avoid this and remained vigorous for two millennia.

Confucius' little school certainly had a far-reaching and very long-term effect in this way, but paradoxically the examination system, which had been established as a practical application of his belief in universal education, killed off any chance that his educational methods would ever be applied in China, at least until some far-off time in the future which still has not yet arrived.

In order to stand any chance of success, candidates for the civil service needed to memorize all 492 of Confucius' *Analects*, yet were not required to discuss them or even understand them. The same applied to the other classics of literature. Whereas Confucius had used the *Book of Songs* and the *Book of History* as a basis for discussion, the education system in the many private schools which sprang up to coach students for the Imperial examinations simply crammed students with quotations and historical facts. This form of teaching has remained the basis of Chinese education right up to the present day. Confucius' method of giving students "one corner" of a topic and allowing the students to arrive at the other three themselves was the first casualty of the Imperial examination system.

Confucius said: "The Superior Person is not a utensil."

Analects, 2:12

By this famous remark Confucius meant that we should think for ourselves, not just be receptacles for other people's ideas, to be used for other people's tasks. Unfortunately utensils are exactly what Chinese students became after the introduction of the examination system, and have remained so ever since. Teachers pour facts into the receptacles of their minds and this material is then spewed out onto examination papers at the due time and students with the most

Nervous candidates waiting to sit the Imperial Examinations during the Song Dynasty. Shanghai Jiading Museum. *Photo: Jonathan Price*

A completed Imperial Examination paper from the Qing Dynasty. Test paper of Zhang Binwu, 1723. As can be clearly seen the questions were of the 'multiple-choice' type, requiring a good memory rather than a keen intelligence. Shanghai Jiading Museum. *Photo: Jonathan Price*

Swotting for the exams: The highest marks of all time in the Imperial Examinations were scored by Zhang Jian in the nineteenth century. He is seen here in a tableau in Shanghai Jiading Museum studying for the exam. *Photo: Jonathan Price*

efficient memories score the highest marks and end up getting the best jobs.

The sort of student Confucius most admired, as exemplified by Zigong and Yan Hui who both thought deeply and creatively about everything and asked a lot of questions, would have fared very badly in these examinations. Students were not encouraged to ask questions but only answer them and this still applies today in China to a great extent. As a result, as the exam system became more and more entrenched and the question papers more rigid and backward-looking, innovation and creativity became stifled.

The other unfortunate result of the examination system was the institutionalization of cheating. With so

much riding on a single exam, students would go to any lengths to pass, including sewing crib-sheets into their clothes, blatantly copying the next student in the examination room, or when all else failed bribing the examiner or getting somebody else to sit the exam for them. All these methods of achieving success still occur all over China every time an exam is held. Naturally Confucius would be horrified since cheating is clearly unethical, but although Confucianism remained the official philosophy for thousands of years, most of his ethical precepts were conveniently ignored.

By the time of the Ming Dynasty a Confucian was not somebody who acted in a humanitarian way but a person who could recite all 492 of the *Analects* without stopping. In the Qing Dynasty—the final one—a Confucian could find no conflict between his worship of Confucius and the fact that he bound his wife's (or more usually wives') feet. Although Confucius was later blamed even for this inhuman practice, it is covered quite clearly in the *Analects*: "Don't do to others what you would not have them do to you."

Another very negative feature of Chinese society under the dynasties which was ultimately blamed on Confucius was the backwardness which eventually left China in a fossilized state while the rest of the world moved into the industrial age. In the first millennium AD China unquestionably led the world in the field of scientific advances. Paper, printing, gunpowder, rockets, the compass, even the humble wheelbarrow were all Chinese inventions which were used for hundreds of years before their adoption in the West. Then it all just stopped. The Confucian scholars who became ever more powerful decreed that scientific enquiry was anti-

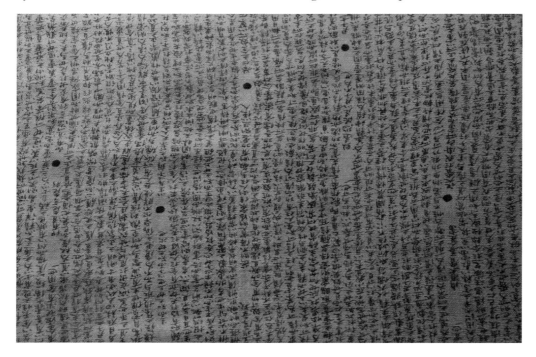

Crib sheet: Cheating in the exams was widespread despite official measures to prevent it. Seen here is an example from the Ming Dynasty—a "cheating-silk" with all the answers minutely transcribed, which was concealed under the candidate's clothes.
Photo: Jonathan Price

The 'Confucius Theme Park'. Despite the invention of photography, these descendants of Confucius in the later Qing period (nineteenth century) had their photographic likenesses pasted onto paintings of ancient costumes – exactly like modern tourists sticking their heads through holes in cardboard cut-outs. Left: Kong Lingyi, 76th generation Confucius descendant. Right: His mother Madam Peng, wife of the 75th descendant.

The Emperor Gao Zu of the Han Dynasty offering sacrifices to Confucius in front of his old school house. Confucius' hat and other possessions can be seen on display just inside. Ming Dynasty painting. *Qilu Press*

Confucian, and then went on also to decree that commerce was not the occupation of a gentleman so that all trade was taken out of private hands and was conducted by a government agency called the *Cohong*.

This conveniently gave the Emperor the monopoly on all trade, apparently with the blessing of Confucius himself, and for several hundred years all exports and imports virtually stopped although silk was still smuggled illegally. When the British arrived in the eighteenth century they were politely welcomed but denied trading rights. The justification that the scholars used for the prohibition of trade were the remarks Confucius made in the *Analects* in which he condemned the worship of money-making, but they conveniently forgot that he also said that if he could find a sure-fire way of making money he would do it, and he also went on record in admiration of Zigong's business acumen. China could have made a killing exporting tea, which it had done for centuries to neighboring countries along the "tea roads" which crossed the Himalayas, but by the time tea had become very big business worldwide Confucian China had practically ceased trading with any other country, and indeed had more or less shut itself off from all contact with the outside world.

While the rest of the globe industrialized, China turned into a vast theme park, a quaint re-enactment of life in the fifth century BC (they even wore more or less the same clothes) and into this Confucian Disneyland came the gunboats and machine guns of the Western powers and very quickly, after 2,000 years, it was all over.

Rivalry from the West: The increasing popularity of Buddhism threatened for a time to totally eclipse Confucianism. 5th Century A.D. relief. Capital Museum Beijing. *Photo: Jonathan Price*

When the last dynasty, the Qing, finally fell in 1911, Confucius was worshipped as a god, as he had effectively been for many centuries. This would perhaps have amused him had he known, or more likely enraged him since he never even claimed to be a sage. His deification originally came about as a reaction to the threat from Buddhism, which reached China in a big way in the second century AD, but had probably started filtering in across the Himalayas and down the Silk Road much earlier than that. The new religion immediately became popular, threatening for a time to eclipse Confucianism totally. The rulers of the Han and Song Dynasties, who had invested heavily in Confucius as the basis of their regimes, were extremely worried and ordered the Confucian scholars to revamp the philosophy completely—literally add bells and whistles in order to make it more colorful and bring the whole thing more in line with popular religion.

Although the tradition of sacrificing an ox, a sheep, and a pig at Confucius' grave every year had been instituted by Zigong and had continued regularly except during the brief reign of Qin Shi Huang the book-burner,

this did not constitute "worshipping" him and was simply following the ancient tradition of honoring the ancestors which was done in every family. Confucius' old school house had been turned into a small museum where his hat, robes, ritual utensils, and even his old travelling wagon were on display. How these things could have survived the purges is not clear so they were probably fakes but nevertheless the little house attracted many "tourists" including the Han emperors themselves and their official historian Sima Qian, who described his visit:

> I went to Lu, and in the mansion of Confucius I contemplated his chariot, his garments, and his ceremonial implements. At a fixed time, scholars performed the rites of his house. So I remained there, full of reverence, and could not tear myself away.
>
> Sima Qian, *Records of the Grand Historian*

How wonderful it would be if we too could visit this place of quiet dignity, as is still possible with Mozart's tiny little house in Salzburg. Another man who was rejected in his own time, Mozart's monument is his

Rich and powerful: Unlike their impoverished and despised ancestor, Confucius' later descendants enjoyed wealth and power beyond imagining. Kong Hongxu, the 61st generation 'Hereditary Sage' from the Ming Dynasty. Ming Dynasty painting. *Qilu Press*

Fabulously wealthy: the sumptuous interior of the Kong Mansion in Qufu (now open to the public) surpassed in magnificence the Imperial Palace in Peking. *Qilu Press*

music, as Confucius' monument should only be the *Analects*, but this was not to be. His little house vanished long ago underneath the monumental temples to Confucianism and the vulgar displays of wealth and power his descendants erected on the site.

With Buddhism sweeping the country, the imperial authorities decided that quiet dignity was not the way to go and what Confucius needed was something more elaborate—chanting monks, bells, incense, and gigantic statues. All over China Buddhist monasteries were being built and colossal statues of the Buddha were being carved into the sides of mountains—the largest in the world still stands, carved into a cliff beside a tributary of the Yangtze River in Sichuan. It was always slightly unclear whether Buddha was actually a god or occupied a sort of halfway house between earth and heaven, but the Confucians could see that their founder had to be considerably upgraded if he was to stand any chance of competing with his Indian rival.

Confucius was accordingly first of all made an official sage, and was then posthumously promoted to the rank of duke (coincidentally one year after Christ was born in Bethlehem on the other side of the world). Confucius' descendants the Kong family had been doing fairly well after their forbear had been nominated official state philosopher, but according to Sima Qian, who lived in the earlier years of the Han Dynasty, by his time they had still only managed to rise to relatively lowly positions as court archaeologists or governors of cities. With their ancestor now elevated to the aristocracy, his descendants clamoured to be made a noble family as well, and they were eventually made the "Dukes of Yansheng" with the responsibility of guarding the shrine of Confucius in perpetuity, while in each generation the head of the household also took the title "Lord Hereditary Sage." After being given large amounts of land and receiving huge donations from successive emperors, the Kong family ended up fabulously wealthy, eventually becoming the second most powerful family in the country, and in terms of wealth they actually reached the

number one spot. This proved embarrassing and when the Qing emperor Qianlong made a state visit to the Kong Mansion in Qufu the family hastily draped one whole wall in red silk in case the emperor noticed that their decorations were more sumptuous than in his own mansion inside the Forbidden City.

Confucius was now big business. His wife, who as far as we know left him after four years, would have been kicking herself in her grave if she could have realized that she had in fact married God. How was she to know? She need not have worried—in the new Confucius complex which arose on the site of the earlier modest

Vamping up the myth: to ward off rivalry from conventional religions like Buddhism, supernatural elements were added to the story of Confucius' birth. In this painting, Confucius' mother, cradling her newborn child, watches as 'four divine sages' play music in the sky. Ming Dynasty Paintings. *Qilu Press*

shrine she was given her own temple just in front of her husband's, so she also became semi-divine, the other half of a husband-and-wife team proudly upholding family values into eternity.

The circumstances of Confucius' strange parentage and bizarre lifestyle were swept under the carpet, and the story of his life was given a much more Buddhist flavour in the many paintings which were now churned out to reinforce the cult of Confucius the demigod. Celestial sages were shown playing music in the sky after his birth; the same beings appeared riding on rainbows just before his death; and in the many paintings depicting his mother and father praying for a son at the hill of Ni they are both invariably shown as being in their late twenties, a typical happy couple. The fact that she was only fifteen and her husband was fifty-five years older was now considered unsuitable for the myth—Buddha's parents had been entirely respectable aristocrats. In the drive to rival the *Bhagavadgita* there was no place for Lolita.

"Confucius Temples" were now hastily constructed all over China in attempt to keep pace with the mushrooming spread of Buddhist shrines, and members of the civil service were obliged to sacrifice at the temples on a regular basis. In 267 AD huge "sacrifices to Confucius" were made compulsory for all civil servants four times a year, and in 492 he was finally upgraded to "venerable"—one stage down from an actual god, so more or less on a par with Buddha.

By this time Confucianism had become so similar to Buddhism that it managed to reassert itself as the dominant ideology, and in fact had become a religion in all but name. Many temples to Confucius survive to this day in China, and inside they are almost identical to the many Buddhist shrines all over the country except that they have no chanting monks. The only other difference is that while the centerpiece of the Buddhist temples is always an effigy of the contemplative sage, the Confucius temples contain a statue of a very tall man sitting in a chair and grinning. The grin perhaps is the only authentic touch, and one always has the impression that the wooden or stone Confucius is about to say: "What, exactly, am I doing here?"

Although Confucianism was now operating as a quasi-religion, those in search of genuine spiritual enlightenment have always preferred the real thing, and Confucianism did not spread widely across the globe in the same way that Buddhism, Christianity, and Islam have done—but then Confucianism was never a religion in the first place so this is hardly surprising. There appear to have been no excited discussions of the *Analects* among travellers journeying westwards along the Silk Road, in the same way that religious and intellectual ideas travelled in the other direction. Chinese

Quasi-religion: From 267 A.D. sacrifices to Confucius – as if he were a god – were made compulsory all over the Chinese Empire. The ceremonies continued unchanged for the next 1648 years until they were finally abolished in 1915. They have now made a come-back and re-enactments take place in Qufu every year on Confucius' birthday in September, as shown in the photos above. *Qilu Press*

"What am I doing here?" Statue of Confucius as a god in the Confucius Temple Qufu. *Qilu Press*

case of the samurai, these would have been his insistence on hierarchy (no problem there for a warrior), filial piety (samurai really respect their fathers), and of course the Chinese Master's belief in the importance of study. The fact that Confucius would hardly approved of the main field of samurai studies—the most efficient way of cutting off other people's heads—was not considered.

Thus in the writings of the seventeenth-century Japanese master Yamaga Soko (1622–85), author of *Way of the Samurai*, a Confucian samurai is presented not as a contradiction in terms but a model for all aspiring warriors to emulate. In one mind-boggling passage Yamaga quotes several of the *Analects*, respectfully giving them their reference numbers as has been done in this book, and then follows with this:

"Within the four seas are we [the Japanese] not supreme in military valour?"

Yamaga Soko, *Autobiography in Exile*

This appears almost as a parody of Confucius' famous statement "All within the four seas will be his brother" (*Analects*, 12:5), and naturally Yamaga does not quote this one. Whereas Confucius was talking about universal peace and brotherhood, the Japanese master seems to be suggesting that his nation is ready for world domination, and one almost expects him to complete the sentence with "Confucius said: 'Attack Pearl Harbor—now.'"

In fact later in the same work Yamaga does almost say this. After a lot more Confucian homilies about the importance or ritual (something that the samurai adored), he goes on to state categorically that the Japanese are superior to the Chinese in every way and it is Japan not China which should be called the "Middle Kingdom."

Millions of ordinary Japanese people have followed Confucius' true teachings over many centuries, and this applies to all the other Asian countries which have been influenced by Confucianism. Nevertheless the militaristic posturing of Yamaga and other scholars eventually formed the ideological basis for Japan's invasion of Manchuria and the horrors inflicted on Nanjing and many other cities in China during the Second World War. It seems that when his ideas get into the hands of whole governments or their toadying scholars they can be twisted to support almost any sort of horror. Confucius of course is not alone in having had his humanitarian ideas distorted into a philosophy of inhumanity: the Holy Inquisition, the Crusaders, and the medieval heretic-burners in France and elsewhere perpetrated their atrocities in the name of Christ in a similar way and were also justified by the theologians

technology like paper and gunpowder eventually made the westward journey but Confucius' ideas never reached the West until much later in history. In the East, Confucian ethics and watered-down versions of his political ideas similar to those adopted in China did spread to one or two neighboring territories, including Burma, Vietnam, Cambodia, and Korea, but all these places were at one time or another part of the Chinese Empire.

The only strictly non-Chinese country to which Confucianism spread was Japan, and it was here that his ideas experienced perhaps their most bizarre distortion of all: the "Way of Confucius" was incorporated into the "Way of the Samurai." It might be wondered how the principles of Confucius, the avowed pacifist, could possibly fit into the fierce code of the samurai warriors, but inconsistency has never deterred those who have set out to twist his ideas to suit their own beliefs. They usually do this by ignoring his main creed—the "golden rule" of humanity, peace, and brotherhood—selecting only those parts of the *Analects* they can live with. In the

and scholars of their day.

Ironically, at almost exactly the same time (the early seventeenth century) that Confucius was being turned into the samurai's favorite philosopher, the first Jesuit Christian missionaries arrived in China itself, and it was of course the Jesuit Matteo Ricci who gave Kong Fu Zi his Latin name. The Jesuits had certainly never heard of Confucius before they made landfall, but they were very excited when they discovered that his teachings appeared to be very similar to those of Jesus. Despite this his ideas still did not have very much impact in Europe, although there was a great flurry of interest in all things Chinese in the nineteenth century and almost all the great classics including the *Analects* were

The Jesuits in China in a 17ᵗʰ century engraving. It was the Jesuit priest Matteo Ricci who gave Kong Fu Zi his Latinized name 'Confucius'.

translated into English. It is only perhaps in our own time, when the ridiculous idea of Confucius as God has finally gone onto the scrapheap where it belongs, that he can finally be truly understood and appreciated in the West.

Although he remained almost completely unknown outside China, posthumous honors continued to be heaped upon him in his own country, and in 1067 Confucius was officially declared "Honorary Emperor in Perpetuity." He must have been pleased about that. The Kong family continued to enlarge his temple as they themselves became richer and richer. Each succeeding

emperor surpassed the last in the lavishness of the gifts that were showered on the family. Some of these beautiful gifts, ranging from exquisitely worked gold and silver ornaments embossed with precious gems to priceless antiques from as far back as the Zhou Dynasty may still be seen on display in the "Kong Fu" or Kong Mansion.

Somewhat bizarrely Confucius was not officially made a god until the year 1906, by which time the imperial dynastic system (not to mention the Confucius bandwagon itself) had almost reached the end of its very long run. Even more bizarrely, the worship of Confucius was continued by the first President of the Republic of China, Yuan Shi Kai, who attempted to put the clock back once again. Failing to see that Confucius was now the wrong horse to back, Yuan got himself killed shortly after he declared himself the new emperor in 1915, and Confucianism as a political and social force, after an uninterrupted run of almost 2,100 years, was finally finished. The theme park had closed for good, and from now on Chinese men would wear trousers and stop behaving as if nothing had changed in China since the first century BC.

Although Confucius himself had condemned injustice and suffering and "people who made the rich richer," Confucianism had been used as window-dressing for the

Ostentatious wealth: valuable treasures on display at the Confucius Mansion in Qufu. The Kong family hung on to their fabulous wealth at a time when most Chinese people were living in poverty. Ironically, Confucius himself would have been on the side of the people - as attested by his many pronouncements against the greedy nobility of his own time. *Qilu Press*

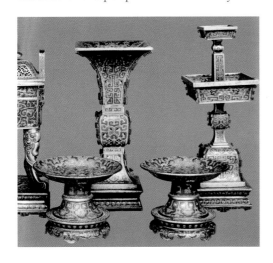

Last Days of the God-Emperor: Confucius enthroned in splendour (and wearing an emperor's hat) inside the Jiading Confucius Temple, Shanghai. Although founded much earlier, most of the interior dates from the final years of the last dynasty, the Qing. *Photo: Jonathan Price*

ruling class for so long that he was now seen as the representative of everything that was wrong with society in China. Nobody really bothered to read his sayings any more: his name was synonymous with oppression, and he would continue to be perceived as such for the next seventy-five years or so.

In the radical writer Lu Xun's most famous story "The Madman's Diary," written in the early twentieth century, a lunatic sees the inscription "Confucian Morality" written on a wall but reads the words as "Eat People." In another of Lu Xun's stories, "The New-Year Sacrifice" a poor working woman's whole life is destroyed by the "iron cage" of society, which is equated with Confucianism. Having been dethroned as a god he was now seen as the devil, and many people genuinely believed that the *Analects* had contained passages saying "Confucius said: 'Eat People'"; "Confucius said: 'Put women in cages where they belong'"; "Confucius said: 'Keep the peasantry in the poverty they deserve,'" and so on.

It might have helped if Confucius' family descendants had made more effort to promote and live by their ancestor's humanitarian principles; as it was the Kong Mansion remains the largest private house ever built in China and the family continued ostentatiously displaying their wealth to the end. Finally accepting that it was all over in 1948, the seventy-seventh generation "Hereditary Sage" and lineal descendant of Confucius through his son Bo Yu fled to Taiwan. The show was at last well and truly over.

Despite Confucius' fall from official grace, his philosophy remained popular among ordinary Chinese people even after the success of the revolution in 1949 and the birth of the new China—to such an extent that he began to be perceived as a threat by the new government just as he had been in his own lifetime. Confucius' idea that society advances through a gradual process of correction, that extremes should be avoided, and that we should learn from the past in order to move into the future, did not sit well with the prevailing mood of the time. In the 1960s the ancient sage was attacked mercilessly in the newspapers and on wall-posters, students were ordered to attend "Criticize Confucius" lectures, and an officially orchestrated "Down with

The Kong Mansion in Qufu – the largest private house ever built in China

Confucius!" campaign gathered momentum all over the country, reaching hysterical levels at the height of the Cultural Revolution.

It is of course astonishing that this obscure teacher from the fifth century BC, whose only public achievement was to have served for three undistinguished years as a junior minister in a tiny mini-state, was continuing to make front-page headlines two and a half thousand years later. Why has Confucius always been so loved or hated over such a long period of time? This can only be because his message remains timeless, and his general philosophy of kindness and decent behavior to one's neighbors has always had a very strong appeal in China, which has remained a basically secular society ever since the Zhou Dynasty. Even today China remains one of the most religiously tolerant nations on earth, and like Confucius most people consider that the god you worship is your own affair but the most important thing is to be a good neighbor.

During the Cultural Revolution all this was turned on its head. Almost all the statues of Buddha, along with those of Confucius, were destroyed. Neighbors were encouraged to inform upon neighbors and children regularly reported their own parents for "incorrect thinking," resulting in their being sent away for a course of "re-education" from which they often never returned. Traditional culture like the Peking Opera was banned and anybody seen reading one of the ancient Chinese classics was immediately arrested as a subversive.

Most ordinary Chinese people supported the revolution, but were horrified by the idea of completely obliterating their ancient culture, which is what they were being ordered to do on the radio every day. Many of the more moderate leaders of the time shared this view and could see no reason why China could not continue to advance towards a just and fair society while retaining its traditional past. These leaders were denounced hysterically and their names linked to the arch-demon: Confucius. One campaign after another was launched and the fanatical youth gangs in their red armbands paraded the streets chanting "Down with

Lu Xun (1881-1936), Chinese novelist of the early 20th century who denounced Confucianism as the mother of all the evils which beset the Chinese people. *Qilu Press*

Confucius! Down with Zhou Enlai!" "Down with Confucius! Down with Deng Xiao Ping!"

The Red Guards—mostly young students in their early twenties—fervently believed that utopia could be achieved if not tomorrow, then certainly the day after, and this could only be done by totally destroying the past. For the second time in 2,000 years, the book burning began: copies of the *Analects* were tossed onto bonfires, schools and libraries were destroyed, and teachers were beaten up. It was an uncanny re-run of what had happened after Qin Shi Huang launched his campaign against the scholars in 221 BC, and once again Confucius was taking the most serious beating.

The young Red Guards enjoyed free rail travel in order to encourage them to move all over China and demonstrate against the old culture. In January 1967 thousands of them took the train to Qufu in Shandong, site of the Confucius temple and of Confucius' little school, where it had all started.

Chanting (and this is possibly the most bizarre touch of all) "Down with Confucius! Down with Confucius' wife!" the mob of Red Guards, led by a young girl student in her early twenties, Tan Houlan, surged into the Confucius Temple, smashing statues of disciples like Yan Hui, Zigong, and Zilu with sledgehammers. At one end of the temple was a huge stone statue of a seated Confucius, erected centuries before in order to rival those of Buddha in the Buddhist shrines. The statue was pulled over with ropes and then smashed to pieces, as the chanting echoed to a crescendo.

> Last week Red Guards went to Shantung province and wrecked the birthplace of Confucius. For 2,400 years, the Chinese have studied his counsels of moderation and non-violence. The zealots who desecrated his shrine at Chu Fu, reported the Peking *People's Daily*, had buried Confucianism "once and for all."
>
> *Time*, January 27th, 1967

Finally it was official. It was in the papers so it must be true. Confucius was dead, Confucianism was finished, and this time it was permanent—the old man would not be standing up again after this. The Red Guards had buried Confucius and all his works "once and for all."

Not quite.

Confucius Today and Tomorrow

Zigong said: "Confucius cannot be slandered … Confucius is like the sun and the moon. There is no way they can be climbed over. Even if you want to cut yourself off from the sun and moon, how can you hurt them?"

Analects, 19:24

Thirty years after the Red Guards smashed the statue of their hated enemy, construction began on a Confucius theme park in Qufu. Although Mao's wife Jiang Qing, the most vocal critic of Confucius and ringleader of the "Gang of Four," committed suicide in 1991, and Tan Houlan, leader of the attack on his temple, was jailed in 1978, many of the former Red Guards would only have been in their early fifties when "Confucius World" (it is actually called "The City of the)Six Arts") finally opened its doors. The center continues to attract thousands of visitors, and many of the life-size models of Confucius and his disciples on display have been featured in this book. There is even a Disneyland-style ride into the past on electric chariots.

How, the ageing survivors of the Great Cultural Revolution must have wondered, could this possibly have happened? What had it all been for—the chanting, the book burning, the parades? Once again the old man had done his phoenix act and staged another spectacular comeback. Thousands of tourists were now queuing up to have themselves photographed beside cardboard cut-outs of Confucius, on the very spot where only a few years before they as young students had screamed "Down with Confucius! Down with Confucius' wife!"

Any student of history could have told them that this was not so very surprising—it had happened before, in the second century BC. The ideas of Confucius, and a kind of long-standing affection for him as a man, are so deeply ingrained into the Chinese soul that he is indeed, as Zigong said so long ago, like the sun and the moon. No amount of book-burning or slogan-chanting is going to stop the sun coming up in the morning, and it was equally foolish to think that the memory of Confucius could be erased by the same methods.

During the Cultural Revolution, the Red Guards had also chanted "Down with Confucius! Down with Deng Xiao Ping!" Deng, who was probably flattered by the comparison, quietly exiled himself to a distant province until the hysteria died down (rather like Confucius had done) and eventually took the reins of power himself after Mao's death. He immediately proceeded to

Huge sculpture of Confucius on his travels in the City of Six Arts, Qufu. *Qilu Press*

Get your official Confucius souvenirs here! – a licensed vendor inside the Confucius Temple complex in Qufu. *Photo: Jonathan Price*

"rectify" the system in such a way that Confucius could have well been his advisor. His aim was to transform China totally from a planned economy to a market economy, and to open up the country to the outside world, but without causing major upheavals or the collapse of the egalitarian social system which he himself had fought to achieve (Deng was a veteran of the Long March but had subsequently been vilified as a moderate and "capitalist roader"). This ideal, to achieve change not by overthrowing a system but by correcting and redirecting it so that the past leads smoothly into the future, derives directly from Confucius.

The transformation happened in stages, adopting a "middle way" to allow everybody to get used to the changes and then see the benefits. State industries were not privatized overnight but instead were restructured gradually and the monolithic enterprises split into sections which were given specific tasks. This was exactly what Confucius had recommended in his most famous pronouncements on management. Although Deng did not cite Confucius (it was too soon after his last fall from grace) the whole process of change which he initiated was carried out in an instinctively Confucian way and the fact that this was achieved without any of the cataclysmic disruptions to the social fabric that occurred for example in the former Soviet Union is directly attributable to the ongoing influence of Confucianism in modern China.

There are many other ways in which Confucius is still alive and well in the country of his birth. Although his first-born heirs fled the country some time ago, there are still millions of people walking about who claim direct descent. It is an almost mathematical certainty that anybody spending more than a few weeks in China will

encounter somebody named "Kong" who claims to be descended from the Sage. Visitors to his home town should be able to score a sighting of a Confucius family member within a few minutes of stepping off the bus or train, since more than a quarter of the entries in the Qufu telephone book are for people with the surname Kong— and they all hotly insist they are descendants.

Some of these families may have changed their name over the centuries in order to cash in on the Confucius bandwagon while others may be entirely unrelated; nevertheless it is still highly likely that anybody named Kong whose family comes from Qufu does in fact carry the philosopher's genes. If one assumes that the number of direct descendants doubles with each generation, this number starts to become really huge after about ten generations and we have now almost reached the twentieth generation of Kongs since the birth of his son Bo Yu in 529 BC.

Apart from filling whole telephone directories with his name, perhaps the most obvious legacy of Confucius in China today is the huge respect accorded to teachers, and the incredible popularity of part-time education. In every Chinese city almost everybody is taking evening courses in something or other, be it English, philosophy, music, hip-hop dancing, or traditional embroidery. More people are taking part-time courses in China than in any other nation on earth, and this goes back to Confucius'

Deng Xiaoping (1904-1997) – survived the Cultural Revolution and carried Confucius' ideal of the 'middle way' into the later 20th century.

Kong Kang, a high school student from Qufu and a direct descendant of Kong Qiu – Confucius. Her facial resemblance to the portraits we have of her ancestor is quite remarkable.
Photo: Jonathan Price

first school in Lu when he first opened education to anybody who wanted to learn.

Foreigners who come to China to teach are always amazed at the respect they receive—teachers in Western countries get their job satisfaction from what they do, not from society as a whole. Students in China consciously use the language of the *Analects*, and will say for example "You are my Great Teacher" (*Fu Zi*—this was Confucius' appellation: Kong Fu Zi, the Great Master). If you are a teacher and you meet a former student later in life, the student will introduce you by saying "He (or she) *is* my teacher"—not "used to be my teacher" as would be said in the West. This again directly derives from the *Analects*—Zilu and Zigong even when they were middle-aged described Confucius as "my teacher" or "my Master." Parents who might themselves have high-status jobs will bow to teachers and say "You are the great teacher of my son/daughter"—it would be inconceivable to imagine a state governor or even the head of a large company doing this at their local primary school in any other part of the world, but it happens regularly in China and it was Confucius who originally gave Chinese teachers the huge respect they still enjoy.

Other direct echoes of the *Analects* also live on. Anybody visiting China will be introduced as "a foreign friend." This is a direct translation of the most often quoted of the *Analects* and in fact it appears as the first of all the sayings of Confucius:

Confucius said: "Isn't it the greatest pleasure when friends visit from distant places?"

Analects, 1:1

Confucius did not invent Chinese hospitality, but gave it voice. His own homeland (now called Shandong Province) has traditionally been held as the friendliest place in China, and any foreigner visiting Confucius' own area will be able to confirm this. If as a foreigner you visit a remote village in Shandong, the inhabitants will often be so overwhelmed by the great honor of a "friend from a distant place" visiting their home that they will refuse to let you pay for anything.

It is perhaps surprising that this kind of welcome still exists after the "friends from distant places" carved up China at the end of the nineteenth century, and the reaction against this, the Boxer Rebellion (in Chinese "the Fists of Righteousness") of the early twentieth century which proclaimed the creed of "kill all foreigners" in fact originated in Shandong. Nevertheless this was just a temporary aberration, and in the end, as always, Confucius triumphs.

The tradition of the "wandering scholars" also lives

Confucius for a day" – a Sunday morning 'English corner' at Black Tiger Spring, Jinan, Shandong – not far from where Confucius himself held his open-air classes for all-comers 2500 years ago. *Photo: Jonathan Price*.

on in the impromptu gatherings known as "English corners" which can be found in almost every town or city in China. Confucius of course became immortalized for continuing his teaching in the open air when he was *persona non grata* in his own state, and during the period of the book-burning under the first emperor people still emulated his example and met in secret to discuss philosophy and literature. Following this tradition, when education practically stopped during the Cultural Revolution and once again most books were unavailable, thousands of ordinary Chinese people who were interested in learning foreign languages and maintaining contact with the outside world risked their lives and met together covertly, sharing tattered copies of banned text books and speaking English with each other.

Today, although China is now largely open to the outside world and language learning has become almost an obsession (not to mention a very big business) these little gatherings have lived on, and every weekend "English Corners" are held in parks or cafés all over the country and still attract large numbers of people of all ages. This is in the direct tradition of Confucius' classes—formal English classes are still relatively expensive and only the lucky few can afford to attend elite schools with native-speaking English teachers, but the "English corners" are free and open to absolutely anybody, just like the Master's classes thousands of years ago.

Visitors to China who want to plug in directly to Confucius' ancient tradition are highly recommended to attend one of these gatherings. You will be treated as a "sage" simply on account of your ability to speak English (it is not necessary to be a native speaker) and because you are a "friend from afar" your opinions on every conceivable subject will be greeted with awed reverence. The open-air classes of so many centuries ago will come to life once more, and you too can be Confucius for a day …

When it comes to formal education in China today, sadly almost nothing remains of Confucius' "advanced" teaching methods. Although his influence has survived in respect of the immense reverence shown to teachers and the huge popularity of part-time study, his teaching methods were abandoned long ago except in a few heroic cases. If you walk down the corridors of any Chinese school and look into the classrooms all you will see is the teacher reading from a textbook while the students passively listen, or you will hear echoed chanting in unison as students recite texts from memory. Only on very rare occasions will you ever observe the teacher actually *talking* to the students, although this does sometimes happen and it is these teachers who are the true heirs of Confucius.

Chinese students of today who go on exchange trips or courses of study in Western schools and universities are usually amazed and delighted that suddenly, instead of being expected to sit quietly and absorb facts, they are encouraged to discuss everything with their teacher and the other students and their opinions are valued. Most of them see this as a feature of modern Western education, and indeed it is, but the ironical truth is that the same method of learning existed in their own culture thousands of years ago, pioneered by Confucius, but has now sadly been lost. The reason this happened, as already discussed, was largely as a result of the introduction of the Imperial examinations in the Song and Tang Dynasties, which shifted the whole focus of the education system onto passing exams.

Recitation, for example, the hallmark of Chinese education for centuries, is indeed the most anti-Confucian of all teaching practices, yet in China remains the most firmly entrenched technique in all classrooms, despite the fact that Confucius many times dismissed learning-by-rote as useless:

Confucius said: "You may be able to recite all the 300 poems from the *Book of Songs*, but when you try to use them in your job, they are not effective … so even though you know a lot of facts off by heart, what good is it?"

Analects, 13:5

The supreme irony is that during the age of the Dynasties, candidates for the Imperial civil service were required to memorize all 492 of the Confucian *Analects*, including the ones about the uselessness of reciting, and even today quite small Chinese children are able to rattle

Confucius revival in China (especially among the young): A young woman bowing before Confucius' grave in Qufu. *Photos: Jonathan Price*

off many of them word-perfect, but are not required to understand what they mean. In the same way many Chinese high-school students can often recite whole chunks of English-language texts and are praised as model students but they are in fact unable to carry on even the simplest conversation with an English speaker. All this is precisely what Confucius meant—what is the good of reciting something if you cannot *use* it?

Chinese students are still noted for being very dedicated and hard-working—more so than their Western counterparts—and this at least derives from the Confucian tradition. Although his classes were lively and inter-active he did not go down the road followed by many modern educationists in making classes "all play and no work" in order to keep the students interested. He still insisted on hard work:

Confucius said: "If you are strict with yourself, your mistakes will be few."

Analects, 4:23

It is naturally this passage from the *Analects* which modern Chinese parents and teachers are most anxious to dun into their children—but they usually leave out the ones about the importance of students thinking for themselves.

Outside mainstream Chinese education, however, where Confucian ideas are only making a slow resurgence, the Master's educational ideals are enjoying increasing popularity in the private "traditional schools"

which have become something of a vogue in recent years. In these schools both teachers and students wear traditional robes from the Song Dynasty and bow to a statue of Confucius at the beginning of each class. Many modern Chinese parents are prepared to pay for their children to have this sort of "old-fashioned" education (Confucius' own school it will be remembered was in effect a "private school"). They do this because they feel that in the modern world their sons and daughters need not only to learn physics and mathematics (of course they study these subjects as well), but also have a grounding in Confucian morality.

Even very small children can enjoy this kind of Confucian education. At the Nanjing Fuzimiao (Confucius Temple) Elementary School in Nanjing, all

Children in ancient dress at a welcoming ceremony for new entrants. Here they receive copies of the *Analects*, an important part of their schooling.

the children dress up in traditional costume (see photos on pages 238–239) for all the important school ceremonies (each little girl and boy proudly holding a copy of the *Analects*) and a study of Confucius is included in the curriculum as well as reading, writing, and arithmetic. The school, which is attached to the Nanjing Confucius Temple, believes that children who absorb Confucian principles at a very young age will be better citizens in the future. This was of course the whole idea of Confucius' first school, and clearly indicates that many parents and teachers—and hopefully the children themselves—believe that Confucius still has a role to play in his own country, not just today but tomorrow.

Surprisingly perhaps, millions of other Chinese people now share this view, and not only in the educational field. Whereas in twentieth-century China Confucius was viewed as "yesterday's man," the twenty-first century has seen him make another remarkable comeback and his ideas are becoming increasingly popular. Paradoxically, Confucius aficionados in China today are mainly young people and (very encouragingly) predominantly female, which finally puts to rest the age-old belief that he only appeals to men.

As the new century gets under way, the older Chinese generation is made up from survivors of the Cultural Revolution, and many retain at least some of the prejudices of that time, believing for example that Confucius was a slave-driver and woman-hater who had no relevance to contemporary life. Their children, born into the era of greater openness, have none of these prejudices and read the *Analects* simply for what they are and can see that they do indeed still have extreme relevance. As China's values become increasingly materialistic, a significant but vocal minority feel that their society is beginning to resemble that of Confucius' own day, and his criticisms of those who worshipped money and would go to any lengths to get it also apply today.

> **"These mean creatures! When they don't have something, they make themselves miserable in getting it. Once they get it, they go crazy about losing it. Once they are worried about losing it, there is nothing they won't do."**
>
> *Analects*, 17:15

The "nothing that they won't do" in order to get their share of today's increasing prosperity includes for many the placing of substantial bribes in the right quarters. In contemporary China contracts are regularly obtained by making a "donation" to the right official, and both

Yu Dan – author of the best-selling book '*Insights into the Analects*', which applies Confucius' ideas to modern China.

university professors and ordinary school teachers augment their incomes by accepting equally substantial donations from parents in order that their children will get high marks. It is not surprising that many Chinese young people feel that the situation is out of control; all around them they can see honesty being penalized and fairness sacrificed to greed, and Confucius' ideas have become suddenly popular among those for whom the Cultural Revolution is remote history.

Yu Dan, a young woman professor at Beijing Normal University, who was only a very small child when the anti-Confucian hysteria of the late 1960s was at its height, has become the major advocate of Confucius' ideals among the younger Chinese, and was completely taken aback by the phenomenal public response to her book *Insights into the Analects*, which was published in December 2006. Following a hugely successful TV series about Confucius which made her an instantly recognisable media personality, Yu brought out a book version which analyzed the relevance of Confucius' ideas to modern society. The book sold more than 3 million copies in four months, making modern Chinese publishing history and beating the previous top seller— the "Harry Potter" series in Chinese translation—into second place. Confucius is more popular in China than Harry Potter? Surely some mistake …

Apparently not. As surprised as everybody else, Yu Dan went on a gruelling book-signing tour all round China during which she autographed 39,000 copies, often having to sit for over ten hours signing book after book, desperately trying to keep smiling as one person after another told her "how much her book meant to them." Interviewed later for an American newspaper, she said with commendable humility: "I saw so many people waiting in line I couldn't refuse. They were not there for me—they were there for Confucius."

A lot of the fan-mail Yu Dan received on her website was from students—mostly girls—who told sad stories of how their prospects in life had suffered because they had refused to pay bribes to their professors in order to get high marks, but after reading *Insights into the Analects* they now knew that Confucius stood behind them on this. Students who protest against corruption both in universities and schools are often vilified by their fellow-students for upsetting the system yet there are still many who dare to do this, and these courageous young people are the finest example of the survival of Confucius' ideals in modern China. After refusing to pay for success they are told (even sometimes by their parents) that they have ruined their chances—and maybe they have done—but they have not compromised their integrity and Confucius is indeed behind them on this:

"I don't worry about not having a good position; I worry about the means I use to gain position."

Analects, 4:14

Many Chinese businesses are also starting to insist that their employees read the *Analects* in order to stem the tide of widespread corruption and unethical practices that continue to make headlines and have blighted the reputation of Chinese companies all over the world. These Confucian businesses are a minority, as are the courageous Confucian students who make a stand against academic corruption, yet their numbers are growing, and once again Confucius is seen as the man of the moment whose ethical precepts can help restore decent standards in business:

Confucius said: "The Superior Person… seeing an opportunity for gain, thinks of what would be Just."

Analects, 16:10

Some have even suggested issuing some sort of certificate along the lines of "We only use recycled materials"—which in this case would read "This company operates according to Confucian standards of Business Ethics."

Unethical business practices are of course a worldwide phenomenon; this is one of the reasons that Confucius is cited so often at business management seminars all over the world and is quoted so frequently in the many publications which appear each year on management in the twenty-first century.

Peter Drucker, the American business guru who started the whole "Confucius for business" bandwagon, always maintained that doing the right thing does not necessarily mean reduced profits, and in the long term Confucian ethics are actually good for business: we only have to look at the series of financial scandals that rocked the business world in both the USA and Australia in the 1990s to see that this is the case. While the high flyers served out their prison sentences or enjoyed exile in reduced circumstances in Spain or South America, those companies which had maintained high ethical standards in all their dealings still kept going strong, and have headed into the twenty-first century even stronger. Drucker died in 2005, but his followers have continued to stress the importance of Confucius' principles for modern business:

Confucianism is a compelling managerial ethic for several reasons:

1. Confucianism is compatible with accepted managerial practices.

2. It requires individuals and organizations to make a positive contribution to society.

3. It recognizes hierarchy as an important organizational principle and demands managerial moral leadership.

Edward J. Romar, College of Management, University of Massachusetts

This idea, that impeccable moral leadership is the key

Peter Drucker (1909-2005), the 'father of modern management', who held that many of Confucius' ideas can be applied to the running of a modern company.

to success, is of course the centerpiece of Confucius' managerial philosophy:

> Confucius said: "If you govern with the power of your virtue, you will be like the North Star. It just stays in its place while all the other stars position themselves around it."

Analects, 2:1

It is not only in the realm of business ethics that Confucius' ideas have been so enthusiastically adopted by the management gurus of today. His more general ideas about the administration of a state are now

frequently quoted in their road-show presentations given to audiences of eager business executives worldwide, and many of the *Analects* are seen to be directly applicable to the running of a modern company—almost word-for-word:

> Confucius said: "If you would govern a state of a thousand chariots you must pay strict attention to business, be true to your word, be economical in expenditure and love the people."

Analects, 1:5

Or alternatively: "If you would govern a company of a thousand employees, you must pay strict attention to business, be true to your word, be economical in expenditure and love your staff."

The man they said should be consigned to the history books has once again proved that his ideas will never be out-dated, and the Confucius-for-business industry is booming. Business management sections in bookshops all over the world and online now contain such titles as: *The Confucius Connection*; *Confucius in the Boardroom*; *How Would Confucius Ask for a Raise? One Hundred Enlightened Solutions for Tough Business Problems*; and my own personal favorite: *How to Achieve Business Success: Confucius Wears a Three-piece Suit*.

Unfortunately, although "Confucius said …" is becoming one of the most popular catch-phrases at management seminars all over the world, he is perhaps still best known outside China for the corpus of largely unfunny Confucius jokes which have been running for years and now even include Mrs Confucius jokes. The jokes have a standard format and always begin with "Confucius he say …" followed by something totally obvious or more often than not scatological or obscene. The humor depends almost entirely on the premise that Confucius cannot speak English properly and instead he delivers his breathtakingly obvious pronouncements in what used to be called pidgin and is now known as Chinglish.

Confucius probably would not mind—he was noted for accepting with great good humor jokes against himself—and perhaps Zigong the astute businessman would have felt that there is no such thing as bad publicity anyway. Here is an example of Confucius enjoying a joke against himself as quoted by Sima Qian:

> In the city of Cheng he and his pupils had lost
> each other. Confucius stood alone at the East Gate
> of the suburb. A man of Cheng said to Zigong, the
> disciple of Confucius: "At the East Gate there
> stands a man with broad shoulders and short legs,
> standing there looking as miserable as a dog in a

house of mourning." Zigong told the story to Confucius. Confucius laughed joyously and said: "I can't help my appearance, but the similarity with a dog in a house of mourning, that fits, that fits!"

Sima Qian, *Records of the Grand Historian*

Since he found the comparison of himself with a miserable dog so amusing, he would be unlikely to be insulted by jokes about his appalling English and constant reference to toilets or sex, and he might even consider the whole thing flattering—there are after all no Socrates jokes. Some comedians specialize in impersonating prominent politicians, imitating their voices and mannerisms exactly and making them say ridiculous things, but in order for their acts to be funny the audience has to know what the original looks and sounds like. So perhaps the most flattering aspect of the whole Confucius jokes phenomenon is that his unique style of speaking is so familiar that it can still be parodied thousands of years later—and in another language. The jokes are not all that funny but they closely mimic the style of the *Analects*.

Joking aside, Confucius and his ideas are attracting more and more interest all over the world among educated people at least, and the Chinese government has recently sponsored the opening of "Confucius Institutes" in many countries around the world. Although these institutes are designed to promote Chinese language and culture in general, it is nevertheless highly significant that it is *his* name which has been chosen to symbolize a whole culture: the same name which was being execrated and vilified in his own country on the front pages of all the newspapers less than forty years before the first institute was opened in Seoul in 2004.

Within two years there were over eighty "Confucius Institutes" in capitals and major cities in every continent; the number is fast growing every year, and there is an ambitious plan to top a thousand institutes by the year 2020. Statues of Confucius dominate the foyers of these institutes in every corner of the globe, not only in the obvious places like London, New York, Tokyo, Melbourne, and Sydney, but in many diverse and sometimes unexpected locations like Cairo, Helsinki, Buenos Aires, and in the Universities of Kansas, Alabama, and Ohio. From public enemy number one to worldwide celebrity in four decades is no mean achievement—the phoenix has indeed risen again.

Of course it is highly unlikely that China itself will ever again adopt Confucianism as the official state philosophy, as the emperors did for almost exactly 2,000 years, but nevertheless many Chinese officials from the president down to local level are once again proud to be seen as following his ethical principles. He will never again be given an official government position, but the opening of the Confucius Institutes all over the world has signaled his complete rehabilitation as the unofficial Chinese cultural ambassador, a posting he would no doubt relish as it is all about promoting peace and friendship and ancient Chinese culture. If there are young people in Kansas City reading the *Book of Songs*, then Confucius must surely be happy.

Outside China, some modern Asian states have made public claims that their governments are run along Confucian lines, but in the same way that the Imperial Chinese dynasties used his philosophy to cloak oppression and injustice, their modern counterparts are once again giving Confucius a bad name—one that he really does not deserve. Confucius always advocated government by example and not by excessive punishment, so he would hardly approve of a state which claims to be proudly Confucian but imposes punitive fines for possession of chewing gum and mercilessly flogs its citizens (and occasionally those of other nations) on a weekly basis for trivial offenses like stealing road signs. The same state shows videos of these floggings to primary-school children in order to make them understand the consequences of disobedience—this is not what Confucius meant by ruling by example. Meanwhile another Asian country which makes a great noise about being Confucian is a byword for massive corporate and government corruption and police brutality. Confucius would not have condoned the use of tear-gas against students. The "Asian tigers" seem to have forgotten that this was the man who said that "an

oppressive government is more to be feared than the fiercest tiger."

To find examples of true Confucianism in our own day we should look toward individuals rather than governments, and it is in any case almost axiomatic that if a government claims to be Confucian it almost certainly is not, and this also applies to individuals. Confucius himself often castigated his students for smugly claiming to be "humane" and "superior people" rather than letting themselves be judged by their actions.

Thus Deng Xiao Ping, who never overtly claimed to be a Confucian, nevertheless acted in a Confucian way, even to the extent of emulating the Master by being exiled twice. Even when the Cultural Revolution was officially over Jiang Qing continued her "criticize Confucius" campaigns until she herself fell from grace, linking the name of the hated ancient sage with both Deng and Zhou Enlai, and Zhou too can be regarded as a modern Confucian who never laid claim to the title. Confucius described his ideal leader as a *junzi*—often translated as "ideal gentleman." Zhou as Foreign Minister was perceived in the West throughout his career as a "gentleman"—not least because of his impeccable dress-sense (he was rumored to have his "peasant" uniform hand-tailored). He attempted—often successfully—to moderate the excesses of the Cultural Revolution, and just before he died engineered the

Zhou Enlai 1898-1976. First Premier and Foreign Minister of the People's Republic of China.
Like Confucius, Zhou worked actively for peace and world brotherhood, achieving friendly relations with many countries including India and most famously the USA. He also shared the Master's firm belief that: "Going too far is the same as not going far enough" (*Analects 11:15*), managing to curb many of the excesses of the 1960's. Perhaps the most universally beloved Chinese figure since Confucius, he was a true *Junzi* – the perfect 'Confucian gentleman', even though he lived at a time when Confucianism was officially anathema.

"Is it not the greatest pleasure when friends visit from distant places?" *Analects 1:1.*
President Nixon and his wife posing on the Great Wall of China in February 1972 with Mao and his wife. Despite Nixon's later troubles he will be remembered for his visit to Confucius' homeland, and this event is considered of such historical significance that it even inspired an opera: 'Nixon in China' (1987) by the American composer John Adams.

historic visit of Nixon to China, which began the opening-up of his country to the West, a process which was continued and accelerated by Deng. Is it not, Confucius had said, the greatest pleasure to welcome friends from afar?

Nixon himself can of course hardly be described as a *junzi*—if as well as being photographed on the Great Wall he had taken time off to read the *Analects* the Watergate break-in might never have happened. His predecessor John F. Kennedy on the other hand certainly conformed to the Confucian model. Many would argue that Kennedy actually achieved very little during his presidency, apart from sending young Americans to dig latrines in Africa and averting the Third World War in 1962, but for the latter achievement alone he should be nominated for the Zigong Peace Prize—Confucius' star student prevented at least two major wars in his own lifetime. Confucius like Kennedy failed to realize most of his dreams, but nevertheless both are perceived as having their hearts in the right place, and in the end this is what matters. Confucius dreamed of the golden age of the Zhou, and it is no coincidence that the Kennedy years are also known as the years of Camelot. In the hearts of American people, the memory of J.F.K. can never be erased, in exactly the same way that Confucius

John F. Kennedy 1917-1963
"Ask not what your country can do for you; ask what you can do for your country". From John F. Kennedy's Inauguration Address, January 20th 1961.
"You should not worry that you have no position in society – you should worry about how to make yourself fit for such a position". Confucius *Analects 4:14*
In many of his speeches JFK echoed not only the ideals of Confucius - but also his style. Although both failed to realize many of their dreams for a better and more peaceful world during their own lifetimes, their dreams have lived on in the hearts of people everywhere.

has lived on in the hearts of Chinese people. They are both, as Zigong said, like the sun and moon, and cannot be slandered. Confucius survived his ill-advised visit to Nanzi the sex-goddess of the state of Wei; the memory of J.F.K will survive Marilyn Monroe.

"Think not what your country can do for you, but what you can do for your country."

John F. Kennedy

This is from the *Analects*? It could well have been, even the style is identical:

"You should not worry that you have no position in society—you should worry about how to make yourself fit for such a position."

Analects, 4:14

Since J.F.K. as far as we know never studied the *Analects*, perhaps we should take a cue from Dante, who included Virgil in his Christian *Paradiso*, and nominate for the Confucian heaven all those who have followed his Way even though they might not have been conscious of doing so. The Way of Confucius is after all the Way of Humanity; he never claimed to have invented it and only urged us to try and follow it.

Thus Princess Diana for example must surely dwell in the Confucian paradise since in her life she was one of the finest examples of his ideal *junzi* who used her position of responsibility to try and make the world a better place, was prompted by feelings of humanity in her public actions—her work for child victims of landmines and many other causes—and "led by example." All these are primary Confucian virtues, and the thousands of people who turned out to lay flowers in memory of Diana all said the same thing when asked why they were doing this: "She was a good person."

The public reaction to Diana's death was also an uncanny echo of Confucius' own passing two and a half millennia before her own. Shunned by the establishment exactly like Diana, Confucius in death was ignored by the government and royal family of the day in exactly the same way, until they too were forced by public opinion to make some sort of gesture. Everybody will have their own selection of other candidates for the status of Confucian *junzi* from among public figures in recent times; Martin Luther King and Nelson Mandela must appear high on everybody's list.

"A *junzi* never leaves humaneness for even the time of a single meal."

Analects, 4:5

Mandela certainly never abandoned his principles, not even for the time of one solitary prison meal, and he certainly ate a lot of those. After finally being released

Nelson Mandela
"A Superior Man never leaves humaneness for even the time of a single meal. If you lack humaneness you can't handle long periods of difficulty". Confucius *Analects* 4:2/ 5
Like Confucius, Mandela endured many years of extreme hardship but never abandoned his principles. He exemplifies the Confucian ideal of the *Junzi*, or 'true gentleman'.

Benigno Aquino 1932-1983, Philippines opposition leader. Like Confucius before him, he championed human values in the face of a corrupt and greedy government; suffering imprisonment, exile, and finally assassination for his principles.

and becoming the leader of his country, he once again chose the Way of Humanity, avoiding revenge and adopting the policy of reconciliation.

Confucius spent much of his life as an outcast, repudiated by the governments of his time, and we can also look for his ideal *junzi* among opposition figures, who even if they never took power nevertheless had a huge influence on the progress of humanitarian ideals, simply by their example of steadfastness. A shining example of a Confucian opposition figure whose refusal to abandon his principles finally led to a bloodless revolution in his own country is Benigno Aquino of the Philippines. Returning from exile in 1986, Aquino was shot dead as he stepped off his plane at Manila airport, and his murder sparked the People Power revolution, when hundreds of thousands of ordinary people took to the streets to face a division of tanks mobilized by President Marcos.

The downfall of Marcos was sealed when Christian nuns stood in front of the tanks offering flowers to the soldiers, who disobeyed orders and refused to open fire, and after this almost the whole military turned against the president. Although the celebrated incident of the flowers was a Christian act it was also a highly Confucian one, since he had always claimed that acts of rightness will shame wrongdoers into the right path. This has always seemed one of his more over-optimistic ideas, yet in Manila in 1986 this is exactly what happened, so maybe the old boy was right after all—it just takes a lot of courage.

Another opposition leader who stood by his principles in a commendably Confucian way was Vaclav Havel, the dissident playwright and activist who eventually became the first president of the independent Czech Republic. By his actions Havel would certainly gain approval not only from Confucius, but also from the music-loving Duke Jing of Qi who had listened to the Master's advice on so many occasions: one of Havel's first acts as president was to invite the American rock star Frank Zappa to Prague to advise him on how to modernize the country. Confucius, who put huge emphasis on the value of music and always insisted that good music inspires good behavior, would be delighted if he could know that at least one leader in the history of the world has invited a *musician* to advise him. Zappa's main advice was: make tourism your top priority. It was good advice, and the beautiful city of Prague is now on the list of must-see destinations for any visitor to Europe.

Zappa himself was something of a Confucius figure in his own country. Universally hated by successive U.S.

Frank Zappa testifies before a Senate committee hearing concerning the possible government regulation of objectionable lyrics in rock music.

John Lennon 1940-1980. *'Give peace a chance'.*
Confucius 551-479 B.C. *'What is the need of killing?'*

administrations for his habit of criticizing them publicly, he perfected a technique of delivering pithy one-liners during interviews in a style remarkably similar to Confucius' own; he uttered so many of these "Zappa-isms" that they could almost be collected into a volume entitled "The Analects of Frank Zappa". Here are a few of them; Confucius could (almost) have made the same remarks:

"Without deviation from the norm, progress is not possible.'
"Stupidity has a certain charm—ignorance does not."
"If you want to get laid, go to college. If you want an education, go to a library."

Frank Zappa

Another musician who publicly espoused Confucian values without ever having necessarily read anything attributed to the Chinese Master (although he may have done since his wife though iconoclastic and avant-garde was also steeped in traditional oriental culture) was of course John Lennon. Although Confucius and his followers made attempts to disarm the barons and Lennon famously stayed in bed with Yoko for three days in London and seven days in Montreal "on behalf of world peace" and in order to stop the Vietnam War, neither succeeded and the killing continued. Their message lives on, however, in their words and their music—and although sadly we will never hear the music of Confucius we should imagine him singing his words too—for that is what he did.

"All we are saying is give peace a chance."

John Lennon, 1969

"What is the need of killing?"

Analects, 12:19 (483 BC)

"All you need is love."

John Lennon / Paul McCartney (lyrics attributed to Lennon), 1967

"Love others—that is the meaning of humanity."

Analects, 12:22 (*ca.* 500 BC)

"No need for greed or hunger, a brotherhood of man—imagine all the people sharing all the world."

John Lennon, "Imagine," 1971

"All within the four seas will be his brothers."

Analects, 12:5 (*ca.* 480 BC)

"You may say I'm a dreamer, but I'm not the only one,
I hope some day you'll join us, And the world will be as one."

John Lennon, "Imagine," 1971

John sang "Imagine there's no heaven," but if we can imagine there *is* a heaven, then Confucius and Lennon are somewhere up there singing together. Confucius is accompanying John on his Chinese zither—no doubt rather annoyingly suggesting improvements, for the *guqin* of two and a half millennia ago is more expressive than the modern guitar. But John does not mind, in fact when he first heard Confucius play he exclaimed, like the Master so long ago when he first heard the music of Qi: "I never knew music could reach this level of excellence!" He does not mind because Confucius has already told him he loves the lyrics, and he could not have put it better himself.

When are we going to start listening to the sweet music of humanity? For that is all it is, the "Way of Confucius," the music of humanity. Not an all-embracing philosophy that explains the world, nor a political creed, and certainly not a religion. It is so simple to understand, apparently so difficult to follow, but we have to try. Many other philosophies are obscure and difficult to comprehend, not so the ideas of Confucius. He said it all two and a half thousand years ago and his message is still breathtakingly simple:

"My Way is penetrated by a single thread ... what you don't want done to yourself, don't do to others."

Analects, 4:15, 12:2

We should perhaps give the last words to Sima Qian, Confucius' first biographer, who, although he misunderstood Confucius in many respects, nevertheless revered him, appreciated the simplicity of both the man and his message, and knew even then that he will live for all time:

There were on earth many princes and sages who, in their lifetime, were famous, but whose names were no longer known after their death. Confucius was a simple man of the people. But after so many generations his doctrine is still handed down, and men of learning honor him as Master. All who practice the arts of humanity in the Middle Kingdom take their decisions and their measure from the Master. That can be designated the highest possible sanctity.

Sima Qian, *Records of the Grand Historian*

The Master is gone, but his spirit will live forever. Confucius' tomb in winter. *Qilu Press*

Timeline

All dates are approximate but are probably accurate to within one or two years—chronology based on Sima Qian's *Records of the Grand Historian*.

Date	Confucius' age	Event
551		Born
536	15	Attends Lord Ji's school.
538	17	Mother Zhengzhai dies.
531	20	Marries. Starts job as steward of grain.
529	22	Birth of his son Bo Yu.
528	23	Promoted to steward in charge of livestock. Birth of his daughter.
527	24	Divorced?
526–524		Working as steward for Lord Ji.
523	28	Visit to Zhou with Nangong Jingshu. Meets Daoists ("Lao Tze").
522	29	Begins teaching nobles. Duke Jing visits Lu and becomes Confucius' student.
521	30	Begins open classes. Zilu becomes his student.
517	34	Ji/Meng coup. Duke Zhao flees to Qi. Confucius' first exile.
516	35	Confucius in exile in Qi. Hears Shao Music.
515	36	Exile in Qi. Political dialogues with Duke Jing
511	40	Still in exile in Qi. Confucius offered an estate by Duke Jing.
510	41	Duke Zhao dies in Qi. Duke Ding becomes Duke. Confucius returns to Lu.
508	43	Daughter married?
506	45	Zigong joins Confucius' classes.
505	46	Lord Ji dies? Yang Huo seizes power.
504	47	Yang Huo dictator of Lu.
503	48	Yang Huo offers power to Confucius, Confucius refuses.
501	50	Yang Huo flees to Qi. Ji Huan first minister. Confucius governor of Chungdu.
500	51	Jiagu Convention—Confucius scores major diplomatic victory.
499	52	Confucius minister of justice.
498	53	Confucius promotes disarmament. Demolition of walls begun.
497	54	Lord Meng reneges on disarmament. Dancing girls incident. Confucius goes into exile. Yan Hui joins Confucius' classes.
496–485		Wandering years.
496	55	Confucius, Zilu, Zigong, and Yan Hui in exile in Wei.
495	56	Confucius arrested on suspicion of being Yang Huo.
494	57	Duke Ding dies. Duke Ai becomes Duke of Lu
493	58	Confucius almost killed in state of Song.
492	59	Confucius in state of Chen.
490	61	Confucius advises on discovery of dinosaur bones?
489	62	Duke Jing of Qi dies. Confucius and disciples in state of Chu—refused estates.
488	63	Confucius advises Duke of Wei. Zigong solves diplomatic crisis in state of Lu.
487	64	Grandson Zisi born in Lu.
484	67	Confucius returns to Lu at invitation of Ji Kangzi. Zengzi joins classes.
483	68	Confucius edits classics. Son Bo Yu dies age 46. Yan Hui dies.
481	70	Duke Chien of Qi assassinated. Confucius urges intervention.
480	71	Zilu killed in coup in Wei.
479	72	Confucius dies.

In the Footsteps of Confucius

Those readers planning a visit to China will find that a Confucius-themed tour will be very rewarding and will take you to places well off the standard Beijing–Xian–Qufu track to places which most tourists never see but are nonetheless unforgettable.

Qufu, Shandong Province

The birthplace and modern center of Confucianism. First stop for Confucius buffs is of course Qufu, where it all started. Like all major world tourist destinations you can't escape the crowds so don't expect any sort of sixth century BC atmosphere—the main attraction is that you are standing on the actual place where Confucius taught his students.

Main Temple Complex

The entry fee is pretty hefty but it also gives you admission to the Confucius Mansion and Confucius Forest (*see below*). Be warned that none of the buildings date from anywhere near the time of Confucius. Almost all the temple buildings were constructed or rebuilt during the Ming Dynasty about 500 years ago (around the time of Shakespeare) and most of the statues are modern as the originals were destroyed during the upheavals of the late 1960s. The Apricot Altar is supposed to be the site of Confucius' classes.

Confucius Mansion

The mansion as it stands was mainly constructed during the last (Qing) Dynasty but gives a good impression of the immense wealth the Kong family accrued over the centuries. In the museum section there are some artifacts from Confucius' period.

Confucius Forest and Cemetery

The forest is quite large and is in fact a huge cemetery containing the graves of not only Confucius but many of his direct descendants over the last two and a half millennia. This is the one place in Qufu which is dripping with Spring-and-Autumn Period atmosphere and is not to be missed. There is even the gnarled remnant of a tree supposedly planted by Zigong immediately after his Master's death. All the original trees in the forest were planted by his main disciples from seedlings they brought from their homes.

City of the Six Arts

In the main city of Qufu. Don't miss it—they really should call it Confucius World! This is a theme park based around the "six arts" of ancient China as applied to the life of Confucius, so there are sections on Literature, History, Ritual, Music, Archery, and Charioteering.

To get there just show a taxi-driver one of the photos from the Six-Arts City in this book—most foreign tourists miss out on it as they don't know anything about it. The City is very popular with Chinese tourists as they all know about Confucius' life history—but if you have read this book you will be their equals so join them!

There are some wonderful life-size tableaux of key events in Confucius' life, which you get to see by riding on electric chariots—his privations in exile all represented by very realistic wooden figures. It's all a bit Disneyland but loads of fun.

Hill of Ni, Shandong Province

Not far from Qufu. The sacred hill where Confucius' father and mother prayed for a son. Full of atmosphere with various temples shaded by trees on the wooded slopes. Nearby is the Cave of Confucius, touted as his actual birthplace although this is unlikely (*see* Chapter 3: "Zhengzai's Child").

Taishan, Shandong Province

Also known as Mount Tai (*see* Chapter 4: "Growing Up"). Confucius would have seen the view from the top of the most sacred mountain in China. You can take a cable car if you can't face the hundreds of steps to the summit. It was at the base of the mountain that he encountered the woman whose whole family had been eaten by tigers. As a side trip, Chinese tigers (which roamed in the forests in this area during Confucius' time) may still be seen in a wild environment at the Jinan Wildlife Park which is not far from Taishan.

The Great Wall of Qi, Shandong Province

Many centuries older than the more famous Great Wall of China, this is the only building still standing intact which Confucius saw with his own eyes. Much of the wall still survives, and well-preserved sections may be visited in many tourist sites easily accessible from the cities of Jinan and Zibo. However, if you want to see the best bit (as shown in the photos in this book) you are going to have to do some serious hiking!

To get to this section you have to travel southwest from Jinan, the capital of Shandong, to the small city of Chanqing. Take the road directly south from here (about 12 miles/20 km) to the small village of Dazhuang and ask the villagers. There are no signposts; the site seems to be a well-kept secret and this is why it has survived so well. The hike to the mountaintop takes just under an hour. You need to be fit: wear stout boots and long pants (there are many brambles as you go up).

The effort will be rewarding. As you reach the summit there it is—untouched for two and a half thousand years. No restoration, no tourists, just you and the ancient battlements and guardhouses exactly as they were at the time of Confucius, while hawks and eagles hover in the sky above you. This is the nearest thing you're going to get to a time-machine in the whole of China and it won't cost you a cent—apart from sore feet. But hurry—there is talk of "restoring" the wall and this will destroy the atmosphere completely exactly like the most popular parts of the more famous Great Wall.

Linzi, Shandong Province

Site of the original capital of the state of Qi, where Confucius spent many years in exile (*see* Chapter 11: "The Thousand Chariots").

The magnificent Linzi Chariot Museum is built around the famous "chariot burial" site—where Duke Jing of Qi, who was a student and friend of Confucius, had himself buried together with hundreds of his horses and chariots, the fossilized remains of which are on display.

The adjoining museum contains many artifacts from the time of Confucius plus reconstructions of chariots and war implements of the period—which are featured in many of the photos in this book. For anybody wishing to get a real feel for the world in which Confucius lived, this is not to be missed. Once again, most foreign tourists know nothing about Linzi. Of course you have to see the Terracotta Warriors in Xian, but if you are a Confucius fan Linzi is a must-see destination and the skeletons of the horses and the complete chariots are—after so many thousands of intervening years—frankly amazing.

Zhengzhou, Henan Province

Situated in what was the ancient state of Zhou (visited by Confucius in 523 BC when he first encountered the Daoists) Zhengzhou is another must-see destination for committed Confucius fans. The magnificent and very modern Henan Museum not only displays many artefacts from the period of Confucius but has daily performances on ancient instruments including the *guqin*—Confucius' instrument of choice—by musicians in ancient costumes. This is a unique opportunity to travel into the past.

Students of comparative religion will also enjoy the world-famous Longmen Grottos with their huge Buddhist carvings which are a short trip from Zhengzhou. Martial arts fans can also visit the nearby Shaolin Monastery, home of kung-fu (not to be confused with Kong Fu who was of course a philosopher). If you're into Confucius, Buddha, or martial arts, forget the Great Wall of China and head for Zhengzhou—before or after hitting Qufu and Shandong—it's the real thing.

Beijing

Beijing did not exist during Confucius' time as a major city. However, the wonderful Capital Museum in its very recently-built new home is (as might be expected) one of the very best museums in China and many of the photos in this book were taken there. It is the home of some of the very best artefacts from Confucius' period. Whatever else you do in Beijing don't miss out on a visit to the Capital Museum.

Acknowledgements

This has been a pioneering international project and I would like to thank all the many people who have given so much of their time and invaluable help to bring it to fruition.

First of all to my wonderful students who have worked so tirelessly and enthusiastically as picture researchers, P.A.s, photographer's assistants, and historical and literary advisors. I couldn't have done it without you! You were all wonderful so I will thank you alphabetically.

Connie Kong—thanks not only for being descended from Confucius but also for allowing me to put your picture in the book and to your whole family for organizing my research trip to Qufu. Ellen Lei—many many thanks for organizing the photo-shoots in Linzi and Henan, and also for introducing me to the story of Min Ziqian which appears in the book. Betty Liu— fantastically efficient picture research and tremendous thanks also for organizing the photos in Shandong Museum. Jane Wang—thanks a million for organizing everything so smoothly for all the pictures in Beijing. Shirley Zhang—can't thank you enough for all you did, including the really professional research on the bamboo manuscripts, organizing the photo-shoots in Shanghai, Henan, and Nanjing, and also for the invaluable help with the translations. Thanks also to my student Debbie (Wang Meiying) for helping sort out the pictures before they went to London, and to Jeannie Liu for outstanding courier services.

I owe a big debt of gratitude to everybody who has helped with the historical research, both for the pictures and text. Big thanks in this respect to my colleague Wang Hongmei for deciphering the inscriptions on ancient Chinese vases and for all the other invaluable translation work. Also to Wang Hao, another colleague, for helping track down local historical sites, and to Gong Xiaowei of Qilu Press whose specialized knowledge of ancient geography helped immeasurably with the map.

Professor Li Hong and the Huaxia Ancient Music Ensemble, Henan Museum, put on a special performance of music from Confucius' time for the photographs—thanks so much for that, it was wonderful! Thanks also to Peng Li, Professor of Musicology at Shandong College of Arts for arranging this.

Many museums all over China have been immensely helpful and co-operative in allowing me to photograph their exhibits. I would like in particular to thank the Shanghai Museum Department of Manuscripts for allowing us to use photographs from their Bamboo Slip collection, and the extremely helpful staff at the Capital Museum in Beijing, Shandong Museum in Jinan, and the Linzi Museum of Chariots, also in Shandong.

Huge thanks to Paul Richardson in England who has been the Godfather of the whole project from the outset and has been immensely supportive ever since I came on board. Your deep knowledge and love of ancient Chinese culture and desire to share this in the best way possible with readers all over the world has been my inspiration. Also to Alan Greene of Compendium Publishing who got right behind the concept of the book from the word go and this too was an inspiration! It is not often that publishers are so supportive of their authors so I have been very lucky on this one. Special thanks too to Simon Forty, the Publishing Director at Compendium, for holding my hand electronically all the way through the publishing process with unfailing enthusiasm and encouragement. To use one of your favorite words—"Cheers!"

Last but not least, heartfelt thanks to my long-suffering editor in China, Yan Menghui, who gave me the project in the beginning, laid down the main idea for the structure of the book, and has seen the whole project through from start to finish. Especial thanks for recommending me as the author of the text in the first place, and for having faith that your daughter's teacher would be able to do justice to your ancient culture. I hope I have not let you down!

Finally I would like to thank Confucius for just having existed.

Index